"I shall speak of nothing of which I have no experience, either in my own life or in observation of others, or which the Lord has not taught me in prayer."   *Prologue*

Almost four centuries have passed since St. Teresa of Avila, the great Spanish mystic and reformer, committed to writing the experiences which brought her to the highest degree of sanctity. Her search for, and eventual union with, God have been recorded in her own world-renowned writings —the autobiographical *Life*, the celebrated masterpiece *Interior Castle* and *The Way of Perfection*—as well as in the other numerous works which flowed from her pen while she lived.

The Way of Perfection was written during the height of controversy which raged over the reforms St. Teresa enacted within the Carmelite Order. Its specific purpose was to serve as a guide in the practice of prayer and it sets forth her counsels and directives for the attainment of spiritual perfection through prayer. It was composed by St. Teresa at the express command of her superiors, and was written during the late hours in order not to interfere with the day's already crowded schedule.

Without doubt it fulfills the tribute given all St. Teresa's works by E. Allison Peers, the outstanding authority on her writings: "Work of a sublime beauty bearing the ineffaceable hallmark of genius."

THE WAY OF PERFECTION

BY

ST. TERESA OF AVILA

TRANSLATED & EDITED BY

E. ALLISON PEERS

FROM THE CRITICAL EDITION OF

P. SILVERIO DE SANTA TERESA, C.D.

IMAGE BOOKS

A DIVISION OF DOUBLEDAY & COMPANY, INC.

GARDEN CITY, NEW YORK

IMAGE BOOKS EDITION 1964
by special arrangement with Sheed & Ward, Inc.
Image Books Edition published September 1964

Nihil Obstat: Georgius Can. Smith, D.D., Ph.D.
Censor Deputatus
Imprimatur: E. Morrogh Bernard
Vic. Gen.
Westmonasterii,
Die 14 Februarii, 1946

Printed in the United States of America

CONTENTS

PRINCIPAL ABBREVIATIONS

A.V.—Authorized Version of the Bible (1611).

D.V.—Douai Version of the Bible (1609).

Letters—Letters of St. Teresa. Unless otherwise stated, the numbering of the Letters follows Vols. VII–IX of P. Silverio. *Letters* (St.) indicates the translation of the Benedictines of Stanbrook (London, 1919–24, 4 vols.).

Lewis—*The Life of St. Teresa of Jesus,* etc., translated by David Lewis, 5th ed., with notes and introductions by the Very Rev. Benedict Zimmerman, O.C.D., London, 1916.

P. Silverio—*Obras de Santa Teresa de Jesús,* editadas y anotadas por el P. Silverio de Santa Teresa, C.D., Durgos, 1915–24, 9 vols.

Ribera—Francisco de Ribera, *Vida de Santa Teresa de Jesús,* Nueva ed. aumentada, con introducción, etc., por el P. Jaime Pons, Barcelona, 1908.

S.S.M.—E. Allison Peers, *Studies of the Spanish Mystics,* London, 1927–30, 2 vols.

St. John of the Cross—*The Complete Works of Saint John of the Cross, Doctor of the Church,* translated from the critical edition of P. Silverio de Santa Teresa, C.D., and edited by E. Allison Peers, London, 1934–35, 3 vols.

Yepes—Diego de Yepes, *Vida de Santa Teresa,* Madrid, 1615.

INTRODUCTION

We owe this book, first and foremost, to the affectionate importunities of the Carmelite nuns of the Primitive Observance at Ávila, and, in the second place, to that outstanding Dominican who was also St. Teresa's confessor, Fray Domingo Báñez. The nuns of St. Joseph's knew something of their Mother Foundress' autobiography, and, though in all probability none of them had actually read it, they would have been aware that it contained valuable counsels to aspirants after religious perfection, of which, had the book been accessible to them, they would have been glad to avail themselves. Such intimate details did it contain, however, about St. Teresa's spiritual life that her superiors thought it should not be put into their hands; so the only way in which she could grant their persistent requests was to write another book dealing expressly with the life of prayer. This P. Báñez was very anxious that she should do.

Through the entire *Way of Perfection* there runs the author's desire to teach her daughters to love prayer, the most effective means of attaining virtue. This principle is responsible for the book's construction. St. Teresa begins by describing the reason which led her to found the first Reformed Carmelite convent—viz., the desire to minimize the ravages being wrought, in France and elsewhere, by Protestantism, and, within the limits of her capacity, to check the passion for a so-called "freedom", which at that time was exceeding all measure. Knowing how effectively such inordinate desires can be restrained by a life of humility and poverty, St. Teresa extols the virtues of poverty and exhorts her daughters to practise it in their own lives. Even the buildings in which they live should be poor: on the Day of Judgment both majestic palaces and humble cottages will fall and she has no desire that the convents of her nuns should do so with a resounding clamour.

In this preamble to her book, which comprises Chapters 1–3, the author also charges her daughters very earnestly to commend to God those who have to defend the Church of Christ—particularly theologians and preachers.

The next part of the book (Chaps. 4–15) stresses the importance of a strict observance of the Rule and Constitutions, and before going on to its main subject—prayer—treats of three essentials of the prayer-filled life—mutual love, detachment from created things and true humility, the last of these being the most important and including all the rest. With the mutual love which nuns should have for one another she deals most minutely, giving what might be termed homely prescriptions for the domestic disorders of convents with the skill which we should expect of a writer with so perfect a knowledge of the psychology of the cloister. Her counsels are the fruit, not of lofty mental speculation, but of mature practical experience. No less aptly does she speak of the relations between nuns and their confessors, so frequently a source of danger.

Since excess is possible even in mutual love, she next turns to detachment. Her nuns must be detached from relatives and friends, from the world, from worldly honour, and—the last and hardest achievement—from themselves. To a large extent their efforts in this direction will involve humility, for, so long as we have an exaggerated opinion of our own merits, detachment is impossible. Humility, to St. Teresa, is nothing more nor less than truth, which will give us the precise estimate of our own worth that we need. Fraternal love, detachment and humility: these three virtues, if they are sought in the way these chapters direct, will make the soul mistress and sovereign over all created things—a "royal soul", in the Saint's happy phrase, the slave of none save of Him Who bought it with His blood.

The next section (Chaps. 16–26) develops these ideas, and leads the reader directly to the themes of prayer and contemplation. It begins with St. Teresa's famous extended simile of the game of chess, in which the soul gives check and mate to the King of love, Jesus. Many people are greatly attracted by the life of contemplation because they have acquired imperfect and misleading notions of the ineffable mystical joys which they believe almost synonymous with contemplation. The Saint protests against such ideas as these and lays it down clearly that, as a general rule, there is no way of attaining to union with the Beloved save by the practice of the "great virtues", which can be acquired only at the cost of continual self-sacrifice and self-conquest. The favours which God grants to contemplatives are only exceptional and of a transitory kind and they are intended to incline them more closely to virtue and to inspire their lives with greater fervour.

And here the Saint propounds a difficult question which has occasioned no little debate among writers on mystical theology. Can a soul in grave sin enjoy supernatural contemplation? At first sight, and judging from what the author says in Chapter 16, the answer would seem to be that, though but rarely and for brief periods, it can. In the original (or Escorial) autograph, however, she expressly denies this, and states that contemplation is not possible for souls in mortal sin, though it may be experienced by those who are so lukewarm, or lacking in fervour, that they fall into venial sins with ease. It would seem that in this respect the Escorial manuscript reflects the Saint's ideas, as we know them, more clearly than the later one of Valladolid; if this be so, her opinions in no way differ from those of mystical theologians as a whole, who refuse to allow that souls in mortal sin can experience contemplation at all.

St. Teresa then examines a number of other questions, on which opinion has also been divided and even now is by no means unanimous. Can all souls attain to contemplation? Is it possible, without experiencing contemplation, to reach the summit of Christian perfection? Have all the servants of God who have been canonized by the Church necessarily been contemplatives? Does the Church ever grant non-contemplatives beatification? On these questions and others often discussed by the mystics much light is shed in the seventeenth and eighteenth chapters.

Then the author crosses swords once more with those who suppose that contemplatives know nothing of suffering and that their lives are one continuous series of favours. On the contrary, she asserts, they suffer more than actives: to imagine that God admits to this closest friendship people whose lives are all favours and no trials is ridiculous. Recalling the doctrine expounded in the nineteenth chapter of her *Life* she gives various counsels for the practice of prayer, using once more the figures of water which she had employed in her first description of the Mystic Way. She consoles those who cannot reason with the understanding, shows how vocal prayer may be combined with mental, and ends by advising those who suffer from aridity in prayer to picture Jesus as within their hearts and thus always beside them—one of her favourite themes.

This leads up to the subject which occupies her for the rest of the book (Chaps. 27–42)—the Lord's Prayer. These chapters, in fact, comprise a commentary on the Paternoster, taken petition by petition, touching incidentally upon the themes of Recollection, Quiet and Union. Though nowhere expounding them as fully as in the *Life* or the *Interior Castle*, she treats them with equal sublimity, profundity and fervour and in language of no less beauty. Consider, for example, the apt and striking simile of the mother and the child (Chap. 31), used to describe the state of the soul in the Prayer of Quiet, which forms one of the most beautiful and expressive expositions of this degree of contemplation to be found in any book on the interior life whatsoever.

In Chapter 38, towards the end of the commentary on the Paternoster, St. Teresa gives a striking synthetic description of the excellences of that Prayer and of its spiritual value. She enters at some length into the temptations to which spiritual people are exposed when they lack humility and discretion. Some of these are due to presumption: they believe they possess virtues which in fact they do not—or, at least, not in sufficient degree to enable them to resist the snares of the enemy. Others come from a mistaken scrupulousness and timidity inspired by a sense of the heinousness of their sins, and may lead them into doubt and despair. There are souls, too, which make overmuch account of spiritual favours: these she counsels to see to it that, however sublime their contemplation may be, they begin and end every period of prayer with self-examination. While others, whose mistrust of themselves makes them restless, are exhorted to trust in the Divine mercy, which never forsakes those who possess true humility.

Finally, St. Teresa writes of the love and fear of God—two mighty castles which the fiercest of the soul's enemies will storm in vain—and begs Him, in the last words of the Prayer, to preserve her daughters, and all other souls who practise the interior life, from the ills and perils which will ever surround them, until they reach the next world, where all will be peace and joy in Jesus Christ.

Such, in briefest outline, is the argument of this book. Of all St. Teresa's writings it is the most easily comprehensible and it can be read with profit by a greater number of people than any of the rest. It is also (if we use the word in its strictest and truest sense) the most ascetic of her treatises; only a few chapters and passages in it, here and there, can be called definitely mystical. It takes up numerous ideas already adumbrated in the *Life* and treats them in a practical and familiar way—objectively, too, with an eye not so much to herself as to her daughters of the Discalced Reform. This last fact necessitates her descending to details which may seem to us trivial but were not in the least so to the religious to whom they were addressed and with whose virtues and failing she was so familiar. Skilfully, then, and in a way profitable to all, she intermingles her teaching on the most rudimentary principles of the religious life, which has all the clarity of any classical treatise, with instruction on the most sublime and elusive tenets of mystical theology.

ESCORIAL AUTOGRAPH – *The Way of perfection* – or *Paternoster*, as its author calls it, from the latter part of its content—was written twice. Both autographs have been preserved in excellent condition, the older of them in the monastery of San Lorenzo el Real, El Escorial, and the other in the convent of the Discalced Carmelite nuns at Valladolid. We have already seen how Philip II acquired a number of Teresan autographs for his new Escorial library, among them that of the *Way of perfection*. The Escorial manuscript bears the title "Treatise of the Way of Perfection", but this is not in St. Teresa's hand. It plunges straight into the prologue: both the title and the brief account of the contents, which are found in most of the editions, are taken from the autograph of Valladolid, and the humble protestation of faith and submission to the Holy Roman Church was dictated by the Saint for the edition of the book made in Évora by Don Teutonio de Braganza — it is found in the Toledo codex, which will be referred to again shortly.

The text, divided into seventy-three short chapters, has no chapter-divisions in the ordinary sense of the phrase, though the author has left interlinear indications showing where each chapter should begin. The chapter-headings form a table of contents at the end of the manuscript and only two of them (55 and 56) are in St. Teresa's own writing. As the remainder, however, are in a feminine hand of the sixteenth century, they may have been dictated by her to one of her nuns: they are almost identical with those which she herself wrote at a later date in the autograph of Valladolid.

There are a considerable number of emendations in this text, most of them made by the Saint herself, whose practice was to obliterate any unwanted word so completely as to make it almost illegible. None of such words or phrases was restored in the autograph of Valladolid—a sure indication that it was she who erased them, or at least that she approved of their having been erased. There are fewer annotations and additions in other hands than in the autographs of any of her remaining works, and those few are of little importance. This may be due to the fact that a later redaction of the work was made for the use of her convents and for publication: the Escorial manuscript would have circulated very little and would never have been subjected to a minute critical examination. Most of what annotations and corrections of this kind there are were made by the Saint's confessor, P. García de Toledo, whom, among others, she asked to examine the manuscript.

There is no direct indication in the manuscript of the date of its composition. We know that it was written at St. Joseph's, Ávila, for the edification and instruction of the first nuns of the Reform, and the prologue tells us that only "a few days" had elapsed between the completion of the *Life* and the beginning of the *Way of perfection*.[1] If, therefore, the *Life* was finished at the end of 1565 [or in the early weeks of 1566][2] we can date the commencement of the *Way of perfection* with some precision. [But even then there is no indication as to how long the composition took and when it was completed.]

A complication occurs in the existence, at the end of a copy of the *Way of perfection* which belongs to the Discalced Carmelite nuns of Salamanca, and contains corrections in St. Teresa's hand, of a note, in the writing of the copyist, which says: "This book was written in the year sixty-two—I mean fifteen hundred and sixty-two." There follow some lines in the writing of St. Teresa, which make no allusion to this date; her silence might be taken as confirming it (though she displays no great interest in chronological exactness) were it not absolutely impossible to reconcile such a date with the early chapters of the book, which make it quite clear that the community of thirteen nuns was fully established when they were written (Chap. 4: p. 55, below). There could not possibly have been so many nuns at St. Joseph's before late in the year 1563, in which María de San Jerónimo and Isabel de Santo Domingo took the habit, and it is doubtful if St. Teresa could conceivably have begun the book before the end of that year. Even, therefore, if the reference in the preface to the *Way of perfection* were to the first draft of the *Life* (1562), and not to that book as we know it, there would still be the insuperable difficulty raised by this piece of internal evidence.[3] We are forced, then, to assume an error in the Salamanca copy and to assign to the beginning of the *Way of perfection* the date 1565–6.

---

[1] [It is in this way that P. Silverio interprets the phrase. For another interpretation of it see p. 35, n. 8, below.]

[2] Cf. Vol. I, pp. 2–5, above.

[3] See also the reference, in the "General Argument" of the Valladolid redaction, to her being Prioress of St. Joseph's when the book was written. Presumably the original draft is meant.

VALLADOLID AUTOGRAPH. In writing for her Ávila nuns, St. Teresa used language much more simple, familiar and homely than in any of her other works. But when she began to establish more foundations and her circle of readers widened, this language must have seemed to her too affectionately intimate, and some of her figures and images may have struck her as too domestic and trivial, for a more general and scattered public. So she conceived the idea of rewriting the book in a more formal style; it is the autograph of this redaction which is in the possession of the Discalced Carmelite nuns of Valladolid.

The additions, omissions and modifications in this new autograph are more considerable than is generally realized. From the preface onwards, there is no chapter without its emendations and in many there are additions of whole paragraphs. The Valladolid autograph, therefore, is in no sense a copy, or even a recast, of the first draft, but a free and bold treatment of it. As a general rule, a second draft, though often more correctly written and logically arranged than its original, is less flexible, fluent and spontaneous. It is hard to say how far this is the case here. Undoubtedly some of the charm of the author's natural simplicity vanishes, but the corresponding gain in clarity and precision is generally considered greater than the loss. Nearly every change she makes is an improvement; and this not only in stylistic matters, for one of the greatest of her improvements is the lengthening of the chapters and their reduction in number from 73 to 42, to the great advantage of the book's symmetry and unity.

It is clear that St. Teresa intended the Valladolid redaction to be the definitive form of her book since she had so large a number of copies of it made for her friends and spiritual daughters: among these were the copy which she sent for publication to Don Teutonio de Braganza and that used for the first collected edition of her works by Fray Luis de León. For the same reason this redaction has always been given preference over its predecessor by the Discalced Carmelites.

TRANSLATOR'S NOTE

In the text of each of the chapters, of the Valladolid autograph there are omissions—some merely verbal, often illus-
trating the author's aim in making the new redaction, others
more fundamental. If the Valladolid manuscript represents
the *Way of perfection* as St. Teresa wrote it in the period
of her fullest powers, the greater freshness and individuality
of the Escorial manuscript are engaging qualities, and there
are many passages in it, omitted from the later version, which
one would be sorry to sacrifice.

In what form, then, should the book be presented to English readers? It is not surprising if this question is difficult to
answer, since varying procedures have been adopted for the
presentation of it in Spain. Most of them amount briefly to
a re-editing of the Valladolid manuscript. The first edition
of the book, published at Évora in the year 1583, follows this
manuscript, apparently using a copy (the so-called "Toledo"
copy) made by Ana de San Pedro and corrected by St. Teresa;
it contains a considerable number of errors, however, and
omits one entire chapter—the thirty-first, which deals with the
Prayer of Quiet, a subject that was arousing some controversy
at the time when the edition was being prepared. In 1585,
a second edition, edited by Fray Jerónimo Gracián, was published at Salamanca: the text of this follows that of the Évora
edition very closely, as apparently does the text of a rare edition published at Valencia in 1586. When Fray Luis de León
used the Valladolid manuscript as the foundation of his
text (1588) he inserted for the first time paragraphs and
phrases from that of El Escorial, as well as admitting variants
from the copies corrected by the author: he is not careful,
however, to indicate how and where his edition differs from
the manuscript.

Since 1588, most of the Spanish editions have followed
Fray Luis de León with greater or less exactness. The principal

2123

exception is the well-known "Biblioteca de Autores Españoles" edition, in which La Fuente followed a copy of the then almost forgotten Escorial manuscript, indicating in footnotes some of the variant readings in the codex of Valladolid. In the edition of 1883, the work of a Canon of Valladolid Cathedral, Francisco Herrero Bayona, the texts of the two manuscripts are reproduced in parallel columns. P. Silverio de Santa Teresa gives the place of honour to the Valladolid codex, on which he bases his text, showing only the principal variants of the Escorial manuscript but printing the Escorial text in full in an appendix as well as the text of the Toledo copy referred to above.

The first translations of this book into English, by Woodhead (1675: reprinted 1901) and Dalton (1852), were based, very naturally, on the text of Luis de León, which in less critical ages than our own enjoyed great prestige and was considered quite authoritative. The edition published in 1911 by the Benedictines of Stanbrook, described on its title-page as "including all the variants" from both the Escorial and the Valladolid manuscript, uses Herrero Bayona and gives an eclectic text based on the two originals but with no indications as to which is which. The editors' original idea of using one text only, and showing variants in footnotes, was rejected in the belief that "such an arrangement would prove bewildering for the generality of readers" and that anyone who could claim the title of "student" would be able to read the original Spanish and would have access to the Herrero Bayona edition. Father Zimmerman, in his introduction, claimed that while the divergences between the manuscripts are sometimes "so great that the [Stanbrook] translation resembles a mosaic composed of a large number of small bits, skilfully combined", "the work has been done most conscientiously, and while nothing has been added to the text of the Saint, nothing has been omitted, except, of course, what would have been mere repetition".

This first edition of the Benedictines' translation furnished the general reader with an attractive version of what many consider St. Teresa's most attractive book, but soon after it was published a much more intelligent and scholarly interest began to be taken in the Spanish mystics and that not only by students with ready access to the Spanish original and ability to read it. So, when a new edition of the Stanbrook translation was called for, the editors decided to indicate the passages from the Escorial edition which had been embodied in the text by enclosing these in square brackets. In 1911, Father Zimmerman, suspecting that the procedure then adopted by the translators would not "meet with the approval of scholars", had justified it by their desire "to benefit the souls of the faithful rather than the intellect of the student"; but now, apparently, he thought it practicable to achieve both these aims at once. This resolution would certainly have had the support of St. Teresa, who in this very book describes intelligence as a useful staff to carry on the way of perfection. The careful comparison of two separate versions of such a work of genius may benefit the soul of an intelligent reader even more than the careful reading of a version compounded of both by someone else.

When I began to consider the preparation of the present translation it seemed to me that an attempt might be made to do a little more for the reader who combined intelligence with devoutness than had been done already. I had no hesitation about basing my version on the Valladolid MS., which is far the better of the two, whether we consider the aptness of its illustrations, the clarity of its expression, the logical development of its argument or its greater suitability for general reading. At the same time, no Teresan who has studied the Escorial text can fail to have an affection for it: its greater intimacy and spontaneity and its appeal to personal experience make it one of the most characteristic of all the Saint's writings—indeed, excepting the *Letters* and a few chapters of the *Foundations*, it reveals her better than any. Passages from the Escorial MS. must therefore be given: thus far I followed the reasoning of the Stanbrook nuns.

Where this translation diverges from theirs is in the method of presentation. On the one hand I desired, as St. Teresa must have desired, that it should be essentially her mature revision of the book that should be read. For this reason I have been extremely conservative as to the interpolations admitted into the text itself: I have rejected, for example, the innumerable phrases which St. Teresa seems to have cut out in making her new redaction because they were trivial or repetitive, because they weaken rather than reinforce her argument, because they say what is better said elsewhere, because they summarize needlessly[1] or because they are mere personal observations which interrupt the author's flow of thought, and sometimes, indeed, are irrelevant to it. I hope it is not impertinent to add that, in the close study which the adoption of this procedure has involved, I have acquired a respect and admiration for St. Teresa as a reviser, to whom, as far as I know, no one who has written upon her has done full justice. Her shrewdness, realism and complete lack of vanity make her an admirable editor of her own work, and, in debating whether or no to incorporate some phrase or passage in my text I have often asked myself: "Would St. Teresa have included or omitted this if she had been making a fresh revision for a world-wide public over a period of centuries?"

At the same time, though admitting only a minimum of interpolations into my text, I have given the reader all the other important variants in footnotes. I cannot think, as Father Zimmerman apparently thought, that anyone can find the presence of a few notes at the foot of each page "bewildering". Those for whom they have no interest may ignore them; others, in studying them, may rest assured that the only variants not included (and this applies to the variants from the Toledo copy as well as from the Escorial MS.) are such as have no significance in a translation. I have been rather less meticulous here than in my edition of St. John of the Cross, where textual problems assumed greater importance. Thus, except where there has been some special reason for doing so, I have not recorded alterations in the order of clauses or words; the almost regular use by E. of the second person of the plural where V. has the first; the frequent and often apparently purposeless changes of tense; such substitutions, in the Valladolid redaction, as those of "Dios"

[1] E.g., at places where a chapter ends in E. but not in V.

or "Señor mío" for "Señor"; or merely verbal paraphrases as (to take an example at random) "Todo esto que he dicho es para . . ." for "En todo esto que he dicho no trato . . .". Where I have given variants which may seem trivial (such as "hermanas" for "hijas", or the insertion of an explanatory word, like "digo") the reason is generally that there seems to me a possibility that some difference in tone is intended, or that the alternative phrase gives some slight turn to the thought which the phrase in the text does not.

The passages from the Escorial version which I have allowed into my text are printed in italics. Thus, without their being given undue prominence (and readers of the Authorized Version of the Bible will know how seldom they can recall what words are italicized even in the passages they know best) it is clear at a glance how much of the book was intended by its author to be read by a wider public than the nuns of St. Joseph's. The interpolations may be as brief as a single expressive word, or as long as a paragraph, or even a chapter: the original Chapter 17 of the Valladolid MS., for example, which contains the famous similitude of the Game of Chess, was torn out of the codex by its author (presumably with the idea that so secular an illustration was out of place) and has been restored from the Escorial MS. as part of Chapter 16 of this translation. No doubt the striking bull-fight metaphor at the end of Chapter 39 was suppressed in the Valladolid codex for the same reason. With these omissions may be classed a number of minor ones—of words or phrases which to the author may have seemed too intimate or colloquial but do not seem so to us. Other words and phrases have apparently been suppressed because St. Teresa thought them redundant, whereas a later reader finds that they make a definite contribution to the sense or give explicitness and detail to what would otherwise be vague, or even obscure.[2] A few suppressions seem to have been due to pure oversight. For the omission of other passages it is diffi-

---

[2] One special case of this class is the suppression in V. of one out of two or three almost but not quite synonymous adjectives referring to the same noun.

cult to find any reason, so good are they: the conclusion of Chapter 38 and the opening of Chapter 41 are cases in point.

The numbering of the chapters, it should be noted, follows neither of the two texts, but is that traditionally employed in the printed editions. The chapter headings are also drawn up on an eclectic basis, though here the Valladolid text is generally followed.

The system I have adopted not only assures the reader that he will be reading everything that St. Teresa wrote and nothing that she did not write, but that he can discern, almost at a glance, what she meant to be read by her little group of nuns at St. Joseph's and also how she intended her work to appear in its more definitive form. Thus we can see her both as the companion and Mother and as the writer and Foundress. In both rôles she is equally the Saint.

But it should be made clear that, while incorporating in my text all important passages from the Escorial draft omitted in that of Valladolid, I have thought it no part of my task to provide a complete translation of the Escorial draft alone, and that, therefore, in order to avoid the multiplication of footnotes, I have indicated only the principal places where some expression in the later draft is not to be found in the earlier. In other words, although, by omitting the italicized portions of my text, one will be able to have as exact a translation of the Valladolid version as it is possible to get, the translation of the Escorial draft will be only approximate. This is the sole concession I have made to the ordinary reader as opposed to the student, and it is hardly conceivable, I think, that any student to whom this could matter would be unable to read the original Spanish.

One final note is necessary on the important Toledo copy, the text of which P. Silverio also prints in full. This text I have collated with that of the Valladolid autograph, from which it derives. In it both St. Teresa herself and others have made corrections and additions—more, in fact, than in any of the other copies extant. No attempt has been made here either to show what the Toledo copy omits or to include those of its corrections and additions—by far the largest number of them—which are merely verbal and unimportant, and many of which, indeed, could not be embodied in a translation at all. But the few additions which are really worth noting have been incorporated in the text (in square brackets, so as to distinguish them from the Escorial additions) and all corrections which have seemed to me of any significance will be found in footnotes.

BOOK CALLED WAY OF PERFECTION[1]

Composed by TERESA OF JESUS, *Nun of the Order of Our Lady of Carmel, addressed to the Discalced Nuns of Our Lady of Carmel of the First Rule.*[2]

General Argument of this Book
J. H. S.

This book treats of maxims and counsels which Teresa of Jesus gives to her daughters and sisters in religion, belonging to the Convents which, with the favour of Our Lord and of the glorious Virgin, Mother of God, Our Lady, she has founded according to the First Rule of Our Lady of Carmel. In particular she addresses it to the sisters of the Convent of Saint Joseph of Ávila, which was the first Convent, and of which she was Prioress when she wrote it.[3]

---

[1] With few exceptions, the footnotes to the *Way of perfection* are the translator's. Square brackets are therefore not used to distinguish them from those of P. Silverio, as elsewhere. Ordinary brackets, in the footnote translations, are placed round words inserted to complete the sense.

[2] This title, in St. Teresa's hand, appears on the first page of the Valladolid autograph (V.) which, as we have said in the Introduction, is the basis of the text here used. The Escorial autograph (E.) has the words "Treatise of the Way of Perfection" in an unknown hand, followed by the Prologue, in St. Teresa's. The Toledo copy (T.) begins with the Protestation.

[3] These lines, also in St. Teresa's hand, follow the title in the Valladolid autograph. P. Báñez added, in his own writing, the words: "I have seen this book and my opinion of it is written at the end and signed with my name." Cf. pp. 279–280, below.

PROTESTATION[1]

In all that I shall say in this Book, I submit to what is taught by Our Mother, the Holy Roman Church; if there is anything in it contrary to this, it will be without my knowledge. Therefore, for the love of Our Lord, I beg the learned men who are to revise it to look at it very carefully and to amend any faults of this nature which there may be in it and the many others which it will have of other kinds. If there is anything good in it, let this be to the glory and honour of God and in the service of His most sacred Mother, our Patroness and Lady, whose habit, though all unworthily, I wear.

[1] This Protestation, taken from T., was dictated by St. Teresa for the edition of the *Way of perfection* published at Évora in 1583 by D. Teutonio de Braganza.

THE WAY OF PERFECTION

PROLOGUE

J. H. S.

The sisters of this Convent of Saint Joseph, knowing that I
had had leave from Father Presentado Fray Domingo Bañes,[1]
of the Order of the glorious Saint Dominic, who at present is
my confessor, to write certain things about prayer, which it
seems I may be able to succeed in doing since I have had to
do with many holy and spiritual persons, have, *out of their
great love for me*, so earnestly begged me to say something to
them about this[2] that I have resolved to obey them. I realize
that the great love which they have for me may render the
imperfection and the poverty of my style in what I shall say
to them more acceptable than other books which are very
ably written by those who[3] have known what they are writing
about. I rely upon their prayers, by means of which the Lord
may be pleased to enable me to say something concerning
the way and method of life which it is fitting should be prac-

[1] The words "Fray Domingo Bañes" are crossed out, probably by
P. Báñez himself. T. has: "from the Father Master Fray Domingo
Báñez, Professor at Salamanca." Báñez was appointed to a Chair
at Salamanca University in 1577.

[2] E. continues: "that, although there are many books which treat
of this and persons with a good knowledge of what they write,
good-will seems to make certain things which are imperfect and
faulty more acceptable than others which are quite perfect; and, as
I say, their wishes and their importunity have been such as to de-
termine me to do it, for their prayers and their humility have made
me believe that it is the Lord's will to enable me to say something
profitable to them and to give me what I am to say. If I do not succeed, etc."

[3] The pronoun (*quien*) in the Spanish is singular, but in the sixteenth century it could have plural force and the context would
favour this. A manuscript note in V., however (not by P. Báñez, as
the Paris Carmelites—*Oeuvres*, V, 30—suggest), evidently takes the
reference to be to St. Gregory, for it says: "And he wrote something on Job, and the *Morals*, importuned by servants of God, and
trusting in their prayers, as he himself says."

tised in this house. If I do not succeed in doing this, Father Presentado, who will first read what I have written, will either put it right or burn it,[4] so that I shall have lost nothing by obeying these servants of God, and they will see how useless I am when His Majesty does not help me.

My intent is to suggest a few remedies for a number of small temptations which come from the devil, and which, because they are so slight, are apt to pass unnoticed. I shall also write[5] of other things, according as the Lord reveals them to me and as they come to my mind; since I do not know what I am going to say I cannot set it down in suitable order; and I think it is better for me not to do so, for it is quite unsuitable that I should be writing in this way at all. May the Lord lay His hand on all that I do so that it may be in accordance with His holy will;[6] this is always my desire, although my actions may be as imperfect as I myself am.

I know that I am[7] lacking neither in love nor in desire to do all I can to help the souls of my sisters to make great progress in the service of the Lord. It may be that this love, together with my years and the experience which I have of a number of convents, will make me more successful in writing about small matters than learned men can be. For these, being themselves strong and having other and more important occupations, do not always pay such heed to things which in themselves seem of no importance but which may do great harm to persons as weak as we women are. For the snares laid by the devil for strictly cloistered nuns are numerous and he finds that he needs new weapons if he is to do them harm. I, being a wicked woman, have defended myself but ill, and so I should like my sisters to take warning by me. I shall speak of nothing of which I have no experience, either in my own

---

[4] E.: "will burn it." T.: "the learned men who will first read what I have written will tear it up."
[5] E.: "I am thinking of suggesting a few remedies for temptations which come to nuns and of describing my motives for the foundation of this house—I mean, in the perfection which is observed here, quite independently of our Constitution. I shall also write, etc."
[6] E. omits: "holy."
[7] T.: "I hope in God that I shall be."

life or in the observation of others, *or which the Lord has not taught me in prayer.*

A few days ago I was commanded to write an account of my life in which I also dealt with certain matters concerning prayer.[8] It may be that my confessor will not wish you to see this,[9] for which reason I shall set down here some of the things which I said in that book and others which may also seem to me necessary.[10] May the Lord direct this, as I have begged Him to do, and order it for His greater glory. Amen.

[8] E.: "A few days ago I wrote an account of my life." [This phrase is generally taken as indicating that the *Way of perfection* was written immediately after the *Life.* If "wrote", in E., means "completed", we can take "a few days" literally; otherwise it must be equivalent to "a short time", as it frequently is in St. Teresa—this will in any case, be its meaning in the context of V. Cf. pp. 18–19, above.]

[9] T. adds: "so quickly", but these words are crossed out in the manuscript.

[10] E.: "As my confessor may not wish you to read this, I shall set down certain matters concerning prayer, which will be in agreement with the things I have said there, together with other things that may seem to me necessary."

CHAPTER 1

Of the reason which moved me to found this convent in such strict observance.

When this convent[1] was originally founded, for the reasons set down in the book which, as I say, I have already written, and also because of certain wonderful revelations by which the Lord showed me how well He would be served in this house, it was not my intention that there should be so much austerity in external matters, nor that it should have no regular income: on the contrary, I should have liked there to be no possibility of want. I acted, in short, like the weak and wretched woman that I am, although I did so with good intentions and not out of consideration for my own comfort.

At about this time there came to my notice the harm and havoc that were being wrought in France by these Lutherans and the way in which their unhappy sect was increasing.[2] This troubled me very much,[3] and, as though I could do anything, or be of any help in the matter, I wept before the Lord and entreated Him to remedy this great evil. I felt that I would have laid down a thousand lives to save a single one of all the souls that were being lost there. And, seeing that I was a woman, and a sinner,[4] and incapable of doing all I should like in the Lord's service, and as my whole yearning was, and still is, that, as He has so many enemies and so few friends, these last should be trusty ones, I determined to do the little that was in me—namely, to follow the evangelical counsels as perfectly as I could, and to see that these few nuns who are here should do the same, confiding in the great

[1] "Of St. Joseph's, Ávila," adds T.
[2] French Protestantism, which had been repressed during the reigns of Francis I and Henry II, increased after the latter's death in 1559, and was still doing so at the time of the foundation of St. Joseph's.
[3] T. omits: "This . . . much."
[4] *Lit.*: "and bad"—which T. omits.

goodness of God, Who never fails to help those who resolve to forsake everything for His sake. As they are all that I have ever painted them[5] as being in my desires, I hoped that their virtues would more than counteract my defects, and I should thus be able to give the Lord some pleasure, and all of us, by busying ourselves in prayer for those who are defenders of the Church, and for the preachers and learned men who defend her, should do everything we could to aid this Lord of mine Who is so much oppressed by those to whom He has shown so much good that it seems as though these traitors[6] would send Him to the Cross again and that He would have nowhere to lay His head.

Oh, my Redeemer, my heart cannot conceive this without being sorely distressed! What has become of Christians now? Must those who owe Thee most always be those who distress Thee?[7] Those to whom Thou doest the greatest kindnesses, whom Thou dost choose for Thy friends, among whom Thou dost move, communicating Thyself to them through the Sacraments? Do they not think, *Lord of my soul*, that they have made Thee endure more than sufficient torments?[8]

It is certain, my Lord, that in these days withdrawal from the world means no sacrifice at all. Since worldly people have so little respect for Thee, what can we expect them to have for us? Can it be that we deserve that they should treat us any better than they have treated Thee? Have we done more for them than Thou hast done that they[9] should be friendly to us? What then? What can we expect—we who, through the goodness of the Lord, are free from that pestilential infection, and do not, like those others, belong to the devil? They have won severe punishment at his hands[10] and their pleasures have richly earned them eternal fire. So to eternal fire they will have to go,[11] though none the less it breaks my heart to

---

[5] T.: "imagined them."
[6] T.: "as though they."
[7] E.: "Must it always be they who distress Thee most"?
[8] E. reads: "the Jews have" for "they have."
[9] E.: "that Christians."
[10] T. omits: "at his hands."
[11] *Allá se lo hayan.* "And serve them right!" would, in most con-

see so many souls travelling to perdition. I would the evil
were not so great and I did not see[12] more being lost every
day.

Oh, my sisters in Christ! Help me to entreat this of the
Lord, Who has[13] brought you together here for that very purpose. This is your vocation; this must be your business; these
must be your desires; these your tears; these your petitions.
Let us not pray for worldly things, my sisters. It makes me
laugh, and yet[14] it makes me sad, when I hear of the things
which people come here to beg us to pray to God for; we are
to ask His Majesty to give them money and to provide them
with incomes—I wish that some of these people would entreat[15] God to enable them to trample all such things beneath
their feet. Their intentions are quite good, and I do as they
ask because I see that they are really devout people, though
I do not myself believe that God ever hears me when I pray
for such things.[16] The world is on fire. Men try to condemn
Christ once again, as it were,[17] for they bring a thousand
false witnesses against Him. They would raze His Church to
the ground[18]—and are we to waste our time upon things
which, if God were to grant them, would perhaps bring one
soul less to Heaven? No, my sisters, this is no time to treat
with God for things of little importance.

Were it not necessary to consider human frailty, which
finds satisfaction in every kind of help—and it is always a

---

texts, be a more exact rendering of this colloquial phrase, but there
is no suspicion of *Schadenfreude* here.
[12] T.: "I would I did not see."
[13] E.: "Help me to entreat this, for the Lord has."
[14] T. has "Certainly" for "It makes me laugh, and yet".
[15] E.: "which people come here to commend to us, until we pray
God for their business affairs and for their lawsuits about money—
I wish that they would entreat God." In T., the words "I wish . . .
feet" are crossed out.
[16] E.: "and I commend it [i.e., their affairs] to God, so that I may
be telling the truth [i.e., when I tell them I will], but I do not myself believe that He ever hears me."
[17] T.: "Men would like, if they could, to condemn Christ once
again."
[18] In T., St. Teresa has substituted for this phrase: "His Church,
with heresies."

good thing if we can be of any help to people[19]—I should like it to be understood that it is not for things like these that God should be importuned with such anxiety.[20]

CHAPTER 2

Treats of how the necessities of the body should be disregarded and of the good that comes from poverty.

Do not think, my sisters, that because you do not go about trying to please people in the world[1] you will lack food. You will not, I assure you: never try to sustain yourselves by human artifices, or you will die of hunger, and rightly so. Keep your eyes fixed upon your Spouse: it is for Him to sustain you; and, if He is pleased with you, even those who like you least will give you food, if unwillingly, as you have found by experience. If you should do as I say and yet die of hunger, then happy are the nuns of Saint Joseph's![2] For the love of the Lord, let us not forget this: you have forgone a regular income; forgo worry about food as well, or you will lose everything. Let those whom the Lord wishes to live on an income do so: if that is their vocation,[3] they are perfectly justified; but for us to do so, sisters, would be inconsistent.

Worrying about getting money from other people seems to me like thinking about what other people enjoy. However much you worry, you will not make them change their minds nor will they become desirous of giving you alms. Leave these anxieties to Him Who can move everyone,[4] Who is the Lord

19 E. omits the words in parenthesis.
20 E. reads: "importuned at Saint Joseph's."
1 E.: "that for this reason."
2 E. adds: "I tell you here that your prayers will be accepted and we shall do something of what we are trying to do."
3 In T.: "vocation" is altered to "office", but not in St. Teresa's hand.
4 T.: "can move us all."

of all money and of all who possess money. It is by His command that we have come here and His words are true—they cannot fail: Heaven and earth will fail first.[5] Let us not fail Him, and let us have no fear that He will fail us; if He should ever do so it will be for our greater good, just as the saints failed to keep their lives[6] when they were slain for the Lord's sake, and their bliss was increased through their martyrdom. We should be making a good exchange if we could have done with this life quickly and enjoy everlasting satiety.

Remember, sisters, that this will be important when I am dead; and that is why I am leaving it to you in writing. For, *with God's help*, as long as I live, I will remind you of it myself, as I know by experience what a great help it will be to you. It is when I possess least that I have the fewest worries and the Lord knows that, as far as I can tell, I am more afflicted when there is excess of anything than when there is lack of it;[7] I am not sure if that is the Lord's doing, but I have noticed that He provides for us immediately. To act otherwise would be to deceive the world by pretending to be poor when we are not poor in spirit but only outwardly.[8] My conscience would give me a bad time. It seems to me it would be like stealing what was being given us, as one might say; for I should feel[9] as if we were rich people asking alms: please God this may never be so. Those who worry too much about the alms that they are likely to be given[10] will find that sooner or later this bad habit will lead them to go and ask for something which they do not need, and perhaps from someone who needs it more than they do. Such a person[11] would gain rather than lose by giving it us but we should certainly be the worse off for having it. God forbid this should ever happen, my daughters; if it were likely to do so, I should prefer you to have a regular income.

[5] An apparent reference to St. Mark xiii, 31.
[6] E. ends the sentence: "and they cut off their heads, in order to give them more and to make them martyrs."
[7] E.: "when they give us more than when there is nothing."
[8] T. ends this sentence at "spirit".
[9] E.: "for it would be."
[10] E. adds parenthetically: "I mean, if anyone did so."
[11] T.: "Those who give it."

I beg you, for the love of God, just as if I were begging alms for you, never to allow this to occupy your thoughts. If the very least of you ever hears of such a thing happening in this house, cry out about it to His Majesty and speak to your Superior. Tell her humbly that she is doing wrong; this is so serious a matter that it may cause true poverty gradually to disappear. I hope in the Lord that this will not be so and that He will not forsake His servants; and for that reason, if for no other, what you have told me to write may be useful to you as a reminder.[12]

My daughters must believe that it is for their own good that the Lord has enabled me to realize in some small degree[13] what blessings are to be found in holy poverty.[14] Those of them who practise it will also realize this, though perhaps not as clearly as I do;[15] for, although I had professed poverty, I was not only without poverty of spirit, but my spirit was devoid of all restraint. Poverty is good and contains within itself all the good things in the world.[16] It is a great domain—I mean that he who cares nothing for the good things of the world has dominion over them all.[17] What do kings and lords matter to me if I have no desire to possess their money, or to please them, if by so doing I should cause the least displeasure to God? And what do their honours mean to

---

[12] E. reads: "and for that reason, as I have been told to write this, the advice of this miserable sinner may be useful as a reminder." In T. all this paragraph, except the words "Never allow this to occupy your thoughts," is crossed out.

[13] T. omits: "in some small degree."

[14] E. has: "in poverty of spirit", and continues: "and you, if you give heed to it, will understand it, though not as clearly as I do."

[15] E. continues: "for my spirit had been devoid of all restraint, and not poor, though I had made the profession of being so." In T., St. Teresa has crossed out the words: "for although . . . restraint" and substituted: "for I have proved the contrary."

[16] E. adds: "and, I believe, much of what good there is in all the virtues. I do not affirm this, for I do not know the worth of each, and I shall not speak of what I think I do not properly understand: still, I am sure it embraces many virtues."

[17] E. adds: "and if I were to say that he has dominion over them all I should not be lying."

me if I have realized that the chief honour of a poor man consists in his being truly poor?[18]

For my own part, I believe that honour and money nearly always go together, and that he who desires honour never hates money, while he who hates money cares little for honour. Understand this clearly, for I think this concern about honour always implies some *slight* regard for endowments or money:[19] seldom *or never* is a poor man honoured by the world; however worthy of honour he may be, he is apt rather to be despised by it. With true poverty there goes a different kind of honour to[20] which nobody can take objection. I mean that, if poverty is embraced for God's sake alone, no one has to be pleased save God. It is certain that a man who has no need of anyone has many friends: in my own experience I have found this to be very true.

A great deal has been written about this virtue which I cannot understand, still less express,[21] and I should only be making things worse if I were to eulogize it, so I will say no more about it now. I have only spoken of what I have myself experienced and I confess that I have been so much absorbed that until now I have hardly[22] realized what I have been writing. However, it has been said now. Our arms are holy poverty, which was so greatly esteemed and so strictly observed by our holy Fathers at the beginning of the foundation of[23] our Order. (Someone who knows[24] about this tells me that they never kept anything from one day to the next.)

---

[18] E. omits this sentence, after varying the preceding one slightly, and continues: "We shall spoil everything; for I believe for my own part that, etc."

[19] T. omits: "for . . . money."

[20] T. reads *honra* (honour: cf. Vol. I, p. 14, n. 2 above) for *honraza*, translated above as "different kind of honour".

[21] E. omits from "and I should . . ." to "experienced and". T. reads, after "this virtue": "and I do not know why I speak of it, for I cannot understand it" and omits following words down to "experienced and".

[22] E. continues: "realized how foolish I was being to speak of it: now that I have realized this, I shall be silent. But, as it has been said, let it remain said if it is said well. However, etc."

[23] E. omits: "the foundation of."

[24] E.: "who has read."

For the love of the Lord, then, [I beg you] now that the rule of poverty is less perfectly observed as regards outward things, let us strive to observe it inwardly. Our life lasts only for a couple of hours; our reward is boundless; and, if there were no reward but to follow the counsels given us by the Lord,[25] to imitate His Majesty in any degree would bring us a great recompense.

These arms must appear on our banners and at all costs we must keep this rule—as regards our house, our clothes, our speech, and (which is much more important) our thoughts. So long as this is done, there need be no fear, with the help of God, that[26] religious observances in this house will decline, for, as Saint Clare said, the walls of poverty are very strong. It was with these walls, she said, and with those of humility,[27] that she wished to surround her convents;[28] and assuredly, if the rule of poverty is truly kept, both chastity and all the other virtues are fortified much better than by the most sumptuous edifices. Have a care to this, for the love of God; and this I beg of you by His blood. If I may say what my conscience bids me, I should wish that, on the day when you build such edifices, they[29] may fall down *and kill you all*.[30]

It seems very wrong, my daughters, that great houses should be built with the money of the poor; may God forbid that this should be done; let our houses be small and poor in every way.[31] Let us to some extent resemble our King, Who had no house save the porch in Bethlehem where He was born and the Cross on which He died. These were houses where little comfort could be found.[32] Those who erect large houses will no doubt have good reasons for doing so. *I do*

25 E. ends this paragraph by adding: "it would be a great one."

26 T. reads: "So long as we do this, I hope in God that."

27 E. omits: "and with those of humility."

28 E.: "her convent."

29 In the Spanish the subject is in the singular: P. Báñez inserted "the house", but crossed this out later.

30 E. further adds: "I say this with a good conscience and I shall entreat it of God." As will be observed, she softens the expression greatly in V.

31 T.: "let us be poor in every way and let our house be small."

32 E. omits: "and the Cross . . . found."

not utterly condemn them: they are moved by various holy[33] intentions. But any corner is sufficient for thirteen poor women.[34] If grounds should be thought necessary, on account of the strictness of the enclosure, and also as an aid to prayer and devotion, *and because our miserable nature needs such things*, well and good; and let there be a few hermitages[35] in them in which the sisters may go to pray.[36] But as for a large ornate convent, with a lot of buildings—God preserve us from that![37] Always remember that these things will all fall down on the Day of Judgment, and who knows how soon that will be?[38]

It would hardly look well if the house of thirteen[39] poor women made a great noise when it fell, for those who are really poor must make no noise:[40] unless they[41] live a noiseless life people will never take pity on them. And how happy my sisters will be if they see someone freed from hell by means of the alms which he has given them; and this is quite possible, since they are strictly bound to offer continual prayer for persons who[42] give them food. It is also God's will that, although the food comes from Him,[43] we should thank the persons by whose means He gives it to us:[44] let there be no neglect of this.

I do not remember what I had begun to say, for I have strayed from my subject. But I think this must have been the Lord's will, for I never intended to write what I have said

[33] E. omits: "holy."
[34] T.: "for one [*fem.*] who is truly poor."
[35] St. Teresa liked to have hermitages in the grounds of her convents to give the nuns opportunity for solitude.
[36] E. abbreviates verbally.
[37] T., less dramatically: "But God preserve us from a large, etc."
[38] T.: "and we do not know if that will be soon."
[39] E.: "of twelve."
[40] E.: "for the poor never make a noise."
[41] E.: "unless the really poor."
[42] The MS. has: "for they are strictly bound, continually, since they". This has been corrected by P. García de Toledo to read as translated above. E. reads as in the text above except that it has "for *the souls of* persons."
[43] E.: "although it is He Who gives it to us."
[44] E.: "we should pray for those who give it to us on His behalf."

here.[45] May His Majesty always keep us in His hand so that we may never fall. Amen.

CHAPTER 3

Continues the subject begun in the first chapter and persuades the sisters to busy themselves constantly in beseeching God to help those who work for the Church. Ends with an exclamatory prayer.

Let us now return to the principal reason for which the Lord has brought us together in this house, for which reason I am most desirous that we may be able to please His Majesty. Seeing how great are the evils of the present day and how no human strength will suffice to quench the fire kindled by these heretics[1] (though attempts have been made to organize opposition to them, as though such a great and rapidly spreading evil could be remedied by force of arms),[2] it seems to me that it is like a war in which the enemy has overrun the whole country, and the Lord of the country, hard pressed, retires into a city, which he causes to be well fortified, and whence from time to time he is able to attack. Those who are in the city[3] are picked men who can do more by themselves than they could do with the aid of many soldiers if they were cowards. Often this method gains the victory; or, if the garrison does not conquer, it is at least not conquered; for, as it contains no traitors, *but picked men*, it can be reduced only by hunger.[4] In our own conflict, however, we cannot be forced to surrender by hunger; we can die but we cannot be conquered.

45 E.: "to write this."
1 E.: "to quench this fire."
2 T. omits the parenthetical clause and continues: "which is spreading so much, it seems to me like a war, etc."
3 E. has "in the castle" here, but "city" just above.
4 T. adds: "This hunger may be sufficient to kill them, but it will not lead them to be conquered."

Now why have I said this? So that you may understand, my sisters, that what we have to ask of God is that, in this little castle of ours, inhabited as it is by good Christians,[5] none of us may go over to the enemy. We must ask God, too, to make the captains in this castle or city—that is, the preachers and theologians—highly proficient in the way of the Lord. And as most of these are religious, we must pray that they may advance in perfection,[6] and in the fulfilment of their vocation, for this is very needful. For, as I have already said, it is the ecclesiastical and not the secular arm which must defend us. And as we can do nothing by either of these means to help our King, let us strive to live in such a way that our prayers may be of avail to help these servants of God, who, at the cost of so much toil, have fortified themselves with learning and virtuous living and have laboured to help the Lord.[7]

You may ask why I emphasize this[8] so much and why I say we must help people who are better than ourselves. I will tell you, for I am not sure if you properly understand as yet how much we owe to the Lord for bringing us to a place where we are so free from business matters, occasions of sin and the society of worldly people. This is a very great favour and one which is not granted to the persons of whom I have been speaking, nor is it fitting that it should be granted to them; it would be less so now, indeed, than at any other time, for it is they who must strengthen the weak[9] and give courage to God's little ones. A fine thing it would be for soldiers if they lost their captains! These preachers and theologians have to live among men and associate with men and stay in palaces and sometimes even behave as people in palaces do[10] in out-

[5] E. continues, after "Christians": "no traitor may rise up, but God may have [us] all in His hands, and also that the captains in this castle or city—that is, the preachers and theologians—may be highly proficient, etc."
[6] T.: "in religion."
[7] E.: "and labours."
[8] E.: "why I charge this."
[9] E.: "strengthen people."
[10] This is the reading of E. V.: "as they do."

ward matters. Do you think, my daughters, that it is an easy matter to have to do business with the world, to live in the world, to engage in the affairs of the world, and, as I have said, to live as worldly men do, and yet inwardly to be strangers to the world, and enemies of the world, like persons who are in exile—to be, in short, not men but angels? Yet unless these persons act thus, they neither deserve to bear the title of captain nor to be allowed by the Lord to leave their cells, for they would do more harm than good. This is no time for imperfections in those whose duty it is to teach.

And if these teachers are not inwardly fortified by realizing the great[11] importance of spurning everything beneath their feet and by being detached from things which come to an end on earth, and attached to things eternal, they will betray this defect in themselves, however much they may try to hide it.[12] For with whom are they dealing but with the world?[13] They need not fear: the world will not pardon them or fail to observe their imperfections. Of the good things they do many will pass unnoticed, or will even not be considered good at all;[14] but they need not fear that any evil or imperfect thing they do will be overlooked. I am amazed when I wonder from whom they learned about perfection, when, instead of practising it themselves (for they think they have no obligation to do that and have done quite enough by a reasonable observance of the Commandments),[15] they condemn others, and at times mistake virtue for indulgence. Do not think, then, that they need but little Divine favour in this great battle upon which they have entered; on the contrary, they need a great deal.

I beg you to try to live in such a way as to be worthy to obtain two things from God. First, that there may be many of these very learned and religious men who have the qualifications for their task which I have described; and that the Lord may prepare those who are not completely prepared al-

---

11 E. omits: "great."
12 E.: "however much they do."
13 T. continues: "which never fails to observe their imperfections."
14 E.: "or will even be considered bad."
15 E. adds: "as if they had not the obligation to please God."

ready *and who lack anything*, for a single one who is perfect will do more than many who are not.[16] Secondly, that after they have entered upon this struggle, which, as I say, is not light, *but a very heavy one*, the Lord may have them in His hand so that they may be delivered from all the dangers[17] that are in the world, and, while sailing on this perilous sea, may shut their ears to the song of the sirens. If we can prevail with God in the smallest degree about this, we shall be fighting His battle even while living a cloistered life and I shall consider as well spent all the trouble to which I have gone in founding this retreat,[18] where I have also tried to ensure that this Rule of Our Lady and Empress shall be kept in its original perfection.[19]

Do not think that offering this petition continually[20] is useless. Some people think it a hardship not to be praying all the time for their own souls. Yet what better prayer could there be than this?[21] You may be worried because you think it will do nothing to lessen your pains in Purgatory, but actually praying in this way will relieve you of some of them and anything else that is left—well, let it remain. After all, what does it matter if I am in Purgatory until the Day of Judgment provided a single soul should be saved[22] through my prayer? And how much less does it matter if many souls profit by it and the Lord is honoured! Make no account of any pain which has an end if by means of it any greater service can be rendered to Him Who bore such pains for us. Always try to find out wherein lies the greatest perfection.[23] And for the

[16] E.: "than many imperfect."
[17] E.: "from the dangers."
[18] *Lit.*: "making this corner." The reference is to St. Joseph's, Ávila.
[19] E.: "shall be kept as it began." "And Empress" is not found in E.
[20] E.: "always."
[21] E. continues: "If you think it is necessary for the lessening of the pains which you will have to suffer in Purgatory for your sins, praying so righteously does in fact lessen them, and what is left will have to remain."
[22] E.: "is saved."
[23] E. continues: "You must always treat [i.e., about spiritual matters] with learned men: I shall often ask you (to do this) and give you my reasons, for you must have reasons given you. What I now beg

love of the Lord I beg you to beseech His Majesty to hear us in this; I, miserable creature though I am, beseech this of His Majesty, since it is for His glory and the good of His Church, which are my only wishes.

It seems over-bold of me to think that I can do anything towards obtaining this. But I have confidence, my Lord, in these servants of Thine who are here, knowing that they neither desire nor strive after anything but to please Thee. For Thy sake they have left the little they possessed, wishing they had more so that they might serve Thee with it. Since Thou, my Creator, art not ungrateful, I do not think Thou wilt fail to do what they beseech of Thee,[24] for when Thou wert in the world, Lord,[25] Thou didst not despise women, but didst always help them and show them great compassion.[26] *Thou didst find more faith and no less love in them than in men, and one of them was Thy most sacred Mother, from whose merits we derive merit, and whose habit we wear, though our sins make us unworthy to do so.[27] We can do nothing in public that is of any use to Thee, nor dare we speak of some of the truths over which we weep in secret, lest Thou shouldst not hear this our just petition.* Yet, Lord, I cannot believe this of Thy goodness and righteousness, for Thou art a righteous Judge, not like judges in the world, who, being, after all, men and sons of Adam, refuse to consider any woman's virtue as above suspicion. Yes, my King, but the day will come when all will be known. I am not speaking on my own account, for the whole world is already aware of my wickedness, and I am glad that it should become known; but, when I see what the times are like, I feel it is not right to

---

you to do is to beseech God (about this), and I, miserable creature, etc."

24 E.: "Thou wilt give less than they beseech of Thee, but rather much more."

25 E.: "Lord of my soul."

26 The italicized lines which follow, and are in the nature of a digression, do not appear in V., and in E. they have been crossed out.

27 Here follow two erased lines which are illegible but for the words "Thou didst honour the world". The exact sense of the following words ("We can . . . in secret") is affected by these illegible lines and must be considered uncertain.

*repel spirits which are virtuous and brave, even though they
be the spirits of women.*

Hear us not when we ask Thee for honours, endowments,[28]
money, or anything that has to do with the world; but why
shouldst Thou not hear us, Eternal Father, when we ask only
for the honour of Thy Son, when we would forfeit a thousand
honours and a thousand lives for Thy sake? Not for ourselves,
Lord, for we do not deserve to be heard, but for the blood of
Thy Son and for His merits.

Oh, Eternal Father![29] Surely all these scourgings and insults and grievous tortures will not be forgotten. How, then,
my Creator, can a heart so [merciful and] loving as Thine
endure that an act which was performed by Thy Son in order
to please Thee the more (for He loved Thee most deeply and
Thou didst command Him to love us) should be treated as
lightly as those heretics treat the Most Holy Sacrament to-
day, in taking it from its resting-place when they destroy the
churches? Could it be that [Thy Son and our Redeemer][30]
had failed to do something to please Thee? No: He fulfilled
everything. Was it not enough, Eternal Father, that while He
lived He had no place to lay His head and had always to endure so many trials? Must they now deprive Him of the
places[31] to which He can invite His friends,[32] seeing how
weak we are and knowing[33] that those who have to labour
need such food to sustain them? Had He not already more
than sufficiently paid for the sin of Adam? Has this most
loving Lamb to pay once more whenever we relapse into sin?
Permit it not, my Emperor; let Thy Majesty be appeased;
look not upon our sins but upon our redemption by Thy Most

---

28 E. omits this word.
29 T.: "Oh, our Lord!"
30 V.: "that He." T. has "He left everything fulfilled" for "He fulfilled everything".
31 *Lit.*: "of those." P. Báñez wrote in the margin "of the mansions"
using the word which is thus translated in the titles of the seven
main divisions of the *Interior Castle*. T. has: "of the houses."
32 "And give them the precious food of His Body and Blood," adds
T.
33 T.: "which He wishes to give us because He sees how weak we are
and knows."

Sacred Son, upon His merits and upon those of His glorious Mother and of all the saints and martyrs who have died for Thee.

Alas, Lord, who is it that has dared to make this petition in the name of all? What a poor mediator am I, my daughters, to gain a hearing for you and to present your petition! When this Sovereign Judge sees how bold I am it may well move Him to anger, as would be both right and just. But behold, Lord, Thou art a God of mercy; have mercy upon this poor sinner, this miserable worm who is so bold with Thee. Behold my desires, my God, and the tears with which I beg this of Thee; forget my deeds, for Thy name's sake, and have pity upon all these souls who are being lost, and help Thy Church. Do not permit more harm to be wrought to Christendom, Lord; give light to this darkness.

For the love of the Lord, my sisters, I beg you[34] to commend this poor sinner[35] to His Majesty and to beseech Him to give her humility, as you are bound to do.[36] I do not charge you to pray particularly for kings and prelates of the Church, especially for our Bishop,[37] for I know that those of you now here are very careful about this and so I think it is needless for me to say more. Let those who are to come remember that, if they have a prelate who is holy, those under him will be holy too, and let them realize how important it is to bring him continually before the Lord. If your prayers and desires and disciplines and fasts are not performed for the intentions of which I have spoken, reflect [and believe] that you are not carrying out the work or fulfilling the object[38] for which the Lord has brought you here.

---

34 E.: "I beg all."
35 Lit.: "poor little one." E.: "poor little daring one."
36 E. omits the next two sentences and continues: "And if your prayers . . ."
37 Don Álvaro de Mendoza, then Bishop of Ávila. T. adds: "and for this Order of the most sacred Virgin and the other (Orders)." But this interpolation breaks the sense.
38 E. ends: ". . . the object for which you came together here, and may the Lord never allow this to depart from your memory, for His Majesty's own sake."

CHAPTER 4

Exhorts the nuns to keep their Rule and names three things which are important for the spiritual life. Describes the first of these three things, which is love of one's neighbour, and speaks of the harm which can be done by individual friendships.

Now, daughters, you have looked at the great enterprise which we are trying to carry out. What kind of persons shall we have to be if we are not to be considered over-bold in the eyes of God and of the world?[1] It is clear that we need to labour hard and it will be a great help to us if we have sublime thoughts so that we may strive to make our actions sublime also. If we endeavour to observe our Rule and Constitutions in the fullest sense, and with great care, I hope in the Lord that He will grant our requests.[2] I am not asking anything new of you, my daughters—only that we should hold to our profession, which, as it is our vocation, we are bound to do, although there are many ways of holding to it.

Our Primitive Rule[3] tells us to pray without ceasing. Provided we do this with all possible care (and it is the most important thing of all) we shall not fail to observe the fasts, disciplines and periods of silence which the Order commands; for, as you know, if prayer is to be genuine it must be reinforced with these things—prayer cannot be accompanied by self-indulgence.

[1] E. begins: "Now you have looked at the great enterprise which you are going to carry out for the sake of your Superior and your Bishop (for he is your Superior), and for that of the Order, as is to be understood from what has been said, for all is for the good of the Church, and this is of obligation. Well, as I say, when a person has had the boldness to carry out such an enterprise, what kind of person will she have to be if she is not to be considered over-bold in the eyes of God and of the world?"

[2] T.: "our prayers."

[3] E.: "The beginning of our Rule."

It is about prayer that you have asked me to say something to you. As an acknowledgment of what I shall say, I beg you to read frequently and with a good will what I have said about it thus far, and to put this into practice. Before speaking of the interior life—that is, of prayer—I shall speak of certain things which those who attempt to walk along the way of prayer[4] must of necessity practise. So necessary are these that, even though not greatly given to contemplation, people who have them can advance a long way in the Lord's service, while, unless they have them, they cannot possibly be great contemplatives, and, if they think they are, they are much mistaken. May the Lord help me in this task and teach me[5] what I must say, so that it may be to His glory. Amen.

Do not suppose, my friends and sisters,[6] that I am going to charge you to do a great many things; may it please the Lord that[7] we do the things which our holy Fathers ordained and practised and by doing which they merited that name.[8] It would be wrong of us to look for any other way or to learn from anyone else. There are only three things which I will explain at some length and which are taken from our Constitution itself. It is essential that we should understand how very important they are to us in helping us to preserve that peace, both inward and outward, which the Lord so earnestly recommended to us. One of these is love for each other; the second, detachment from all created things; the third, true humility, which, although I put it last, is the most important of the three and embraces all the rest.[9]

---

4 E.: "to practise prayer."
5 E.: "and tell me."
6 T.: "my sisters."
7 In T. St. Teresa has substituted for this: "I only desire that."
8 E.: "the things which our Fathers duly ordained in the Rule and Constitutions, through which virtue is altogether fulfilled." It omits the following sentence ("It would . . . else.")
9 Here, in both E. and V., the chapter ends; but T. has a marginal note in St. Teresa's hand: "There should not be a new chapter here." All the editions have observed this injunction. The heading to this chapter given above comprises those prefixed in V. to Chapters 4 and 5.

With regard to the first—namely, love for each other[10]—this is of very great importance; for there is nothing, however annoying, that cannot easily[11] be borne by those who love each other, and anything which causes annoyance must be quite exceptional. If this commandment were kept in the world, as it should be, I believe it would take us a long way towards the keeping of the rest; but, what with having too much love for each other or too little, we never manage to keep it perfectly. It may seem that for us to have too much love for each other cannot be wrong, but I do not think anyone who had not been an eye-witness of it[12] would believe how much evil and how many imperfections can result from this. The devil sets many snares here which the consciences of those who aim only in a rough-and-ready way at pleasing God seldom observe—indeed, they think they are acting virtuously—but those who are aiming at perfection understand what they are very well: little by little they deprive the will of the strength which it needs if it is to employ itself wholly in the love of God.

This is even more applicable to women than to men and the harm which it does to community life is very serious. One result of it is that all the nuns do not love each other equally: some injury done to a friend is resented; a nun desires to have something to give to her friend or tries to make time for talking to her, and often her object in doing this is to tell her how fond she is of her, and other irrelevant things,[13] rather than how much she loves God. These intimate friendships are seldom calculated[14] to make for the love of God; I am more inclined to believe that the devil initiates them so as to create factions within religious Orders.[15] When a

[10] E.: "namely, great love."
[11] E.: "quickly."
[12] T. adds: "as I have elsewhere." But this reads awkwardly in the Spanish and it is not found in the Évora edition.
[13] E. omits: "and other irrelevant things."
[14] *Lit.*: "are seldom ordered in such a way as."
[15] E.: "These intimate friendships are never ordered by the devil for the greater service of the Lord, but for the creation of factions within religious Orders."

friendship has for its object the service of His Majesty,[16] it at once becomes clear that the will is devoid of passion and indeed is helping to conquer other passions.

Where a convent is large I should like to see many friendships of that type; but in this house, where there are not, and can never be, more than thirteen nuns,[17] all must be friends with each other, love each other, be fond of each other and help each other. For the love of the Lord, refrain from making individual friendships, however holy, for even among brothers and sisters such things are apt to be poisonous and I can see no advantage in them;[18] when they are between other relatives,[19] they are much more dangerous and become a pest. Believe me, sisters, though I may seem to you extreme in this, great perfection and great peace come of doing what I say and many occasions of sin may be avoided by those who are not very strong. If our will becomes inclined more to one person than to another (this cannot be helped, because it is natural—it often leads us to love[20] the person who has the most faults if she is the most richly endowed by nature), we must exercise a firm restraint on ourselves and not allow ourselves to be conquered by our affection. Let us love the virtues and inward goodness, and let us always apply ourselves and take care to avoid attaching importance to externals.[21]

Let us not allow our will to be the slave of any, sisters, save of Him Who bought it with His blood. Otherwise, before we know where we are, we shall find ourselves trapped, and unable to move. God help me![22] The puerilities which

[16] E.: "its object to help us to serve Him."

[17] E.: "of that type. In Saint Joseph's, where there are not, and can never be, more than thirteen nuns, (there must be) none of them. All, etc." T.: "in this house, where there are few (of us), all, etc."

[18] "Consider the case of Joseph," adds E., parenthetically: the reference is presumably to the treatment of Joseph by his brothers, recorded in Genesis xxxvii.

[19] "Other" is not in the Spanish. "When they are only between", is the reading of T., which also omits: "and become a pest."

[20] T.: "because our nature often leads us to love."

[21] T. omits: "apply ourselves and" and ends: "to be successful in not attaching importance to externals."

[22] E. omits: "God help me!" and continues: "The puerilities which

result from this are innumerable. And, because they are so trivial that only those who see how bad they are will realize and believe it, there is no point in speaking of them here except to say that they are wrong in anyone, and, in a prioress, pestilential.

In checking these preferences[23] we must be strictly on the alert from the moment that such a friendship begins[24] and we must proceed diligently and lovingly rather than severely. One effective precaution against this is that the sisters should not be together except at the prescribed hours, and that they should follow our present custom in not talking with one another, or being alone together, as is laid down in the Rule:[25] each one should be alone in her cell. There must be no workroom at Saint Joseph's;[26] for, although it is a praiseworthy custom to have one, it is easier to keep silence if one is alone,[27] and getting used to solitude is a great help to prayer. Since prayer must be the foundation on which this house is built, it is necessary for us to learn to like whatever gives us the greatest help in it.

Returning to the question of our love for one another, it

---

result from this are, I think, innumerable. Lest those who know nothing about women's weaknesses should learn about them and come to realize (how bad they are), I will not describe them in detail. But it used sometimes really to amaze me to see them; for, by the goodness of God, and perhaps because I was so much worse in other respects, I never had many attachments of this kind. But, as I say, I often observed them in others, and I am afraid they exist in the majority of religious houses, for I have seen them in some, and I know that, wherever they occur, they are the worst thing for strict religious observance and perfection, and in a prioress they would be pestilential. This has already been said."

[23] T.: "In putting from us these private (affections)."

[24] E.: "But in removing these preferences, we must be on the alert from the moment that we become aware of them."

[25] E.: "in our Constitution."

[26] E. adds: "to bring them together."

[27] E. continues: "and solitude is a great thing when one has got used to it, and it is a great blessing for persons given to prayer to get used to it. Since prayer must be the foundation on which this house is built, and it is for this purpose that we have come together, we must learn, more than anything else, to like whatever gives us the greatest profit in it."

seems quite unnecessary to commend this to you, for where are there people so brutish as not to love one another when they live together, are continually in one another's company,[28] indulge in no conversation, association or recreation with any outside their house and believe that God loves us and that they themselves love God since they are leaving everything for His Majesty? More especially is this so as virtue always attracts love, and I hope in God that, with the help of His Majesty, there will always be love in the sisters of this house. It seems to me, therefore, that there is no reason for me to commend this to you any further.

With regard to the nature of this mutual love and what is meant by the virtuous love which I wish you to have here, and how we shall know when we have this virtue, which is a very great one, since Our Lord[29] has so strongly commended it to us and so straitly enjoined it upon His Apostles—about all this I should like to say a little now as well as my lack of skill will allow me; if you find this explained in great detail in other books, take no notice of what I am saying here, for it may be that I do not understand what I am talking about.[30]

There are two kinds of love which I am describing.[31] The one is *purely* spiritual, and apparently has nothing to do with sensuality or the tenderness of our nature, either of which might stain its purity.[32] The other is also spiritual, but mingled with it are our sensuality and weakness;[33] yet it is a worthy love, which, as between relatives and friends, seems lawful. Of this I have already said sufficient.

It is of the first kind of spiritual love that I would now speak. It is untainted by any sort of passion, for such a thing would completely spoil its harmony. If it leads us to treat

28 T.: "for I think people will love one another if they are together in one company."
29 E.: "this exceeding great virtue, for it is a very great one, since Christ, our Master and Lord, etc."
30 E. adds: "unless the Lord gives me light."
31 E.: "which I now want to describe."
32 T. has "its charity." E. omits: "either of which might stain its purity."
33 Here begins the passage reproduced in the Appendix to Chapter 4 (pp. 60-1, below).

virtuous people, especially confessors, with moderation and discretion, it is profitable; but, if the confessor is seen to be tending in any way towards vanity, he should be regarded with grave suspicion, and, in such a case, conversation with him, however edifying, should be avoided, and the sister should make her confession briefly and say nothing more. It would be best for her, indeed, to tell the superior that she does not get on with him and go elsewhere; this is the safest way, providing it can be done without injuring his reputation.[34]

In such cases, and in other difficulties with which the devil might ensnare us, so that we have no idea where to turn, the safest thing will be for the sister to try to speak with some learned person; if necessary, permission to do this can be given her, and she can make her confession to him and act in the matter as he directs her. For he cannot fail to give her some good advice about it, without which she might go very far astray. How often people stray through not taking advice, especially when there is a risk of doing someone harm! The course that must on no account be followed is to do nothing at all; for, when the devil begins to make trouble in this way, he will do a great deal of harm if he is not stopped quickly; the plan I have suggested, then, of trying to consult another confessor is the safest one if it is practicable, and I hope in the Lord that it will be so.[35]

Reflect upon the great importance of this, for it is a dangerous matter, and can be a veritable hell, and a source of harm to everyone. I advise you not to wait until a great deal of harm has been done but to take every possible step that you can think of and stop the trouble at the outset;[36] this you may do with a good conscience. But I hope in the Lord that He will not allow persons who are to spend their lives in prayer[37] to have any attachment save to one who is a great servant of God;[38] and I am quite certain He will not, unless

---

[34] *Honra.* Cf. Vol. I, p. 14, n. 2, above.
[35] "And . . . be so" is crossed out in T.
[36] E. is more emphatic: "at the very outset" (*muy al principio*).
[37] E.: "to spend so much time in prayer."
[38] E.: "who has a great attachment to God and is very virtuous."

they have no love for prayer and for striving after perfection in the way we try to do here. For, unless they see that he understands their language and likes to speak to them of God,[39] they cannot possibly love him, as he is not like them. If he is such a person, he will have very few opportunities of doing any harm, and, unless he is very simple,[40] he will not seek to disturb his own peace of mind and that of the servants of God.[41]

As I have begun to speak about this, I will repeat that the devil can do a great deal of harm here,[42] which will long remain undiscovered, and thus the soul that is striving after perfection can be gradually ruined[43] without knowing how.[44] For, if a confessor gives occasion for vanity through being vain himself, he will be very tolerant with it in [the consciences of] others. May God, for His Majesty's own sake, deliver us from things of this kind. It would be enough to unsettle all the nuns[45] if their consciences and their confessor[46] should give them exactly opposite advice; and, if it is insisted that they must have one confessor only, they will not know what to do, nor how to pacify their minds, since the very person who should be calming them and helping them is the source of the harm. In some places there must be a great deal of trouble of this kind: I always feel very sorry about it and so you must not be surprised if I attach great importance to your understanding this danger.[47]

---

39 E.: "no love for prayer. For if they have such love and see that he does not understand their language or like to speak to them of God."
40 E.: "exceedingly simple."
41 E. adds: "(in a place) where their desires can have so little satisfaction, or even none at all."
42 E.: "can do the very greatest harm in convents so strictly enclosed."
43 E.: "is gradually ruined."
44 E.: "how or by what means."
45 E.: "It is enough to unsettle all the sisters."
46 T. omits: "and their confessor."
47 The last sentence in E. is more definite and personal: "I have seen much trouble of this kind in religious houses, though not in my own, and these cases have moved me to great compassion." T. ends: "if I take great care about some of these things."

APPENDIX TO CHAPTER 4

The following variant reading of the Escorial Manuscript seems too important to be relegated to a footnote. It occurs at p. 57 (cf. n. 33), and deals, as will be seen, with the qualifications and character of the confessor. Many editors substitute it in their text for the corresponding passage in V. As will be seen, however, by comparing it with pp. 57–58, it is not a pure addition; we therefore reproduce it separately.

The important thing is that these two kinds of mutual love should be untainted by any sort of passion, for such a thing would completely spoil this harmony. If we exercise this love, of which I have spoken, with moderation and discretion, it is wholly meritorious, because what seems to us sensuality is turned into virtue. But the two may be so closely intertwined with one another that it is sometimes impossible to distinguish them, especially where a confessor is concerned. For if persons who are practising prayer find that their confessor is a holy man and understands the way they behave, they become greatly attached to him. And then forthwith the devil lets loose upon them a whole battery of scruples which produce a terrible disturbance within the soul, this being what he is aiming at. In particular, if the confessor is guiding such persons to greater perfection, they become so depressed that they will go so far as to leave him for another and yet another, only to be tormented by the same temptation every time.

What you can do here is not to let your minds dwell upon whether you like your confessor or not, but just to like him if you feel so inclined. For, if we grow fond of people who are kind to our bodies, why should we not love those who are always striving and toiling to help our souls? Actually, if my confessor is a holy and spiritual man and I see that he is taking great pains for the benefit of my soul, I think it will be a real help to my progress for me to like him. For so weak are we that such affection sometimes helps us a great deal to undertake very great things in God's service.

But, if your confessor is not such a person as I have described, there is a possibility of danger, and for him to know that you like him may do the greatest harm, most of all in houses where the nuns are very strictly enclosed. And as it is a difficult thing to get to know which confessors are good, great care and caution are necessary. The best advice to give would be that you should see he has no idea of your affection for him and is not told about it. But the devil is so active that this is not practicable: you feel as if this is the only thing you have to confess and imagine you are obliged to confess it. For this reason I should like you to think that your affection for him is of no importance and to take no more notice of it.

Follow this advice if you find that everything your confessor says to you profits your soul; if you neither see nor hear him indulge in any vanity (and such things are always noticed except by one who is wilfully dull) and if you know him to be a God-fearing man, do not be distressed over any temptation about being too fond of him, and the devil will then grow tired and stop tempting you. But if you notice that the confessor is tending in any way towards vanity in what he says to you, you should regard him with grave suspicion; in such a case conversation with him, even about prayer and about God, should be avoided—the sister should make her confession briefly and say nothing more. It would be best for her to tell the Mother (Superior) that she does not get on with him and go elsewhere. This is the safest way if it is practicable, and I hope in God that it will be, and that you will do all you possibly can to have no relations with him, though this may be very painful for you.

Reflect upon the great importance of this, etc. (pp. 58–9).

CHAPTER 5

Continues speaking of confessors. Explains why it is important that they should be learned men.

May the Lord grant, for His Majesty's own sake, that no one in this house shall experience the trials that have been described, or find herself oppressed in this way in soul and body. I hope the superior will never be so intimate with the confessor that no one will dare to say anything about him to her or about her to him. For this will tempt *unfortunate* penitents to leave very grave sins unconfessed because they will feel uncomfortable about confessing them. God help me! What trouble the devil can make here[1] and how dearly people have to pay for their *miserable* worries and concern about honour! If they consult only one confessor, they think they are acting in the interests of their Order and for the *greater* honour of their convent: and that is the way the devil lays his snares for souls when he can find no other. If the *poor* sisters ask for another confessor, they are told that this would mean the *complete* end of all discipline in the convent; and, if he is not a priest of their Order, even though he be a saint,[2] they are led to believe that they would be disgracing their entire Order[3] by consulting him.

Give great praise to God, Daughters, for this liberty that you have, for, though there are not a great many priests whom you can consult, there are a few, other than your ordinary confessors, who can give you light upon everything. I beg every superior,[4] for the love of the Lord, to allow a

---

[1] E.: "How many souls the devil must catch in this way!"
[2] E.: "even if he were a Saint Jerome."
[3] So E. V. has, more vaguely, "disgracing them."
[4] *Lit.:* "I beg her who is in the position of a senior (*mayor*)" Mayor was the title given to the superior at the Incarnation, Ávila, and many other convents in Spain, at that time.

holy liberty here: let the Bishop[5] or Provincial be approached for leave for the sisters to go from time to time beyond their ordinary confessors and talk about their souls with persons of learning, especially if the confessors, though good men, have no learning; for learning is a great help in giving light upon everything. It should be possible to find a number of people who combine both learning and spirituality, and the more favours the Lord grants you in prayer, the more needful is it that your good works and your prayers should have a sure foundation.[6]

You already know that the first stone of this foundation must be a good conscience and that you must make every effort to free yourselves from even[7] venial sins and follow the greatest possible perfection. You might suppose that any confessor would know this, but you would be wrong:[8] it happened that I had to go about matters of conscience[9] to a man who had taken a complete course in theology; and he did me a great deal of mischief by telling me[10] that certain things were of no importance.[11] I know that he had no intention of deceiving me, or any reason for doing so: it was

[5] In T. St. Teresa alters "Bishop" to "Prelate"—no doubt because St. Joseph's was, in August 1577, transferred from the jurisdiction of the Bishop to that of the Order.

[6] E.: "I beg every superior, for the love of God, to try always to consult persons of learning and to see that her nuns do so. God preserve them from being directed entirely by one person, if he be not a learned man, however spiritual they may think him, or he may in fact be; for, the most favours the Lord grants them in prayer, the more needful is it that their devotions, and their prayers, and all their good works, should have a sure foundation."

[7] E. omits: "even."

[8] E.: "be quite wrong." In the margin of V. P. García de Toledo has written: "This is well (said), for there are some spiritual masters who, in order not to err, condemn all the spirits there are as demons, and they err more in (doing) this, as they quench the spirits of the Lord, as the Apostle says." T. has: "It seems that every confessor knows this, but it is not so, because it happened, etc."

[9] E. omits: "about matters of conscience."

[10] E.: "by making me think."

[11] E.: "were not wrong."

simply that he knew no better. And in addition to this instance I have met with two or three similar ones.[12]

Everything depends on our having[13] true light to keep the law of God perfectly. This is a firm basis for prayer; but without this strong foundation the whole building will go awry.[14] In making their confessions, then, the nuns must be free to discuss spiritual matters with such persons as I have described. I will even go farther and say that they should sometimes do as I have said even if their confessor has all these good qualities, for he may quite easily make mistakes and it is a pity that he should be the cause of their going astray. They must try, however, never to act in any way against obedience, for they will find ways of getting all the help they need: it is of great importance to them that they should, and so they must make every possible effort to do so.[15]

All this that I have said has to do with the superior. Since there are no consolations but spiritual ones to be had here, I would beg her once again to see[16] that the sisters get these consolations,[17] for God leads [His handmaidens] by different ways and it is impossible that one confessor should be acquainted with them all.[18] I assure you that, if your souls are as they ought to be, there is no lack of holy persons who

[12] E. omits this sentence.

[13] In T. St. Teresa substituted for this: "It is a great thing to have."

[14] T. has "every building" for "the whole building". E. continues: "so it is necessary for the nuns to consult people of spirituality and learning. If they cannot find a confessor who has both, they may from time to time go to others; and, if by any chance they have been instructed to make their confessions only to one priest, let them talk about their souls to such persons as I have described without making their confessions to them. I will even go farther, etc."

[15] E.: "it is of great importance that every possible effort should be made to secure the good of a soul—much more the good of a great many."

[16] E. reads "let her see" for "I would beg her once again to see".

[17] E.: "the sisters are not without consolations."

[18] E. continues: "So (the superior) must see that they obtain consolations from such persons as these. She need not fear that there will be any lack of such persons if the nuns are what they ought to be, even though they are poor. As God maintains them and gives food to their bodies, which is less necessary, He will provide them

will be glad to advise and console you, even though you are poor. For He Who sustains our bodies will awaken and encourage someone to give light to our souls, and thus this evil of which I am so much afraid will be remedied. For if the devil should tempt the confessor, with the result that he leads you astray on any point of doctrine,[19] he will go slowly and be more careful about all he is doing when he knows that the penitent is also consulting others.[20]

If the devil is prevented from entering convents in this way, I hope in God that he will never get into this house at all; so, for love of the Lord, I beg whoever is Bishop[21] to allow the sisters this liberty and not to withdraw it so long as the confessors are persons both of learning and of good lives, a fact which will soon come to be known in a little place like this.[22]

In what I have said here, I am speaking from experience of things that I have seen and heard *in many convents* and gathered from conversation with learned and holy people[23]

---

with persons who will be most willing to give light to their souls, and thus this evil of which, as has been said, I am so much afraid, will be remedied."

19 E.: "tempt the confessor to any vanity."

20 E.: "he will go slowly, and the devil will be prevented from entering convents in this way—I hope in God he will never get into this house at all."

21 "Bishop or Provincial," says T.; and someone, probably the author, has crossed out "Bishop or", no doubt for the reason given on p. 63, n. 5 above.

22 E. begins: "So, for love . . ." and, after "liberty", continues: "being sure that, with the help of God, he will have good subjects; and he must never withdraw it so long as the confessors are persons both of learning and of good lives, a fact which, in such a little place, will soon come to be known. He should not forbid them to make their confessions occasionally to such persons, and to discuss their method of prayer with them, even if they have their own confessors, for I know that for many reasons this is a good thing, and the harm it may cause is nothing by comparison with the grave, secret and almost irremediable harm which will result from the contrary procedure. For the life of a religious house is such that what is good soon disappears, unless it is most carefully preserved, whereas if once anything bad gets a foothold, it is most difficult to eradicate: in details of imperfection custom very soon becomes habit and second nature."

23 E.: "with prudent and spiritual people."

who have considered what is most fitting for this house, so that it may advance in perfection. Among the perils which exist everywhere, for as long as life lasts, we shall find that this is the least. No vicar should be free to go in and out of the convent, and no confessor should have this freedom either.[24] They are there to watch over the recollectedness and good living of the house and its progress in both interior and exterior matters,[25] so that they may report to the superior whenever needful, but they are never to be superiors themselves. *As I say, excellent reasons have been found why, everything considered, this is the best course, and why, if any priest hears confessions frequently, it should be the chaplain; but, if the nuns think it necessary, they can make their confessions to such persons as have been described, provided the superior is informed of it, and the prioress is such that the Bishop can trust her discretion. As there are very few nuns here, this will not take up much time.*

This is our present practice; and it is not followed merely on my advice.[26] Our present Bishop, Don Álvaro de Mendoza, under whose obedience we live (since for many reasons we have not been placed under the jurisdiction of the Order), is greatly attached to holiness and the religious life, and,

---

[24] E.: "should have power to go in and out of the convent or to give orders, nor should a confessor give orders."

[25] E.: "over the good living of the house and its interior and exterior recollectedness."

[26] T. goes on: "but on that of the prelate whom we now have", and omits the passage about Don Álvaro de Mendoza, which follows. E. continues and ends the chapter thus: "This decision was made after much prayer by many people, including myself, miserable though I am, and they were persons of great learning and understanding and prayer, so I hope in the Lord it is for the best.

"It seemed so to the Lord Bishop, who is now Don Álvaro de Mendoza, a person very glad to further the well-being of this house, both spiritual and temporal. He considered it very carefully, as he desires the house to make still further progress in what is good, and I believe God will not allow it to go astray since the Bishop is in His place and desires nothing but His greater glory. I think future superiors, with the help of God, will not wish to oppose a thing which has been so carefully considered and is for many reasons of such great importance."

besides being of most noble extraction, is a great servant of God. He is always very glad to help this house in every way, and to this very end he brought together persons of learning, spirituality and experience, and this decision was then come to. It will be only right that future superiors should conform to his opinion, since it has been decided on by such good men, and after so many prayers to the Lord that He would enlighten them in every possible way, which, so far as we can at present see, He has certainly done. May the Lord be pleased to promote the advancement of this to His greater glory. Amen.

CHAPTER 6

Returns to the subject of perfect love, already begun.

I have digressed a great deal but no one will blame me who understands the importance of what has been said.[1] Let us now return to the love which it is good[2] [and lawful] for us to feel. This I have described as purely[3] spiritual; I am not sure if I know what I am talking about, but it seems to me that there is no need to speak much of it, since so few, I fear, possess it; let any one of you to whom the Lord has given it praise Him fervently, for she must be a person of the greatest perfection. It is about this that I now wish to write.[4] Perhaps what I say may be of some profit, for if you look at a

[1] E.: "but what has been said is of the greatest importance if this is not lost through its having been said by me."
[2] E.: "is good and lawful, my sisters." V. also adds "and lawful", but the two words have been crossed out by the author. T. restores them.
[3] E.: "wholly."
[4] E. reads: "Let anyone who has it praise God", and adds: "and He will be well praised. (Such a person) must be of the greatest perfection. Perhaps we shall profit by it. Let us say something (about it)."

virtue you desire it and try to gain it, and so become attached to it.[5]

God grant that I may be able to understand this, and even more that I may be able to describe it, for I am not sure that I know when love is spiritual and when there is sensuality mingled with it, or how to begin speaking about it. I am like one who hears a person speaking in the distance and, *though he can hear that he is speaking*, cannot distinguish what he is saying. It is just like that with me: sometimes I cannot understand what I am saying, yet the Lord is pleased to enable me to say it well. If at other times what I say is [ridiculous and] nonsensical, it is only natural for me to go completely astray.

Now it seems to me that, when God has brought someone to a clear knowledge of the world, and of its nature, and of the fact that another world (*or, let us say, another kingdom*) exists, and that there is a great difference between the one and the other, the one being eternal and the other only a dream; and of what it is to love the Creator and what to love the creature (this must be discovered by experience, for it is a very different matter from merely thinking about it and believing it);[6] when one understands by sight and experience[7] what can be gained by the one practice and lost by the other, and what the Creator is and what the creature, and many other things which the Lord teaches to those who are willing to devote themselves to being taught by Him in prayer, or whom His Majesty wishes to teach[8]—then one loves[9] very differently from those of us who have not advanced thus far.

It may be, sisters, that you think it irrelevant for me to

[5] E. renders this sentence as in the last note and then continues: "But it is this other (love) which we must most often feel, and, though I say there is something sensual about it, this may not be so, for I am not sure that I know when love is sensual, and when spiritual, or how to begin speaking about it."

[6] E. omits the parenthetical clause.

[7] T. omits: "and experience."

[8] E.: "teaches truly and clearly to those whom His Majesty wishes to teach."

[9] T.: "then these souls love each other."

treat of this, and you may say that you already know every-thing that I have said.[10] God grant that this may be so, and that you may indeed know it in the only way which has any meaning,[11] and that it may be graven upon your inmost be-ing, *and that you may never for a moment depart from it*; for, if you know it, you will see that I am telling nothing but the truth when I say that he whom the Lord brings thus far possesses this love.[12] Those whom God brings to this state are, *I think*, generous and royal souls; they are not content with loving anything so miserable as these bodies, however beautiful they be[13] and however numerous the graces they possess. If the sight of the body gives them pleasure they praise the Creator, but as for dwelling upon it *for more than just a moment*—no! When I use that phrase "dwelling upon it", I refer to having love for such things. If they had such love, they would think they were loving something insub-stantial and were conceiving fondness for a shadow; they would feel shame for themselves and would not have the effrontery to tell God that they love Him,[14] without feeling great confusion.

You will answer me that such persons cannot love or repay the affection shown to them by others.[15] Certainly they care little about having this affection. They may from time to time experience a natural and momentary pleasure at being loved; yet, as soon as they return to their normal condition, they realize that such pleasure is folly save when the persons concerned can benefit their souls, either by instruction or by prayer. Any other kind of affection wearies them, for they

10 E.: "that you think this some nonsense of mine and say that you all know it."
11 E.: "in the way it should be known."
12 T. adds: "which I shall describe."
13 T. interpolates, parenthetically: "I mean love which subjects and binds."
14 T. ends the sentence here.
15 E. continues: "For by what are they attracted save by what they see? They (do) love much more, and with greater passion, with a more genuine love and with a love which brings more profit. This, in a word, is love, and those other base affections have robbed it of the name. They do love what they see, etc." (p. 71, below).

know it can bring them no profit and may well do them harm; none the less they are grateful for it and recompense it by commending those who love them to God. They take this affection as something for which those who love them lay the responsibility upon the Lord,[16] from Whom, since they can see nothing lovable in themselves, they suppose the love comes, and think that others love them because God loves them; and so they leave His Majesty to recompense them for this and beg Him to do so, thus freeing themselves and feeling they have no more responsibility. When I ponder it carefully, I sometimes think this desire for affection is sheer blindness, except when, as I say, it relates to persons who can lead us to do good so that we may gain blessings in perfection.

It should be noted here that, when we desire anyone's affection, we always seek it because of some interest, profit or pleasure of our own. Those who are perfect, however, have trodden all these things beneath their feet—[and have despised] the blessings which may come to them in this world, and its pleasures and delights—in such a way that, even if they wanted to, so to say, they could not love anything outside God, or unless it had to do with God. What profit, then, can come to them from being loved themselves?[17]

When this truth is put to them, they laugh at the distress which had been assailing them in the past as to whether their affection was being returned or no. Of course, however pure our affection may be, it is quite natural for us to wish it to be returned. But, when we come to evaluate the return of affection, we realize that it is insubstantial, like a thing of straw, as light as air and easily carried away by the wind. For, however dearly we have been loved, what is there that remains to us? Such persons, then, except for the advantage that the affection may bring to their souls (because they realize that our nature is such that we soon tire of life without love), care nothing whether they are loved or not. Do you think that such persons will love none and delight in

---

[16] T.: "Taking this affection as if those who loved them were laying the responsibility (for doing so) upon the Lord."
[17] "By lovers of the world," adds T.

none save God? No; they will love others much[18] more than they did, with a more genuine love, with greater passion and with a love which brings more profit; that, in a word, is what love really is. And such souls are always much fonder of giving than of receiving, even in their relations with the Creator Himself. This [holy affection], I say, merits the name of love, which name has been usurped from it by those other base affections.

Do you ask, again, by what they are attracted if they do not love things they see? They do love what they see[19] and they are greatly attracted by what they hear; but the things which they see are everlasting. If they love anyone[20] they immediately look right beyond the body (*on which, as I say, they cannot dwell*), fix their eyes on the soul[21] and see what there is to be loved in that. If there is nothing, but they see any suggestion or inclination which shows them that, if they dig deep, they will find gold within this mine, they think nothing of the labour of digging, since they have love. There is nothing that suggests itself to them which they will not willingly do for the good of that soul since they desire their love for it to be lasting,[22] and they know quite well that that is impossible unless the loved one has certain good qualities and a great love for God. I really mean that it is impossible, however great their obligations and even if that soul were to die for love of them[23] and do them all the kind actions in its power; even had it all the natural graces joined in one, their wills would not have strength enough to love it nor would they remain fixed upon it. They know and have learned and experienced the worth of all this; no false dice can deceive them.[24] They see that they are not in unison with that soul and that their love for it cannot possibly last; for,

18 T. omits: "much."
19 E. picks up the thread here (cf. p. 69, n. 15, above).
20 E.: "If they love a friend."
21 E.: "pass to the soul."
22 E.: "they desire to love it."
23 E.: "I really mean that it is impossible, even if that soul were to die for them."
24 E.: "yet their wills would not have strength enough (to love it), for they are wise wills, which know by experience the worth of all this, and no false dice can deceive them."

unless that soul keeps the law of God, their love will end with life[25]—they know that unless it loves Him they will go to different places.

Those into whose souls the Lord has already infused true wisdom do not esteem this love, which lasts only on earth, at more than its true worth—if, indeed, at so much. Those who like to take pleasure in[26] worldly things, delights, honours and riches, will account it of some worth if their friend is rich and able to afford them pastime *and pleasure* and recreation; but those who already hate all this[27] will care little or nothing[28] for such things. If they have any love for such a person, then, it will be a passion[29] that he may love God so as to be loved by Him;[30] for, as I say, they know that no other kind of affection but this can last,[31] and that this kind will cost them dear, for which reason they do all they possibly can for their friend's profit;[32] they would lose a thousand lives to bring him a small blessing. Oh, precious love, forever imitating the Captain of Love, Jesus, our Good!

CHAPTER 7

Treats of the same subject of spiritual love and gives certain counsels for gaining it.

It is strange to see how impassioned this love is; how many tears, penances and prayers it costs; how careful is the loving

[25] E.: "cannot possibly last, and they fear that their enjoyment will end with life."
[26] T.: "Those who seek pleasures (consisting) in."
[27] E.: "but those who have this already beneath their feet."
[28] E. omits: "or nothing."
[29] In T. the author has emended "passion" to "affection". T. also omits: "that he may love God".
[30] The words "that he may love God" are interlinear.
[31] E.: "for, as I say, they know that, if (their love) is not (like) this, they will have to forsake it."
[32] E. adds, for greater emphasis, the redundant phrase: "as far as in them lies."

soul to commend the object of its affection to all who it thinks may prevail with God and to ask them to intercede with Him for it; and how constant is its longing, so that it cannot be happy unless it sees that its loved one is making progress.[1] If that soul seems to have advanced,[2] and is then seen to fall some way back, her friend seems to have no more pleasure in life: she neither eats nor sleeps, is never free from this fear and is always afraid[3] that the soul whom she loves so much may be lost, and that the two may be parted for ever. She cares nothing for[4] physical death, but she will not suffer herself to be attached to something which a puff of wind may carry away so that she is unable to retain her hold upon it. This, as I have said, is love without any degree whatsoever of self-interest;[5] all that this soul wishes and desires is to see[6] the soul [it loves] enriched with blessings from Heaven. This is love, quite unlike our ill-starred earthly affections[7]—to say nothing of illicit affections, from which may God keep us free.

These last affections are a very hell, and it is needless for us to weary ourselves by saying how evil they are, for the least of the evils which they bring are terrible beyond exaggeration. There is no need for us ever to take such things upon our lips, sisters, *or even to think of them*, or to remember that they exist anywhere in the world; you must never listen to anyone speaking of such affections, either in jest or in earnest, nor allow them to be mentioned or discussed in your presence. No good can come from our doing this and it might do us harm even to hear them mentioned.[8] But with

---

[1] E. omits: "unless . . . progress."
[2] E.: "to be advancing."
[3] "It must not be understood that it is with interior disquiet," adds T., parenthetically.
[4] E.: "She cares not two farthings (*maravedis*) for."
[5] E. omits: "as I have said" and "self-". T. omits: "any degree whatsoever of."
[6] E.: "all its interest consists in seeing."
[7] E.: "This, in short, is love which grows ever more like the love which Christ had for us. It deserves the name of love and is quite different from our petty, ill-starred, frivolous earthly affections."
[8] E.: "There is no profit in this, nor is there any reason (for us to do it) and it might do us harm."

regard to the lawful affections which, as I have said, we may have for each other, or for relatives and friends, it is different. Our whole desire is that they should not die:[9] if their heads ache, our souls seem to ache too; if we see them in distress, we are unable (as people say) to sit still under it;[10] and so on.

This is not so with spiritual affection. Although the weakness of our nature may at first allow us to feel something of all this, our reason soon begins to reflect whether our friend's trials are not good for her, and to wonder if they are making her richer in virtue and how she is bearing them, and then we shall ask God to give her patience so that they may win her merit. If we see that she is being patient, we feel[11] no distress—indeed, we are gladdened and consoled. If all the merit and gain which suffering is capable of producing[12] could be made over to her, we should still prefer suffering her trial ourselves to seeing her suffer it, but we are not worried or disquieted.[13]

I repeat once more that this love is a similitude and copy of that which was borne for us by the good Lover, Jesus. It is for that reason that it brings us such immense benefits, for it makes us embrace[14] every kind of suffering, so that others, without having to endure the suffering, may gain its advantages. The recipients of this friendship, then, profit greatly, but their friends should realize that either this intercourse— I mean, this exclusive friendship—must come to an end or that they must prevail upon Our Lord that their friend may walk in the same way as themselves, as Saint Monica prevailed with Him for Saint Augustine. Their heart does not

[9] T.: "Let our desire be such that it will not rob us of our peace and liberty, so that, if their heads ache, etc."
[10] *Lit.*: "There remains, as people say, no patience"; but, as the phrase "as people say" (which E. omits) suggests that this was a popular phrase, I have translated rather more freely and picturesquely. T. has (after "ache too"): "and it upsets us, and so on."
[11] E.: "it causes us."
[12] E.: "if all the merit and the good which remain."
[13] E.: "killed" [i.e., "worried to death"].
[14] T.: "want to embrace."

allow them to practise duplicity: if they see their friend straying from the road, or committing any faults, they will speak to her about it; they cannot allow themselves to do anything else. And if after this the loved one does not amend, they will not flatter her or hide anything from her. Either, then, she will amend or their friendship will cease; for otherwise they would be unable to endure it, nor is it in fact endurable. It would mean continual war for both parties. A person may be indifferent to all other people in the world and not worry whether they are serving God or not, since the person she has to worry about is herself.[15] But she cannot take this attitude with her friends: nothing they do can be hidden from her; she sees the smallest mote in them. This, I repeat, is a very heavy cross for her to bear.[16]

Happy the souls that are loved by such as these! Happy the day on which they came to know them! O my Lord, wilt Thou not grant me the favour of giving me many who have such love for me? Truly, Lord, I would rather have this than be loved by all the kings and lords of the world—and rightly so, for such friends use every means in their power to make us lords of the whole world and to have all that is in it subject

---

15 T. omits: "and not worry . . . herself."

16 In E. this paragraph reads: "I repeat that this is love without (self-)interest, like that which Christ bore us. It is for that reason that it brings so much advantage to those who reach this state, for they would like to do nothing but undertake every kind of suffering so that others might profit and rejoice in its benefits. Those, then, who have this friendship profit greatly, for it is evident that they would like to teach by deeds rather than by words, although they may not actually do so. I say they may not do so, meaning that there may be things which they cannot do; in so far as they are able, they would like to be always working for those they love and bringing them profit. Their heart does not allow them to practise duplicity or to see their friends lack anything if they think such a thing will be for their good. Very often they do not even stop to think of this, so earnestly do they desire to see them very rich, though they do not tell them so. What roundabout paths they take to gain their end! They may be indifferent to everyone else in the world and not worry if they are serving God or not, for they have only to worry about themselves. But nothing that their friends do can be hidden from them: they see the smallest mote in them."

to us. *When you make the acquaintance of any such persons, sisters, the Mother Prioress should employ every possible effort to keep you in touch with them. Love such persons as much as you like. There can be very few of them, but none the less it is the Lord's will that their goodness should be known. When one of you is striving after perfection, she will at once be told that she has no need to know such people—that it is enough for her to have God. But to get to know God's friends is a very good way of "having" Him; as I have discovered by experience, it is most helpful. For, under the Lord, I owe it to such persons that I am not in hell; I was always very fond of asking them to commend me to God, and so I prevailed upon them to do so.*

Let us now return to what we were saying. It is this kind of love which I should like us to have; at first it may not be perfect but the Lord will make it increasingly so.[17] Let us begin with the methods of obtaining it. At first it may be mingled with emotion,[18] but this, as a rule, will do no harm. It is sometimes good and necessary[19] for us to show emotion in our love, and also to feel it,[20] and to be distressed by

---

[17] E.: "us to have, but at first this will not be possible."

[18] *Ternura. Lit.:* "tenderness."

[19] E.: "It is quite good and in part necessary."

[20] E. continues: "and to be distressed by any of the weaknesses and trials of a sister, for sometimes people are troubled at mere nothings which others would laugh at. But we must not be dismayed, for the devil may well have worked at this with all his might, much more so than he did to make you distressed at great trials and griefs. To take your recreation with your sisters, when they are taking theirs, though you may not be enjoying it, is real charity, for all considerate treatment of them will grow into perfect love. I had been wanting to say something of love which is less perfect, but I find no reason for thinking that it will be good for us to have any of it among us in this house: if our love is real, as I say, it will all be referred to its source, which is the love that I have described.

"I had thought of saying a great deal about that other love, but, now that I come to the point, I do not think it can possibly exist here, with the kind of life that we lead. For that reason I will add nothing to what I have said, hoping in God that, although you may not always be quite perfect, there will be no suggestion in this house of your loving each other in any other way than the best. It is a very good thing for us to take compassion on one another's needs, though some of our sisters' trials and weaknesses, however trivial they may be. For on one occasion as much distress may be caused by quite a small matter as would be caused on another by some great trial, and there are people whose nature it is to be very much cast down by small things. If you are not like this, do not neglect to have compassion on others; it may be that Our Lord wishes to spare us these sufferings and will give us sufferings of another kind which will seem heavy to us, though to the person already mentioned they may seem light. In these matters, then, we must not judge others by ourselves, nor think of ourselves as we have been at some time when, perhaps without any effort on our part, the Lord has made us stronger than they; let us think of what we were like at the times when we have been weakest.

Note the importance of this advice for those of us who would learn to sympathize with our neighbours' trials, however trivial these may be. It is especially important for such souls as have been described, for, desiring trials as they do, they make light of them all. They must therefore try hard to recall what they were like when they were weak, and reflect that, if they are no longer so, it is not due to themselves. For otherwise, little by little, the devil could easily cool our charity toward our neighbours and make us think that what is really a failing on our part is perfection. In every respect we must be careful and alert, for the devil never slumbers. And the nearer we are to perfection, the more careful we must be, since his temptations are then much more cunning because there are no others that he dare send us; and if, as I say, we are not cautious, the harm is done before we realize it. In short, we must always watch and pray, for there is no better way than prayer of revealing these hidden wiles of the devil and making him declare his presence.

Contrive always, even if you do not care for it, to take part in your sisters' necessary recreation and to do so for the whole of the allotted time, for all considerate treatment of

---

we must show no lack of discretion. I mean, lack of discretion in anything contrary to obedience—that is to say, against the prioress's orders. Though you may think these orders harsh ones, and say so to yourself privately, do not tell anyone about it, etc." (p. 78, below).

them is a part of perfect love.[21] It is a very good thing for us to take compassion on each others' needs. See that you show no lack of discretion about things which are contrary to obedience. Though privately you may think the prioress' orders harsh ones, do not allow this to be noticed or tell anyone about it (except that you may speak of it, with all humility, to the prioress herself), for if you did so you would be doing a great deal of harm. Get to know what are the things in your sisters which you should be sorry to see and those about which you should sympathize with them; and always show your grief at any notorious fault which you may see in one of them. It is a good proof and test of our love if we can bear with such faults[22] and not be shocked by them. Others, in their turn, will bear with your[23] faults, which, if you include those of which you are not aware, must be much more numerous. Often commend to God any sister who is at fault and strive for your own part to practise the virtue which is the opposite of her fault with great perfection. Make determined efforts to do this[24] so that you may teach your sister by your deeds what perhaps she could never learn by words nor gain by punishment.[25]

The habit of performing some conspicuously virtuous action through seeing it performed by another is one which very easily takes root. This is good advice: do not forget it.[26] Oh, how true and genuine will be the love of a sister who can bring profit to everyone by sacrificing her own profit to that of the rest! She will make a great advance in each of the virtues and keep her Rule with great perfection. This will be a much truer kind of friendship than one which uses every possible loving expression (such as are not used, and

---

[21] T. omits: "perfect."

[22] E.: "the things which you should be sorry to see in your sisters, and always show your grief at any fault. This is love, when we can bear with such faults."

[23] E. has "my", and uses the first person to the end of the sentence.

[24] E. continues: "so that, through your being with her, (your sister) cannot fail to learn better than by suffering all the reproofs and punishments that might be inflicted upon her."

[25] Thus T. V. reads, more awkwardly: "nor gain, nor punishment."

[26] E. omits: "The habit . . . forget it."

must not be used,[27] in this house): "My life!" "My love!"
"My darling!"[28] and suchlike things, one or another of which
people are always saying. Let such endearing words be kept
for your Spouse,[29] for you will be so often and so much alone
with Him[30] that you will want to make use of them all, and
this His Majesty permits you. If you use them among yourselves they will not move the Lord so much; and, quite apart
from that, there is no reason why you should do so. They
are very effeminate; and I should not like you to be that, or
even to appear to be that, in any way, my daughters;[31] I
want you to be strong men. If you do all that is in you, the
Lord will make you so manly that men themselves will be
amazed at you. And how easy is this for His Majesty, Who
made us out of nothing at all![32]

It is also a very clear sign of love to try[33] to spare others
household work by taking it upon oneself and also to rejoice
and give great praise to the Lord if you see[34] any increase
in their virtues. All such things, quite apart from the intrinsic good they bring, add greatly to the peace and concord
which we have among ourselves, as, through the goodness of
God, we can now see by experience. May His Majesty be
pleased ever to increase it, for it would be terrible if it did not
exist, and very awkward if, when there are so few of us, we
got on badly together. May God forbid that.[35]

---

27 E. omits: "and must not be used."
28 *Lit.*: "My life!" "My soul!" "My good!" E. omits the last of
these phrases. T. ends the sentence at "suchlike things".
29 E.: "for the Lord."
30 E.: "for you will be with Him so many times a day, and sometimes so much alone."
31 E.: "like my daughters to appear in any way to be that." T.
reads: "I should not like you to be that, in any way, my daughters,
but to appear to be men."
32 *Nonada*. T. has simply *nada* ("nothing").
33 T. omits: "to try."
34 T.: "if He gives."
35 T. omits: "May God forbid that." E. reads: "It is also a sign of
love, as has been said, to try to spare others work, and for each to
take it herself, and to rejoice in the increase in another's virtues as
though they were her own. In many other ways (the sisters) will
know if they have this virtue, which is very great, for in it resides all

If one of you should be cross with another because of some hasty word, the matter must at once be put right and you must betake yourselves to earnest prayer.[36] The same applies to the harbouring of any grudge, or to party strife, or to the desire to be greatest, or to any nice point concerning your honour. (My blood seems to run cold,[37] as I write[38] this, at the very idea that this can ever happen,[39] but I know it is the chief trouble in convents.) If it should happen to you, consider yourselves lost. Just reflect and realize that you have driven your Spouse from His home:[40] He will have to go and seek another abode, since you are driving Him from His own house. Cry aloud to His Majesty and try to put things right; and if frequent confessions and communions do not mend them, you may well fear that there is some Judas among you.

For the love of God, let the prioress be most careful not to allow this to occur. She must put a stop to it from the very outset,[41] *and, if love will not suffice, she must use heavy punishments*, for here we have the whole of the mischief and the remedy. If you gather that any of the nuns is making trouble, see that she is sent to some other convent and God will provide them with a dowry for her. Drive away this plague; cut off the branches as well as you can; and, if that

---

mutual peace, which is so necessary in religious houses. I hope in the Lord we shall always have it in this convent, for, if we did not have it, it would be a terrible thing for there to be so few of us getting on badly together. May God forbid that. But all the good that has been begun here by the Lord's hand would have to be lost before so great an evil could happen."

[36] E.: "put right. If it is not, and you see that (the trouble) is getting worse, you must betake yourselves to earnest prayer."

[37] E. adds: "so to speak."

[38] T.: "as I say and write."

[39] E. omits: "at . . . happen."

[40] E. reads: "driven your Lord," and omits: "He will . . . own house." In T. a page is missing here which comprises the rest of the chapter. P. Silverio inserts the corresponding passage from the Évora edition, which differs considerably from both E. and V.

[41] E. reads: "careful to put a stop to this quickly", and later omits: "for here we have the whole of the mischief and the remedy." The sense of this phrase, which in the Spanish has "or" for "and," is not very clear.

is not sufficient, pull up the roots. If you cannot do this, shut up anyone who is guilty of such things and forbid her to leave her cell; far better this than that all the nuns should catch so incurable a plague. Oh, what a great evil is this! God deliver us from a convent into which it enters: I would rather our convent caught fire and we were all burned alive. As this is so important I think I shall say a little more about it elsewhere, so I will not write at greater length here,[42] *except to say that, provided they treat each other equally, I would rather that the nuns showed a tender and affectionate love and regard for each other, even though there is less perfection in this than in the love I have described, than that there were a single note of discord to be heard among them. May the Lord forbid this, for His own sake. Amen.*

CHAPTER 8

Treats of the great benefit of self-detachment, both interior and exterior, from all things created.

Let us now come to the detachment which we must practise, for if this is carried out perfectly it includes everything else. I say "it includes everything else" because, if we care nothing for any created things, but embrace the Creator alone, His Majesty will infuse the virtues into us in such a way that, provided we labour to the best of our abilities day by day, we shall not have to wage war much longer, for the Lord will take our defence in hand against the devils and against the whole world. Do you suppose, daughters, that it is a small benefit to obtain for ourselves this blessing of giving ourselves wholly to Him,[1] and keeping nothing for our-

---

42 E.: "As I shall deal with this again elsewhere, I say no more here."
1 Lit.: *de darnos todas a Él todo*: "giving ourselves wholly to Him wholly." But E. reads *al todo*, "to the All", which, though more like St. John of the Cross's phraseology than St. Teresa's, may represent more exactly the idea in her mind.

selves? Since, as I say, all blessings are in Him, let us give Him hearty praise, sisters, for having brought us together here,[2] where we are occupied in this alone. I do not know why I am saying this, when all of you here are capable of teaching me, for I confess that, in this important respect, I am not as perfect as I should like to be and as I know I ought to be;[3] and I must say the same about all the virtues and about all that I am dealing with here, for it is easier to write of such things than to practise them. I may not even be able to write of them effectively, for sometimes ability to do this comes only from experience—[that is to say, if I have any success, it must be because] I explain the nature of these virtues by describing the contraries of the qualities I myself possess.[4]

As far as exterior matters are concerned, you know how completely cut off we are from everything.[5] *Oh, my Creator and Lord! When have I merited so great an honour? Thou seemest to have searched everywhere for means of drawing nearer to us. May it please Thy goodness that we lose not this through our own fault.* Oh, sisters, for the love of God, try to realize what a great favour the Lord has bestowed on those of us whom He has brought here.[6] Let each of you apply this to herself, since there are only twelve of us[7] and His Majesty has been pleased for you to be one. How many people—*what a multitude of people!*—do I know who are better than myself and would gladly take this place of mine, yet the Lord has granted it to me who so ill deserve it! Blessed

[2] E.: "let us give many thanks to the Lord, Who brought us together here."

[3] T. continues: "because it is easier, etc."

[4] E.: "I confess that, in this important respect, I am the most imperfect; but, as you order me to do so, I will touch upon a few things that occur to me."

[5] E.: "how completely cut off (we are): it seems as if in bringing (*traer*) us here it is the Lord's will to cut us off from everything, so that His Majesty should get us (*llegarnos*) here without hindrance." In all the editions this sentence closes the preceding paragraph but it seems more properly to belong to this.

[6] E.: "try to realize fully the greatness of this favour."

[7] The thirteenth was St. Teresa. See Vol. I, p. 260, above.

be Thou, my God, and let *the angels and* all created things praise Thee, for I can no more repay this favour than all the others Thou hast shown me. It was a wonderful thing to give me the vocation to be a nun; but I have been so wicked, Lord, that Thou couldst not trust me. In a place where there were many good women living together my wickedness would not *perhaps* have been noticed right down to the end of my life: *I should have concealed it, as I did for so many years.* So Thou didst bring me[8] here, where, as there are so few of us that it would seem impossible for it to remain unnoticed, Thou dost remove occasions of sin from me so that I may walk the more carefully.[9] There is no excuse for me, then, O Lord, I confess it, and so I have need of Thy mercy, that Thou mayest pardon me.

Remember, my sisters, that if we are not good we are much more to blame than others.[10] What I earnestly beg of you is that anyone who knows she will be unable to follow our customs will say so [before she is professed]: there are other convents in which the Lord is also well served and she should not remain here and disturb these few of us whom His Majesty has brought together *for His service.* In other convents nuns are free to have the pleasure of seeing their relatives, whereas here, if relatives are ever admitted, it is only for their own pleasure. A nun who [very much] wishes[11] to see her relatives in order to please herself, *and does not get tired of them after the second visit,* must, unless they are spiritual persons *and do her soul some good,* consider herself imperfect and realize that she is neither detached nor healthy, and will have no freedom of spirit or perfect peace.

---

8 E.: "So Thou bringest me."

9 E.: "from me, so that on the Day of Judgment I may have no room for excuse if I should not do as I ought." E. also omits the last sentence of this paragraph.

10 E. continues: "and so I earnestly charge anyone who, after making the attempt, finds that she has not sufficient spiritual strength to observe what is observed here, to say so; there are other convents, in which perhaps the Lord is served much better. She should not remain here, etc."

11 E.: "needs."

She needs a physician[12]—and I consider that if this desire does not leave her, and she is not cured, she is not intended for this house.[13]

The best remedy, I think, is that she should not see her relatives again until she feels free in spirit and has obtained this freedom from God by many prayers. When she looks upon such visits as crosses, let her receive them by all means, for then they will do the visitors good and herself no harm.[14] *But if she is fond of the visitors, if their troubles are a great distress to her and if she delights in listening to the stories which they tell her about the world, she may be sure that she will do herself harm and do them no good.*

CHAPTER 9

Treats of the great blessing that shunning their relatives brings to those who have left the world and shows how by doing so they will find truer friends.

Oh, if we religious understood what harm we get from having so much to do with our relatives,[1] how we should shun them! I do not see what pleasure they can give us, or how, quite apart from *the harm they do us as touching* our obligations to God, they can bring us any peace or tranquillity.[2] For we cannot take part in their recreations, as it is

[12] E. continues: "and I know of no other better cure than never to see them again until she feels free in spirit and has gained (this) for herself. When she looks, etc."

[13] T. substitutes for this clause: "her spirituality will not grow very much."

[14] E.: "by all means, in order to do the visitors good, as she certainly will."

[1] E. has: "comes to us from this", but in the next sentence reads "the relatives" where the text has "they".

[2] T.: "what pleasure or tranquillity they can give us."

not lawful for us to do so;[3] and, though we can certainly share their troubles, we can never help weeping for them,[4] sometimes more than they do themselves. If they bring us any bodily comforts, there is no doubt that our[5] spiritual life *and our poor souls* will pay for it. From this you are [quite] free here; for, as you have everything in common and none of you may accept any private gift, all the alms given us being held by the community, you are under no obligation to entertain your relatives in return for what they give you, since, as you know, the Lord will provide for us all in common.[6]

I am astounded at the harm which intercourse with our relatives does us: I do not think anyone who had not experience of it would believe it.[7] And how our religious Orders nowadays, *or most of them, at any rate,* seem to be forgetting about perfection, *though all, or most, of the saints wrote about it!*[8] I do not know how much of the world we really leave when we say that we are leaving everything for God's sake, if we do not withdraw ourselves from[9] the chief thing of all—namely, our kinsfolk. The matter has reached such a pitch that some people think, when religious are not fond of their relatives and do not see much of them, it shows a want of virtue in them. And they not only assert this but allege reasons for it.

In this house, daughters,[10] we must be most careful to commend our relatives to God,[11] for that is only right. For

---

[3] E. omits: "as it . . . do so."
[4] E. abbreviates: "and we can never help weeping for their troubles."
[5] St. Teresa substitutes for this, in T.: "So that, if they bring us any physical pleasure, our, etc."
[6] E.: "and no one (of you) may have anything private, you have no need of gifts from relatives."
[7] E.: "I should not believe it if I had not experience (of it)."
[8] T. simplifies farther even than V.: "And how our religious Orders have forgotten about perfection!"
[9] E.: "do not leave."
[10] E.: "my daughter."
[11] E. adds the not very lucid phrase: "after what has been said touching His Church"—meaning, presumably, "after praying for the Church". In T. the sentence reads: "In this house, daughters, we

the rest, we must keep them out of our minds as much as we can, as it is natural that our desires should be attached to them more than to other people.[12] My own relatives were very fond of me, or so they used to say, and I was so fond of them that I would not let them forget me.[13] But I have learned, by my own experience and by that of others, that it is God's servants who have helped me in trouble;[14] my relatives, apart from my parents, have helped me very little. Parents are different, for they very rarely fail to help their children, and it is right that when they need our comfort we should not refuse it them: if we find our main purpose[15] is not harmed by our so doing we can give it them and yet be completely detached; and this also applies to brothers and sisters.[16]

Believe me, sisters,[17] if you serve God as you should, you will find no better relatives[18] than those [of His servants] whom His Majesty sends you. I know this is so,[19] and, if you keep on as you are doing *here*, and realize that by doing otherwise you will be failing[20] your true Friend and Spouse,[21] you may be sure that you will very soon gain this freedom. Then you will be able to trust those who love you for His sake alone more than all your relatives, and they will not fail you, so that you will find parents and brothers and sisters where you had never expected to find them. For these help us and look for their reward only from God; those who look for rewards from us soon grow tired of helping us when

must care about our relatives only in order to commend them to God."

[12] E. omits: "as . . . people."
[13] E. omits: "and I . . . forget me."
[14] T. omits: "it is God's . . . in trouble," reading: "that my relatives, etc."
[15] E.: "if we find our soul." In T., the clause "if . . . so doing" is crossed out.
[16] E. omits: "and this . . . sisters."
[17] E.: "friends" [*amigas*, fem.].
[18] E.: "friends" [*amigos*, masc. or com.].
[19] E. omits: "I know this is so."
[20] T.: "displeasing."
[21] E.: "Friend, Christ."

they see that we are poor and can do nothing for them. This cannot be taken as a generalization, but it is the most usual thing to happen in the world, for it is the world all over! If anyone tells you otherwise, and says it is a virtue to do such things,[22] do not believe him. I should have to write at great length, *in view of my lack of skill and my imperfection*, if I were to tell you of all the harm that comes from it;[23] as others have written about it who know what they are talking about better than I, what I have said will suffice. If, imperfect as I am, I have been able to grasp as much as this, how much better will those who are perfect do so!

All the advice which the saints give us about fleeing[24] from the world is, of course, good. Believe me, then, attachment to our relatives is, as I have said, the thing which sticks to us most closely and is hardest to get rid of. People are right, therefore, when they flee from their own part of the country[25]—if it helps them, I mean, for I do not think we are helped so much by fleeing from any place in a physical sense as by resolutely embracing the good Jesus, Our Lord, with the soul. Just as we find everything in Him, so for His sake we forget everything.[26] Still, it is a great help, until we have learned this truth, to keep apart from our kinsfolk; later on, it may be that the Lord will wish us to see them again, so that what used to give us pleasure may be a cross to us.[27]

[22] E. omits: "Then you will . . . all over!" and continues: "If anyone tells you that the rest is virtue."
[23] E. continues, and ends the paragraph, thus: "How much more would (it be explained by) those who are different [i.e., more skilful than I]. In many places, as I have said, you will find it written: most books treat of nothing else but of how good it is to flee from the world." E. also omits: "All . . . good" from the next paragraph.
[24] T.: "about withdrawing."
[25] *De sus tierras*. The phrase will also bear the interpretation: "from their own countries."
[26] T. adds: "that we [*lit.* "it"—i.e., the soul] had here [i.e., on earth]."
[27] E.: "see them again, so as to give us a cross."

CHAPTER 10

Teaches that detachment from the things aforementioned is insufficient if we are not detached
from our own selves and that this virtue and humility go together.

Once we have detached ourselves from the world, and from
our kinsfolk, and are cloistered here, in the conditions already described,[1] it must look as if we have done everything
and there is nothing left with which we have to contend.
But, oh, my sisters,[2] do not feel secure and fall asleep, or
you will be like a man who goes to bed quite peacefully,[3]
after bolting all his doors for fear of thieves, when the thieves
are already in the house. And you know[4] there is no worse
thief *than one who lives in the house*. We ourselves are always the same;[5] unless we take great care and each of us
looks well to it that she renounces her self-will, which is the
most important business of all,[6] there will be many things
to deprive us of the holy freedom of spirit *which our souls
seek* in order to soar to their Maker unburdened by the
leaden weight of the earth.

It will be a great help towards this if we keep constantly
in our thoughts[7] the vanity of all things and the rapidity

[1] E.: "Once we have detached ourselves from this, and taken great
pains to do so, in view of its great importance—you should consider
how important it is—and are cloistered here, without possessing anything."
[2] E.: "my daughters."
[3] E.: "who remains (at home) quite peacefully."
[4] E.: "And have you not heard that . . . ?"
[5] The sense of this passage, especially without the phrase from E.
which V. omits, is not very clear. T. remodels thus: "You know
there is no worse thief for the perfection of the soul than the love
of ourselves; for unless, etc."
[6] E.: "and each of us looks well to herself, which is the chief thing
that she has to do."
[7] E.: "if we keep a very constant care concerning."

with which they pass away, so that we may withdraw our affections from things which are so trivial[8] and fix them upon what will never come to an end.[9] This may seem a poor kind of help but it will have the effect of greatly fortifying the soul. With regard to small things, we must be very careful, as soon as we begin to grow fond of them, to withdraw our thoughts from them and turn them to God.[10] His Majesty will help us to do this. He has granted us the great favour of providing that, in this house, most of it is done already; *but it remains for us to become detached from our own selves* and it is a hard thing to withdraw from ourselves and oppose ourselves, because we are very close to ourselves and love ourselves very dearly.[11]

It is here that true humility can enter,[12] for this virtue and that of detachment from self, I think, always[13] go together. They are two sisters, who are inseparable. These are not the kinsfolk whom I counsel[14] you to avoid: no, you must embrace them, and love them, and never be seen without them. Oh, how sovereign are these virtues, mistresses of all created things, empresses of the world, our deliverers from all the snares and entanglements laid by the devil, so dearly loved by our Teacher, Christ,[15] Who was never for a moment without them! He that possesses them can safely go out and fight all the united forces of hell and the whole world and its temptations.[16] Let him fear none, for his is the kingdom of the Heavens. There is none whom he need fear, for he cares nothing if he loses everything, nor does he

---

[8] E.: "from everything."
[9] E.: "what is to last for ever."
[10] E.: "to think no more of them, but turn our thoughts to God."
[11] E. continues, after the italicized phrase: "This retiring is hard, for we are very close to ourselves and are very fond of each other."
[12] Here, in the margin, is written: "Humility and mortification, very great virtues."
[13] T. omits "always."
[14] E.: "I tell."
[15] E. omits: "Christ." T. has: "our Lord Jesus Christ", and ends the sentence here.
[16] E. adds: "and against the flesh", but these words have been crossed out, probably by St. Teresa herself.

count this as loss: his sole fear is that he may displease his
God and he begs Him to nourish[17] these virtues within him
lest he lose them through any fault of his own.

These virtues, it is true, have the property of hiding themselves from one who possesses them, in such a way that he
never sees them nor can believe that he has any of them,
even if he be told so. But he esteems them so much that he
is for ever trying to obtain them, and thus he perfects them
in himself more and more. And those who possess them soon
make the fact clear, even against their will, to any with whom
they have intercourse. But how inappropriate it is for a person like myself to begin to praise humility and mortification,[18] when these virtues are so highly praised by the King
of Glory—a praise exemplified in all the trials He suffered.[19]
It is to possess these virtues, then, my daughters,[20] that you
must labour if you would leave the land of Egypt, for, when
you have obtained them, you will also obtain the manna; all
things will taste well to you; and, however much the world
may dislike their savour,[21] to you they will be sweet.

The first thing, then, that we have to do, *and that at once*,
is to rid ourselves of love for this body of ours—and some of
us pamper our natures so much that this will cause us no
little labour, *while others* are so concerned about their health
that the trouble these things give us (this is especially so of
poor nuns, but it applies to others as well)[22] is amazing.
Some of us, however, seem to think that we embraced the
religious life for no other reason than to keep ourselves
alive[23] and each nun does all she can to that end. In this
house, as a matter of fact, there is very little chance for us to

[17] E.: "There is none whom he need fear, but he must beg God to
nourish." E. begins the next paragraph at: "But how inappropriate . . ."
[18] E. adds, redundantly: "or mortification and humility."
[19] T.: "in all His trials."
[20] E.: "my sisters."
[21] E.: "however bad they may be in the eyes of the world."
[22] E.: "the trouble these two things give us."
[23] *Lit.*: "to contrive not to die." But the reading of E. ("to think
that we came to the convent for no other reason than to serve our
bodies and look after them") suggests that this is what is meant.

act on such a principle, but I should be sorry if we even wanted to. Resolve, sisters,[24] that it is to die for Christ, and not to practise self-indulgence for Christ, that you have come here. The devil tells us that self-indulgence is necessary if we are to carry out and keep the Rule of our Order, and so many of us, forsooth, try to keep our Rule by looking after our health[25] that we die without having kept it for as long as a month—perhaps even for a day. I really do not know what we are coming to.

No one need be afraid of our committing[26] excesses here, by any chance—for as soon as we do any penances our confessors begin to fear that we shall kill ourselves with them.[27] We are so horrified at our own possible excesses—if only we were as conscientious about everything else! Those who tend to the opposite extreme will, I know, not mind[28] my saying this, nor shall I mind if they say I am judging others by myself, for they will be quite right.[29] *I believe—indeed, I am sure—that more nuns are of my way of thinking than are offended by me because they do just the opposite.* My own belief is that it is for this reason that the Lord is pleased to make us such weakly creatures; at least He has shown me great mercy in making me so; for, as I was sure to be self-indulgent in any case, He was pleased to provide me with an excuse for this. It is really amusing to see how[30] some people torture themselves about it, when the real reason lies in themselves; sometimes they get a desire[31] to do penances, as one might say, without rhyme or reason; they go on doing

24 E.: "my daughters."
25 E.: "try to keep [i.e., indulge] ourselves in order to keep it [i.e., our Rule]."
26 E.: "that nuns will commit." In T. St. Teresa has substituted for the opening words of the paragraph: "It is certain that we shall not commit."
27 E.: "nor must our confessors be afraid of this and at once start thinking that we shall kill ourselves with penances."
28 E.: "must not mind."
29 E. omits: "for they will be quite right."
30 T. alters *donosa* ["amusing"] to *dañosa* and reads: "It is harmful when."
31 E.: "a frenzy."

them for a couple of days; and then the devil puts it into their heads that they have been doing themselves harm and so he makes them afraid of penances, after which they dare not do even those that the Order requires—they have tried them once![32] They[33] do not keep the smallest points in the Rule, such as silence, which is quite incapable of harming us. Hardly have we begun to imagine that our heads are aching[34] than we stay away from choir, though that would not kill us either. *One day we are absent because we had a headache some time ago; another day, because our head has just been aching again; and on the next three days in case it should ache once more.*[35] Then we want to invent penances of our own, with the result that we do neither the one thing nor the other. Sometimes there is very little the matter with us, yet we think that it should dispense us from all our obligations and that if we ask to be excused from them we are doing all we need.[36]

But why, you will say, does the Prioress excuse us?[37] Perhaps she would not if she knew what was going on inside us; but *she sees one of you wailing about a mere nothing as if your heart were breaking, and you come and ask her to excuse you from keeping the whole of your Rule, saying it is a matter of great necessity, and, when there is any substance in what you say,*[38] there is always a physician at hand to confirm it[39] or some friend or relative weeping at your side. *Some-*

---

[32] E.: "and so—no more penances, not even those that the Order requires: they have tried them once!"

[33] I follow E. here: V. has "We".

[34] So E. V. has: "Hardly have our heads ached."

[35] E. ends the paragraph here.

[36] T. had: "if we comply with (the demands of) obedience", for which St. Teresa substituted, in her own hand: "if we ask the superior (*fem.*) to excuse us from them."

[37] E. reads: "You will say, friends, that the superior (*mayor*: see p. 62, n. 4, above) should not allow it," and omits the following "perhaps".

[38] I follow E. here. V. omits the italicized phrase as far as "breaking" and then reads: "you tell her about it and say it is necessary, and there is always a physician at hand, etc." E. is more picturesque and trenchant throughout the latter part of this chapter: the Saint evidently wrote it with specific incidents in mind.

[39] E.: "to confirm the account you give."

times the poor Prioress sees that your request is excessive, but what can she do? She feels a scruple if she thinks she has been lacking in charity and she would rather the fault were yours than hers: *she thinks, too, that it would be unjust of her to judge you harshly.*

Oh, God help me! That there should be complaining like this among nuns! May He forgive me for saying so, but I am afraid it has become quite a habit. I happened to observe this incident once myself: a nun began complaining about her headaches and she went on complaining to me for a long time. In the end I made enquiries and found she had no headache whatever, but was suffering from some pain or other elsewhere.

These are things which may sometimes happen and I put them down here so that you may guard against them; for if once the devil begins to frighten us about losing our health, we shall never get anywhere. The Lord give us light so that we may act rightly in everything! Amen.

CHAPTER 11

Continues to treat of mortification and describes how it may be attained in times of sickness.

These continual moanings which we make about trifling ailments, my sisters, seem to me a sign of imperfection:[1] if you can bear a thing, say nothing about it. When the ailment is serious, it proclaims itself; that is quite another kind of moaning, which draws attention to itself immediately. Remember, there are only a few of you, and if one of you gets into this habit she will worry all the rest—that is, assuming you love each other and there is charity among you. On the other hand, if one of you is really ill, she should

[1] E.: "This constant talking and moaning and whining as if we were ill, my sisters, seems to me a sign of great imperfection. Do not do this, for the love of God, if you can avoid it."

say so and take the necessary remedies; and, if you have got rid of your self-love, you will so much regret having to indulge yourselves in any way that there will be no fear of your doing so unnecessarily or of your making[2] a moan without proper cause.[3] When such a reason exists, it would be much worse to say nothing about it than to allow[4] yourselves unnecessary indulgence, and it would be very wrong if everybody were not sorry for you.

However, I am quite sure that where there is *prayer and* charity among you, and your numbers are so small *that you will be aware of each other's needs*,[5] there will never be any lack of care in your being looked after.[6] Do not think of complaining about the weaknesses[7] and minor ailments from which women suffer, for the devil sometimes makes you imagine them. They come and go; and unless you get rid of[8] the habit of talking about them and complaining of everything (except to God) you will never come to the end of them. *I lay great stress on this, for I believe myself it is important, and it is one of the reasons for the relaxation of discipline in religious houses.* For this body of ours has one fault: the more you indulge it, the more things it discovers to be essential to it. It is extraordinary how it likes being indulged; and, if there is any reasonable pretext for indulgence, however little necessity for it there may be, the poor soul is taken in and prevented from making progress. Think how many poor people there must be who are ill and have no one to complain to, for poverty and self-indulgence make

[2] T.: "that you will do so unnecessarily or make."
[3] E., which shows slight variations of detail from V. in the preceding sentence, continues: "When such a reason exists, it would be very bad to say nothing about it, and much worse if everybody were not sorry for you."
[4] T.: "it would be a very good thing to say so and much better than to allow."
[5] T.: "However, where there is charity and your numbers are so small."
[6] E.: "lack of comfort."
[7] E.: "Forget the weaknesses." V. reads, literally: "Forget to complain about the weaknesses."
[8] E. uses the imperative: "Get rid of, etc."

bad company. Think, too, how many married women—people of position, as I know—have serious complaints and sore trials and yet dare not complain to their husbands about them for fear of annoying them. Sinner that I am! Surely we have not come here to indulge ourselves more than they! Oh, how free you are from the great trials of the world! Learn to suffer a little for the love of God without telling everyone about it. When a woman has made an unhappy marriage she does not talk about it or complain of it, lest it should come to her husband's knowledge; she has to endure a great deal of misery and yet has no one to whom she may relieve her mind.[9] Cannot we, then, keep secret between God and ourselves some of the ailments which He sends us because of our sins? The more so since talking about them does nothing whatever to alleviate them.

In nothing that I have said am I referring to serious illnesses, accompanied by high fever, though as to these, too, I beg you to observe moderation and to have patience: I am thinking rather of those minor indispositions which you may have and still keep going[10] *without worrying everybody else to death over them.* What would happen if these lines should be seen outside this house? What would all the nuns[11] say of me? And how willingly would I bear what they said if it helped anyone to live a better life! For when there is one person of this kind,[12] the thing generally comes to such a pass that *some suffer on account of others, and* nobody who

[9] Both E. and V. read: "she talks about it and complains of it without her husband's knowledge; and she has to endure, etc."

If, out of respect for these manuscripts, which agree exactly here, except that E. has "she grows very unhappy and suffers great trials", one translates literally, the passage will make fair sense. T., however, inserts a negative before "talks", enabling us to read: "she does not talk about it or complain of it lest her husband should know"; and some unknown hand has also made this emendation in V. This reading, followed by many later editions and translations, is distinctly preferable as to sense and also agrees better with the sentences preceding and following. I therefore adopt it, though it lacks the authority of the reading of E. and V.

[10] *Lit.*: "which can be suffered on foot."

[11] E.: "the convents" (*monasterios*).

[12] E.: "In the end."

says she is ill will be believed, however serious her ailment.[13] *As this book is meant only for my daughters, they will put up with everything I say.* Let us remember our holy Fathers of past days, the hermits[14] whose lives we attempt to imitate. What sufferings they bore, what solitude, cold, [thirst] and hunger, what burning sun and heat![15] And yet they had no one to complain to except God. Do you suppose they were made of iron? No: they were as frail as we are. Believe me, daughters, once we begin[16] to subdue these miserable bodies of ours, they give us much less trouble. There will be quite sufficient people to see to what you really need,[17] so take no thought for yourselves except when you know it to be necessary. Unless we resolve to put up with death and ill-health once and for all, we shall[18] never accomplish anything.

Try not to fear these and commit yourselves wholly to God, come what may. What does it matter if we die?[19] How many times have our bodies not mocked us? Should we not occasionally mock them in our turn?[20] And, believe me, *slight as it may seem by comparison with other things,* this resolution is much more important than we may think;[21]

[13] E. (after "others, and"): "if anyone is suffering (from an illness), the very doctors will not believe her, as they have seen others having very little the matter with them and complaining so much about it."

[14] E.: "Remember our holy Fathers of past days, and the holy hermits."

[15] E.: "how many suns!"

[16] E.: "they were made of flesh as much as we are ourselves, and once we begin."

[17] *Lit.:* "to look at (or to) what is needful"—the phrase is ambiguous and might mean: "to worry about their own needs." The word translated "people" is feminine.

[18] E.: "Unless you . . . you will." The second person is also used for the first in the paragraph following.

[19] E. omits this sentence.

[20] E. uses the imperative, reading: "Mock them yourselves for just one day."

[21] E. continues and ends the chapter thus: "Put it into practice in such a way that it becomes a habit and you will see that I am not lying. May the Lord, Who will help us in all we do, grant (that we may do) this, and may His Majesty do it for His own sake."

for, if we continually make it, day by day, by the grace of the Lord, we shall gain dominion over the body. To conquer such an enemy is a great achievement in the battle of life. May the Lord grant, as He is able, that we may do this. I am quite sure that no one who does not enjoy such a victory, which I believe is a great one, will understand what advantage it brings, and no one will regret having gone through trials in order to attain this tranquillity and self-mastery.

CHAPTER 12

Teaches that the true lover of God must care little for life and honour.

We now come to some other *little* things which are also of very great importance, though they will appear[1] trifling. All this seems a great task,[2] and so it is, for it means warring against ourselves. But once we begin to work, God, too, works in our souls and bestows such favours on them that the most we can do in this life seems to us very little. And we nuns are doing everything we can,[3] by giving up our freedom for the love of God and entrusting it to another, and in putting up with so many trials—fasts, silence, enclosure, service in choir—that however much we may want to indulge[4] ourselves we can do so only occasionally: perhaps, in all the convents I have seen, I am the only nun guilty of self-indulgence.

[1] E.: "they are."
[2] E. ends the sentence here.
[3] E. continues: "giving God the chief thing, which is the will, and entrusting it to another. Why (then) do we shrink from interior (mortification) in what is nothing? We put up with so many trials —fasts, silence, constant service in choir—that, however much we may want to indulge ourselves, we can only do so at times, and not always, and perhaps, etc."
[4] T.: "to excuse." The word "indulge" is crossed out, as is the phrase "and perhaps . . . self-indulgence".

Why, then, do we shrink from interior mortification, since this is the means by which every other kind of mortification[5] may become much more meritorious and perfect,[6] so that it can then be practised with greater tranquillity and ease? This, as I have said, is acquired by gradual progress and by never indulging our own will and desire, even in small things, until we have succeeded in subduing the body to the spirit.[7]

I repeat that this consists mainly or entirely in our ceasing to care about ourselves and our own pleasures, for the least that anyone who is beginning to serve the Lord truly can offer Him is his life. Once he has surrendered his will to Him, what has he to fear?[8] It is evident that if he is a true religious and a real man of prayer and aspires to the enjoyment of Divine consolations, he must not [turn back or] shrink from desiring to die and suffer martyrdom for His sake. And do you not know, sisters, that the life of a good[9] religious, who wishes to be among the closest friends of God, is one long martyrdom? I say "long", for, by comparison with decapitation, which is over very quickly, it may well be termed so, though life itself is short and some lives are short in the extreme.[10] How do we know but that ours will be so short that it may end only one hour or one moment after the time of our resolving to render our entire service to God? This would be quite possible; and so we must not set store by anything that comes to an end, *least of all by life, since not a*

---

[5] T.: "by which everything—everything, even this other (kind of mortification)—"

[6] T. continues: "I mean everything, so that it can be." These words are St. Teresa's own interlinear substitution for "them", which she deletes.

[7] E. repeats: "Why, then, do we shrink from mortifying these bodies as to mere trifles (*naderías*)—that is, giving them pleasure in nothing, and carefully taking them where they have no wish to go, until we have subdued them to the spirit?"

[8] E. begins: "I think, when anyone begins to serve God truly, the least he can offer Him, after surrendering his will, is his life, (which is) a mere nothing (*nonada*)."

[9] E.: "a true."

[10] E. continues: "Briefly, we must not set store, etc."

day of it is secure. Who, if he thought that each hour[11] might be his last, would not spend it in labour?[12]

Believe me, it is safest to think that this is so;[13] by so doing we shall learn to subdue our wills in everything; for if, as I have said, you are very careful *about your prayer,* you will *soon* find yourselves gradually reaching the summit of the mountain without knowing how.[14] But how harsh it sounds to say that we must take pleasure in nothing, unless we also say what consolations and delights[15] this renunciation brings in its train, and what a great gain it is,[16] even in this life! What security it gives us![17] Here, as you all practise this, you have done the principal part; each of you encourages[18] and helps the rest; and each of you must try to outstrip her sisters.

Be very careful about your interior thoughts, especially if they have to do with precedence. May God, by His Passion, keep us from expressing, or dwelling upon, such thoughts as these:[19] "But I am her senior [in the Order]"; "But I am older"; "But I have worked harder"; "But that other sister is being better treated than I am". If these thoughts come, you must quickly check them;[20] if you allow yourselves to dwell on them, or introduce them into your conversation, they will spread like the plague and *in religious houses* they may give rise to great abuses. *Remember, I know a great deal about this.* If you have a prioress who allows such things, however trifling,[21] you must believe that God has permitted her to

---

11 E.: "each day".
12 E. adds—redundantly, no doubt for emphasis—"if he thought he had no more than that (day) to live."
13 E.: "Reflect, then, sisters: it is safest to believe that that is so."
14 E., which has used the second person from the beginning of the paragraph, here adds words implied in the context: "although this may not happen quickly."
15 E.: "what consolation and pleasure."
16 E.: "and how many delights are gained by it."
17 T. omits this sentence.
18 *Lit.:* "awakens." E.: "reminds." T.: "awakens and enlivens."
19 E.: "keep us from saying."
20 E.: "You must quickly check these first movements."
21 E. adds, redundantly: "whether little or much." T. has "superior" (*fem.*) for "prioress".

be given to you[22] because of your sins and that she will be the beginning of your ruin. *Cry to Him, and let your whole prayer be that He may come to your aid by sending you either a religious or a person given to prayer; for, if anyone prays with the resolve to enjoy the favours and consolations which God bestows in prayer, it is always well that he should have this detachment.*[23]

You may ask[24] why I lay such stress on this, and think that I am being too severe about it, and say that God grants consolations to persons less completely detached than that. I quite believe He does; for, in His infinite wisdom, He sees that this will enable Him to lead them to leave everything for His sake. I do not mean, by "leaving" everything, entering the religious life, for there may be obstacles to this, and the soul that is perfect can be detached and humble anywhere. It will find detachment harder in the world, however, for worldly trappings will be a great impediment to it.[25] Still, believe me in this: questions of honour and *desires for* property can arise within convents[26] as well as outside them, and the more temptations of this kind are removed from us, the more we are to blame if we yield to them. Though persons who do so may have spent years in prayer, or rather in meditation (for perfect prayer eventually destroys [all] these attachments), they will never make great progress or come to enjoy the real fruit of prayer.

Ask yourselves, sisters, if these things, *which seem so insignificant,* mean anything to you, for the only reason you are here is that you may detach yourselves from them. Nobody honours you any the more for having them and they lose you advantages which might have gained you more hon-

---

[22] Thus E. V. reads: "has permitted you to have her."
[23] Thus E., the last clause reading literally: "this (matter) of detachment is fitting for all." V. condenses thus: "Pray fervently, so that He may grant you His help, for you are in great danger." T. follows V., but ends the sentence at "help".
[24] E., more briefly: "Do not tell me that God grants consolations, etc."
[25] E. omits this sentence.
[26] T.: "within religious Orders."

our;[27] the result is that you get both dishonour and loss at the same time. Let each of you ask herself how much humility she has and she will see what progress she has made. If she is really humble, I do not think the devil will dare[28] to tempt her to take even the slightest interest in matters of precedence, for he is so shrewd that he is afraid of the blow she would strike him. If a humble soul is tempted in this way by the devil, that virtue cannot fail to bring her[29] more fortitude and greater profit.[30] For clearly the temptation will cause her to look into her life,[31] to compare the services she has rendered the Lord with what she owes Him and with the marvellous way in which He abased Himself to give us an example of humility, and to think over her sins and remember where she deserves to be on account of them.[32] Exercises like this[33] bring the soul such profit that on the following day Satan will not dare to come back again lest he should get his head broken.

Take this advice from me and do not forget it: you should see to it that your sisters profit by your temptations, not only interiorly (where it would be very wrong if they did not), but exteriorly as well. If you want to avenge yourself on the devil and free yourselves more quickly[34] from temptation, ask the superior, as soon as a temptation comes to you, to give you some lowly office to do, or do some such thing, as best you can, on our own initiative, studying as you do it how to bend your will to perform tasks you dislike. The Lord will show you ways of doing so and this will soon rid you of the temptation.[35]

---

27 E.: "and they lose you profit, as we say."
28 E.: "I consider it certain that the devil will not dare."
29 T.: "that virtue gains her."
30 E.: "and most high degrees of profit."
31 E.: "For she will be bound to review [lit.: "to bring out"] her sins."
32 E. omits: "and to think . . . of them."
33 The Spanish of V. has "The soul profits so much." T. reads: "These considerations bring, etc."
34 E. omits: "more quickly."
35 E.: "from temptation, unburden yourself to the superior, as soon as a temptation comes to you, and ask and beg her to give you some

God deliver us from people who wish to serve Him yet who are mindful of their own honour.[36] Reflect how little they gain from this; for, as I have said, the very act of desiring honour robs us of it, especially in matters of precedence:[37] there is no poison in the world which is so fatal to perfection. You will say that these are little things which have to do with human nature and are not worth troubling about;[38] do not trifle with them, for *in religious houses* they spread like foam on water, and there is no small matter so extremely dangerous as are punctiliousness about honour and sensitiveness to insult.[39] Do you know one reason, apart from many others, why this is so?[40] It may have its root, perhaps, in some trivial slight—hardly anything, in fact—and the devil will then induce someone else to consider it important, so that she will think it a real charity to tell you about it and to ask how you can allow yourself to be insulted so; and she will pray that God may give you patience and that you may offer it to Him, for even a saint could not bear more. The devil is simply putting his deceitfulness into this other person's mouth;[41] and, though you yourself are quite ready to bear the slight, you are tempted to vainglory because you have not resisted something else as perfectly as you should.

This human nature of ours is so *wretchedly* weak that, even while we are telling ourselves that there is nothing for us to make a fuss about, we imagine we are doing something

---

very lowly office, or study as best you can how to bend your will in this matter, for the Lord will show you many things: (you can also make use) of public mortifications, which are used in this house. Flee from such temptations of the devil as from the plague, and see to it that he is with you but little."

[36] E. adds: "or fear dishonour."

[37] E.: "especially in religious Orders."

[38] E.: "little things which are nothing (*nada*)."

[39] E. omits: "as are . . . insult." T. has: "as are these cases and punctiliousness, etc."

[40] *Lit.*: "Do you know why, apart from many other things?" E. has simply: "Do you know why?"

[41] E. ends the paragraph: "you cannot help suffering, but you are tempted to vainglory and told it is a great deal (to bear)."

virtuous, and begin to feel sorry for ourselves,[42] particularly
when we see that other people are sorry for us too.[43] In this
way the soul begins to lose the occasions of merit which it
had gained; it becomes weaker; and thus a door is opened to
the devil by which he can enter on some other occasion with
a temptation worse than the last. It may even happen that,
when you yourself are prepared to suffer an insult, your sisters come and ask you if you are a beast of burden, and say
you ought to be more sensitive about things. Oh, my sisters,
for the love of God, never let charity move you to show pity
for another in anything to do with these fancied insults, for
that is like the pity shown to holy Job by his wife and friends.

CHAPTER 13

Continues to treat of mortification and explains
how one must renounce the world's standards of
wisdom in order to attain to true wisdom.[1]

I often tell you, sisters, and now I want it to be set down in
writing,[2] not to forget that we in this house, and for that
matter anyone who would be perfect,[3] must flee a thousand
leagues from such phrases as: "I had right on my side"; "They

---

[42] E.: "that, even while minimizing the thing to ourselves and saying it is nothing, we are feeling sorry for ourselves."
[43] E. ends the chapter thus: "Thinking we are in the right makes
the trouble grow and the soul loses all the occasions of merit which
it had gained, and becomes weaker, so that on the next day the devil
may come with a worse temptation than the last. Often, indeed, it
may happen that, when you yourself are prepared not to feel ag-
grieved, your sisters come and ask you if you are a beast of burden,
and say you ought to be more sensitive about things, Oh, what it is
to have friends!"
[1] E. begins this chapter with the last sentence of the preceding chapter, minus the reference to Job (see previous note), and continues:
"I often tell you, etc."
[2] E.: "and I now write it here."
[3] E.: "and every perfect person."

had no right to do this to me"; "The person who treated me like this was not right".[4] God deliver us from such a false idea of right as that! Do you think that it was right for our good Jesus[5] to have to suffer so many insults, and that those who heaped them on Him[6] were right, and that they had any right to do Him those wrongs? I do not know why anyone is in a convent who is willing to bear only the crosses that she has a perfect right to expect: such a person should return to the world, though even there such rights will not be safeguarded. Do you think you can ever possibly have to bear so much that you ought not to have to bear any more? How does right enter into the matter at all? I really do not know.

Before we begin talking about not having our rights, let us wait until we receive some honour or gratification, or are treated kindly,[7] for it is certainly not right that we should have anything[8] in this life like that. When, on the other hand, some offence is done to us (and we do not feel it an offence to us that it should be so described), I do not see what we can find to complain of. Either we are the brides of this great King or we are not. If we are, what wife is there with a sense of honour who does not accept her share in any dishonour done to her spouse, even though she may do so against her will?[9] Each partner, in fact, shares in the honour and dishonour of the other. To desire to share in the kingdom [of our Spouse Jesus Christ], and to enjoy it, and yet not to be willing to have[10] any part in His dishonours and trials, is ridiculous.

God keep us from being like that! Let the sister who thinks that she is accounted the least among all consider herself the [happiest and] most fortunate, as indeed she *really* is, if she lives her life as she should, for in that case she will, *as a rule,*

[4] E.: "The sister was not right."
[5] E.: "for Christ our Good."
[6] *Lit.*: "did them to Him." E. has "said" for "did".
[7] T. omits: "or are treated kindly."
[8] T.: "any kind treatment."
[9] E. prefaces this last clause to the following sentence.
[10] E.: "To desire to participate in the kingdom of our Spouse, and to be companions with Him in rejoicing, and yet not to have."

have no lack of honour either in this life or in the next. Believe me when I say this[11]—what an absurdity, though, it is for me to say "Believe me" when the words come from Him Who is true Wisdom, *Who is Truth Itself, and from the Queen of the angels*! Let us, my daughters, in some *small* degree, imitate the great humility of the most sacred Virgin,[12] whose habit we wear and whose nuns we are ashamed to call ourselves. *Let us at least imitate this humility of hers in some degree—I say "in some degree"* because, however much we may seem to humble ourselves, we fall far short of being the daughters of such a Mother, and the brides of such a Spouse. If, then, the habits I have described are not sternly checked, what seems nothing to-day will perhaps be a venial sin to-morrow,[13] and that is so infectious a tendency that, if you leave it alone, the sin will not be the only one for long; and that is a very bad thing for communities.

We who live in a community should consider this very carefully, so as not to harm those who labour to benefit us and to set us a good example. If we realize what great harm is done by the formation of a bad habit *of over-punctiliousness about our honour*, we should rather die *a thousand deaths* than be the cause of such a thing. For only the body would die, whereas the loss of a soul is a great loss which is apparently without end; some of us will die, but others will take our places and perhaps they may all be harmed more by the one bad habit which we started than they are benefited by many virtues. For the devil does not allow a single bad habit to disappear and the very weakness of our mortal nature destroys the virtues in us.

[11] E. adds: "for I have experienced it"; but these words were erased by St. Teresa and do not appear in V.
[12] E.: "imitate this most sacred Virgin."
[13] E.: "however much we may abase and humble ourselves, that is nothing for one like myself, who, for her sins, deserves to be abased and despised by the devils, though she might not wish to be, and, while others have not committed so many sins as I, it will be surprising if any of them has failed to commit enough to merit hell. I repeat, then, that you must not consider these things as trifles: unless you are diligent in uprooting them, what was nothing to-day will perhaps be a venial sin to-morrow."

Oh, what a real charity it would be, and what a service would be rendered to God, if any nun who sees that she cannot [endure and] conform to the customs of this house would recognize the fact and go away [before being professed, as I have said elsewhere], *and leave the other sisters in peace! And no convent (at least, if it follows my advice) will take her or allow her to make her profession until they have given her many years' probation to see if she improves. I am not referring to shortcomings affecting penances and fasts, for, although these are wrong, they are not things which do so much harm. I am thinking of nuns who are of such a temperament that they like to be esteemed and made much of; who see the faults of others but never recognize their own; and who are deficient in other ways like these, the true source of which is want of humility. If God does not help such a person by bestowing great spirituality upon her, until after many years she becomes greatly improved, may God preserve you from keeping her in your community. For you must realize that she will neither have peace there herself nor allow you to have any.*

As you do not take dowries, God is very gracious to you in this respect. It grieves me that religious houses should often harbour one who is a thief and robs them of their treasure, either because they are unwilling to return a dowry or out of regard for the relatives. In this house you have risked losing worldly honour and forgone it (for no such honour is paid to those who are poor); do not desire, then, that others should be honoured at such a cost to yourselves. Our honour, sisters, must lie in the service of God, and, if anyone thinks to hinder you in this, she had better keep her honour and stay at home. It was with this in mind that our Fathers ordered a year's probation (which in our Order we are free to extend to four years): personally, I should like it to be prolonged to ten years. A humble nun will mind very little if she is not professed: for she knows that if she is good she will not be sent away, and if she is not, why should she wish to do harm to one of Christ's communities?[14]

By not being good, I do not mean being fond of vanities,

---

[14] Lit.: "to this college of Christ." Cf. p. 181, below.

which, I believe, with the help of God, will be a fault far removed from the nuns in this house. I am referring to a want of mortification and an attachment to worldly things and to self-interest in the matter which I have described. Let anyone who knows that she is not greatly mortified take my advice and not make her profession[15] if she does not wish to suffer a hell on earth, and God grant there may not be another hell awaiting such a nun in the world to come![16] There are many reasons why she should fear there may be[17] and possibly neither she nor her sisters may realize this as well as I do.

Believe what I say here;[18] if you will not, I must leave it to time to prove the truth of my words. For the *whole* manner of life we are trying to live is making us, not only nuns, but hermits [like the holy Fathers our predecessors] and leading us to detachment from all things created. I have observed that anyone whom the Lord has specially chosen[19] for this life is granted that favour. She may not have it in full perfection, but that she has it will be evident from the great joy and gladness that such detachment gives her, and she will never have any more to do with worldly things, for her delight will be in all the practices of the religious life.[20] I say once more that anyone who is inclined to things of the world should leave the convent[21] if she sees she is not making progress. If she still wishes to be a nun she should go to another convent; if she does not, she will see what happens to her. She must not complain of me as the foundress of this convent and say I have not warned her.

This house is another Heaven, if it be possible to have Heaven upon earth. Anyone whose sole pleasure lies in pleas-

---

15 V. reads (after "and go away" p. 106): "Let her see that she carries out her obligations if she does not wish, etc."
16 T. omits: "if she does not . . . to come."
17 E.: "there are many reasons for it in her." T. reads similarly.
18 In T. these words are rather unintelligently deleted.
19 E.: "the Lord specially desires."
20 E. omits: "for her . . . religious life."
21 I.e., St. Joseph's, Ávila. T. reads here: ". . . of the world is not (meant) for these convents [i.e., of the Reform]. If she wishes to be a nun she can go to another; if she does not, etc."

ing God and who cares nothing for her own pleasure will find our life a very good one;[22] if she wants anything more, she will lose everything, for there is nothing more that she can have. A discontented soul is like a person suffering from severe nausea, who rejects all food, however nice it may be; things which persons in good health delight in eating only cause her *the greater* loathing. Such a person will save her soul better elsewhere[23] than here; she may even gradually reach a degree of perfection which she could not have attained here because we expected too much of her all at once. For although we allow time for the attainment of complete detachment and mortification in interior matters, in externals this has to be practised immediately,[24] *because of the harm which may otherwise befall the rest*; and anyone who sees this being done, and spends all her time in such good company, and yet, at the end of *six months* or a year, has made no progress, will, I fear, make none over a great many years, and will even go backward. I do not say that such a nun must be as perfect as the rest, but she must be sure that her soul is gradually growing healthier—and it will soon become clear if her disease is mortal.

CHAPTER 14

Treats of the great importance of not professing anyone whose spirit is contrary to the things aforementioned.

I feel sure that the Lord bestows great help on anyone who makes good resolutions, and for that reason it is necessary to enquire into the intention[1] of anyone who enters [the life

---

[22] T. omits: "will . . . one", and, after "upon earth", reads: "for anyone whose, etc."
[23] E. adds: "in a convent which is not so strict."
[24] E.: "very soon."
[1] E. reads: "gives help to" and: "for that reason it is important to consider what is the talent".

of religion]. She must not come, as many nuns [now] do, simply to further her own interests, although the Lord can perfect even this intention if she is a person of intelligence. If not intelligent, a person of this kind should on no account be admitted; for she will not understand her own reasons for coming, nor will she understand others who attempt subsequently to improve her. For, in general, a person who has this fault always thinks she knows better than the wisest what is good for her; and I believe this evil is incurable, for it is rarely unaccompanied by malice. In a convent where there are a great many *nuns* it may be tolerated, but it cannot be suffered among a few.

When an intelligent person begins to grow fond of what is good, she clings to it manfully, for she sees that it is the best thing for her; this course may not bring her great spirituality but it will help her to give profitable advice, and to make herself useful in many ways, without being a trouble to anybody.[2] But I do not see how a person lacking in intelligence can be of any use in community life, and she may do a great deal of harm. This defect, *like others*, will not become obvious immediately; for many[3] people are good at talking and bad at understanding, while others speak in a sharp and none too refined a tone,[4] and yet they have intelligence and can do a great deal of good. There are also simple, holy people who are *quite* unversed in business matters and worldly conventions but have great skill in converse with God. Many enquiries, therefore, must be made before novices are admitted, and the period of probation before profession should be a long one. The world must understand once and for all that you are free to send them away *again*, as it is often necessary to do in a convent where the life is one of austerity; and then if you use this right no one will take offence.

I say this[5] because these times are so unhappy, and our

---

[2] E. adds: "but rather a recreation" [i.e., a refreshing companion].
[3] E.: "a few."
[4] An untranslatable play upon words: *corto y no muy cortado*—as though "sharpened" could be used in the sense of "refined".
[5] E.: "I say (the world must) understand (this)."

weakness is so great,[6] that we are not content to follow the
instructions of our predecessors and disregard the current
ideas about honour, lest we should give offence to the novices'
relatives.[7] God grant that those of us who admit unsuitable
persons may not pay for it in the world to come! Such persons are never without a pretext for persuading us to accept
them, *though in a matter of such importance no pretext is
valid. If the superior is unaffected by her personal likings
and prejudices, and considers what is for the good of the
house, I do not believe God will ever allow her to go astray.
But if she considers other people's feelings and trivial points
of detail, I feel sure she will be bound to err.*

This is something which everyone must think out for herself; she must commend it to God and encourage her superior *when her courage fails her,* of such great importance
is it. So I beg God to give you light about it. You do very
well not to accept dowries;[8] for, if you were to accept them,
it might happen that, in order not to have to give back money
which you no longer possess, you would keep a thief in the
house who was robbing you of your treasure; and that would
be no small pity.[9] So you must not receive dowries from
anyone, for to do so may be to harm the very person to whom
you desire to bring profit.[10]

[6] E.: "the weakness of nuns is so great—I say this from my own experience—."
[7] E.: "our predecessors, but, lest we should give some slight offence
and in order to stop people from talking—which is of no importance
—we allow virtuous habits to be forgotten."
[8] T. adds: "so that you may be able to choose persons, for this
would be to blind yourselves by self-interest." It varies slightly from
V. in the remaining sentences of the paragraph.
[9] Here St. Teresa is developing an idea found (in E. only) in the
preceding chapter (p. 106, above). As the language, though similar,
is not identical, the passage is allowed to stand.
[10] E. ends the chapter: "since it is a matter of very great importance
to everyone; and so I beg God to give you light about it."

CHAPTER 15

Treats of the great advantage which comes from our not excusing ourselves, even though we find we are unjustly condemned.

But how disconnectedly I am writing! I am just like a person who does not know what she is doing. It is your fault, sisters, for I am doing this at your command. Read it as best you can, for I am writing it as best I can, and, if it is too bad, burn it. I really need leisure, and, as you see, I have so little opportunity for writing that a week passes without my putting down a word, and so I forget what I have said and what I am going to say next. Now what I have just been doing—namely, excusing myself—is very bad for me, and I beg you not to copy it, for to suffer without making excuses is a habit of great perfection, and very edifying and meritorious; and, though I often teach you this, and by God's goodness you practise it, His Majesty has never granted this favour to me. May He be pleased to bestow it on me before I die.[1]

I am greatly confused as I begin to urge this virtue upon you, for I ought myself to have practised at least something of what[2] I am recommending you with regard to it: but actually I must confess I have made very little progress. I never seem unable to find a reason for thinking I am being virtuous when I make excuses for myself. There are times when this is lawful, and when not to do it would be wrong, but I have not the discretion (or, better, the humility) to do it only when fitting. For, indeed, it takes great humility to find oneself unjustly condemned and be silent,[3] and to do this is to

[1] E. opens with this passage and then continues: "I am never unable to find a reason for thinking I am being virtuous, etc." Before taking up the thread of the argument here, however, I give the opening passage from V., which is shorter and equally personal, and, though similar, not identical in thought.

[2] T.: "practised what."

[3] E. omits: "and be silent."

imitate the Lord Who set us free from all our sins. I beg you, then, to study[4] earnestly to do so, for it brings great gain; whereas I can see no gain in our trying to free ourselves from blame: none whatever—save, as I say, in a few cases where hiding the truth might cause offence or scandal. Anyone will understand this who has more discretion than I.

I think it is very important to accustom oneself to practise this virtue and to endeavour to obtain from the Lord the true humility which must result from it. The truly humble person will have a genuine desire to be thought little of, and persecuted, and condemned unjustly, even in serious matters.[5] For, if she desires to imitate the Lord, how can she do so better than in this? And no bodily strength is necessary here, nor the aid of anyone save God.

These are great virtues, my sisters, and I should like us to study them closely, and to make them our penance.[6] As you know, I deprecate [other severe and] excessive penances, which, if practised indiscreetly, may injure the health. Here, however, there is no cause for fear; for, however great the interior virtues may be, they do not weaken the body so that it cannot serve the Order, while at the same time they strengthen the soul;[7] and, furthermore, they can be applied to very little things, and thus, as I have said on other occasions, they accustom one to gain great victories in *very* important matters.[8] I have not, however, been able to test this particular thing myself, for I never heard anything bad said

[4] E.: "I should like strongly to urge upon you to study." T. reads: "to be careful to do so."
[5] T.: "and condemned, although he may have done nothing to justify this."
[6] E.: "and I should like them to be our study and penance." T.: "closely, for they are a good penance."
[7] E.: "As you know, I deprecate other austerities, even good ones, when they are excessive. Great interior virtues do not weaken the body or rob it of strength so that it cannot serve the Order, and at the same time they strengthen the soul."
[8] E. omits: "as I have said on other occasions" and after the end of the sentence goes on: "But how well this can be written down and how badly I put it into practice! In reality I have not been able to test this myself in important matters, for I never, etc."

of me which I did not *clearly* realize fell short of the truth. If I had not *sometimes—often, indeed*—offended God in the ways they referred to, I had done so in many others, and I felt they had treated me far too indulgently in saying nothing about these: I much preferred people to blame me for what was not true than to tell the truth about me. *For I disliked hearing things that were true said about me, whereas these other things, however serious they were, I did not mind at all. In small matters I followed my own inclinations, and I still do so, without paying any attention to what is most perfect. So I should like you to begin to realize this at an early stage, and I want each of you to ponder how much there is to be gained in every way by this virtue, and how, so far as I can see, there is nothing to be lost by it. The chief thing we gain is being able, in some degree, to follow the Lord.*[9]

It is a great help to meditate upon the great gain which in any case this is bound to bring us, and to realize how, properly speaking, we can never be blamed unjustly, since we are always full of faults, and a just man falls seven times a day,[10] so that it would be a falsehood for us to say we have no sin. If, then, we are not to blame for the thing that we are accused of, we are never wholly without blame in the way that our good Jesus was.

Oh, my Lord! When I think in how many ways Thou didst suffer, and in all of them undeservedly, I know not what to say for myself, or what I can have been thinking about when I desired not to suffer, or what I am doing when I make excuses for myself. Thou knowest, my Good, that if there is anything good in me it comes from no other hands than Thine own. For what is it to Thee, Lord, to give much instead of little? True, I do not deserve it, but neither have I deserved the favours which Thou hast shown me already. Can it be that I should wish a thing so evil as myself to be thought well of by anyone, when they have said such wicked

[9] E. continues: "I say 'in some degree' because, as I have said, we are never blamed when we have done nothing wrong at all, for we are always full of faults, since a just man falls seven times a day, etc."
[10] Proverbs xxiv, 16.

things of Thee, Who art good above all other good? It is intolerable, my God, it is intolerable; nor would I that Thou shouldst have to tolerate anything displeasing in Thine eyes being found in Thy handmaiden. For see, Lord, mine eyes are blind and very little pleases them. Do Thou give me light and make me truly to desire that all should hate me, since I have so often left Thee, Who hast loved me with such[11] faithfulness.

What is this, my God? What advantage do we think to gain from giving pleasure to creatures? What does it matter to us if we are blamed by them all, provided we are without blame in the sight of the Lord?[12] Oh, my sisters, we shall never succeed in understanding this truth and we shall never attain perfection[13] unless we think and meditate upon what is real and upon what is not. If there were no other gain than the confusion which will be felt by the person[14] who has blamed you when she sees that you have allowed yourselves to be condemned unjustly, that would be a very great thing. Such an experience uplifts the soul more than ten sermons. And we must all try to be preachers by our deeds,[15] since both the Apostle and our own lack of ability forbid us to be preachers in word.

Never suppose that either the evil or the good that you do will remain secret,[16] however strict may be your enclosure. Do you suppose, daughter,[17] that, if you do not make excuses for yourself, there will not be someone else who will defend you? Remember how the Lord took the Magdalen's part in the Pharisee's house and also when her sister blamed her.[18] He will not treat you as rigorously as He treated Himself:

---

[11] E.: "complete."
[12] E.: "if I am without blame in the sight of my Creator."
[13] E.: "attain the summit of perfection."
[14] E.: "the sister."
[15] E.: "you must . . . your deeds."
[16] E. adds, parenthetically: "I think I have already told you this once and I should like to say it many times more."
[17] E. uses the plural throughout this paragraph.
[18] E. reads: ". . . part when Saint Martha was blaming her," and omits the next sentence ("He will not . . . defend Him.")

it was not until He was on the Cross that He had even a thief to defend Him. His Majesty, then, will put it into somebody's mind to defend you; if He does not, it will be because there is no need. This I have myself seen, and it is a fact, although I should not like[19] you to think too much of it, but rather to be glad when you are blamed, and in due time you will see what profit you experience in your souls.[20] For it is in this way that you will begin to gain freedom; soon you will not care if they speak ill or well of you; it will seem like someone else's business. It will be as if two persons are talking *in your presence* and you are quite uninterested in what they are saying because you are not actually being addressed by them. So here: it becomes such a habit with us not to reply that it seems as if they are not addressing us at all. This may seem impossible to those of us who are very sensitive and not capable of great mortification. It is indeed difficult at first, but I know that, with the Lord's help, the *gradual* attainment of this freedom, and of renunciation and self-detachment, is quite possible.

19 E.: "His Majesty will put it into somebody's mind to defend you when it is necessary. I have the fullest experience of this, although I should not like."
20 E. adds, redundantly: "for a great deal results from this. One kind of profit is that you begin to gain freedom." From here to "at all", E. uses the second person where V. uses the first.

CHAPTER 16

Describes the difference between perfection in the lives of contemplatives and in the lives of those who are content with mental prayer. Explains how it is sometimes possible for God to raise a distracted soul to perfect contemplation and the reason for this. This chapter and that which comes next are to be noted carefully.[1]

I hope you do not think I have written too much about this already; for I have only been placing the board, as they say. You have asked me to tell you about the first steps in prayer; although God did not lead me by them, my daughters, I know no others, and even now I can hardly have acquired these elementary virtues. But you may be sure that anyone who cannot set out the pieces in a game of chess will never be able to play well, and, if he does not know how to give check, he will not be able to bring about a checkmate.[2] Now you will reprove me for talking about games, as we do not play them in this house and are forbidden to do so. That will show you what kind of a mother God has given you—she even knows about vanities like this! However, they say that the game is sometimes legitimate. How legitimate it will be for us to play it in this way, and, if we play it frequently, how quickly we shall give checkmate to this Divine King! He will

[1] The first four paragraphs of this chapter originally formed part of V., but, after writing them, St. Teresa tore them out of the manuscript, as though, on consideration, she had decided not to leave on record her knowledge of such a worldly game as chess. The allegory, however, is so expressive and beautiful that it has rightly become famous, and from the time of Fray Luis de León all the editions have included it. The text here followed is that of E.

[2] Chess was very much in vogue in the Spain of St. Teresa's day and it was only in 1561 that its great exponent Ruy López de Segura had published his celebrated treatise, in Spanish, entitled "Book of the liberal invention and art of the game of chess".

not be able to move out of our check nor will He desire to do so.

It is the queen which gives the king most trouble in this game and all the other pieces support her. There is no queen who can beat this King as well as humility can; for humility brought Him down from Heaven into the Virgin's womb and with humility we can draw Him into our souls by a single hair. Be sure that He will give most humility to him who has most already and least to him who has least. I cannot understand how humility exists, or can exist, without love, or love without humility, and it is impossible for these two virtues to exist save where there is great detachment from all created things.

You will ask, my daughters, why I am talking to you about virtues when you have more than enough books to teach you about them and when you want me to tell you only about contemplation. My reply is that, if you had asked me about meditation, I could have talked to you about it, and advised you all to practise it, even if you do not possess the virtues. For this is the first step to be taken towards the acquisition of the virtues and the very life of all Christians depends upon their beginning it. No one, however lost a soul he may be, should neglect so great a blessing if God inspires him to make use of it. All this I have already written elsewhere, and so have many others who know what they are writing about, which I certainly do not: God knows that.

But contemplation, daughters, is another matter. This is an error which we all make: if a person gets so far as to spend a short time each day in thinking about his sins, as he is bound to do if he is a Christian in anything more than name, people at once call him a great contemplative; and then they expect him to have the rare virtues which a great contemplative is bound to possess; he may even think he has them himself, but he will be quite wrong. In his early stages he did not even know how to set out the chess-board, and thought that, in order to give checkmate, it would be enough to be able to recognize the pieces. But that is impossible, for this King does not allow Himself to be taken except by one who surrenders wholly to Him.

Therefore, daughters, if you want me to tell you the way to attain to contemplation, do allow me to speak at some length about these things, even if at the time they do not seem to you very important,[3] for I think myself that they are.[4] If you have no wish either to hear about them or to practise them, continue your mental prayer all your life;[5] but in that case I assure you, and all persons who desire this blessing,[6] that *in my opinion* you will not attain true contemplation. I may, of course, be wrong about this, as I am judging by my own experience, but I have been striving after contemplation for twenty years.

I will now explain what mental prayer is, as some of you will not understand this. God grant that we may practise it as we should! I am afraid, however, that, if we do not achieve the virtues, this can only be done with great labour, although the virtues are not necessary here in such a high degree as they are for contemplation.[7] I mean that the King of glory will not come to our souls—that is, so as to be united with them—unless we strive to gain the greatest virtues.[8] I will explain this, for if you once catch me out in something which is not the truth, you will believe nothing I say—and if I were to say something untrue intentionally, from which may God preserve me, you would be right;[9] but, if I did, it would be because I knew no better or did not understand what I said. I will tell you, then, that God is sometimes pleased to show great favour to persons who are in an evil

---

[3] E.: "about things which will not seem to you very important."
[4] E.: "for all the things I have said here are (important)."
[5] "All your life" is deleted in T.
[6] E.: "and everybody."
[7] E.: "for that other (exercise)."
[8] *Lit.*: "the great virtues." In V. St. Teresa originally began this sentence thus: "In the last chapter I said that the King of glory, etc.," and ended it: "to gain the virtues which I there described as great." Later she altered it to read as above.
[9] After "that other (exercise)" E. continues: "For I must not forget that I said you must not be afraid of the King's coming: I will explain myself, for if you catch me out in a lie you will not believe me about anything, and you would be right if I knowingly told a lie, from which may God preserve me."

state [and to raise them to perfect contemplation], so that by this means He may snatch them out of the hands of the devil.[10] *It must be understood, I think, that such persons will not be in mortal sin at the time. They may be in an evil state, and yet the Lord will allow them to see a vision, even a very good one, in order to draw them back to Himself. But I cannot believe that He would grant them contemplation. For that is a Divine union, in which the Lord takes His delight in the soul and the soul takes its delight in Him; and there is no way in which the Purity of the Heavens can take pleasure in a soul that is unclean, nor can the Delight of the angels have delight in that which is not His own. And we know that, by committing mortal sin, a soul becomes the property of the devil, and must take its delight in him, since it has given him pleasure; and, as we know, his delights, even in this life, are continuous torture. My Lord will have no lack of children of His own in whom He may rejoice without going and taking the children of others. Yet His Majesty will do what He often does—namely, snatch them out of the devil's hands.*[11]

Oh, my Lord! How often do we cause Thee to wrestle with the devil! Was it not enough that Thou shouldst have allowed him to bear Thee in his arms when he took Thee to the pinnacle of the Temple in order to teach us how to vanquish him? What a sight it would have been, daughters, to see this Sun by the side of the darkness, and what fear that wretched creature must have felt, though he would not have known why, since God did not allow Him to understand!

---

[10] E. reads: "It often happens that the Lord takes a very wretched soul" and then continues "It must be understood . . ." as in the text above. The insertion of this italicized passage necessitates the repetition of the phrase "snatch them out of the devil's hands", in which, after its omissions, V. takes up the thread of E.

[11] *Lit.*: "out of his hands"; but the meaning, made more explicit in V., is evident. On the doctrinal question involved in this paragraph, see Introduction, p. 15, above. P. Silverio (III, 75–6), has a more extensive note on the subject than can be given here and cites a number of Spanish authorities, from P. Juan de Jesús María (*Theologia Mystica*, Chap. III) to P. Seisdedos Sanz (*Principios fundamentales de la mística*, Madrid, 1913, II, 61–77.)

Blessed be such great pity and mercy; we Christians ought to feel great shame at making Him wrestle daily, in the way I have described, with such an unclean beast. Indeed, Lord, Thine arms had need to be strong, but how was it that they were not weakened by the many [trials and] tortures which Thou didst endure upon the Cross? Oh, how quickly all that is borne for love's sake heals again! I really believe that, if Thou hadst lived longer, the very love which Thou hast for us would have healed Thy wounds again and Thou wouldst have needed no other medicine.[12] Oh, my God, who will give me such medicine for all the things which grieve and try me? How eagerly should I desire them if it were certain that I could be cured by such a health-giving ointment!

Returning to what I was saying, there are souls whom God knows He may gain for Himself by this means; seeing that they are completely lost, His Majesty wants to leave no stone unturned to help them; and therefore, though they are in a sad way and lacking in virtues, He gives them consolations, favours and emotions[13] which begin to move their desires, and occasionally even brings them to a state of contemplation, though rarely and not for long at a time.[14] And this, as I say, He does because He is testing them to see if that favour will not make them anxious to prepare themselves to enjoy it often; if it does not, may they be pardoned; pardon Thou us, Lord, for it is a dreadful thing that a soul whom Thou hast brought near to Thyself should approach any earthly thing and become attached to it.

For my own part I believe there are many souls whom God our Lord tests in this way, and few who prepare themselves

---

[12] E. continues: "I seem to be talking nonsense; for I do not act in this way, and yet Divine love does greater things than these. But, lest I should seem over-fond of detail (*curiosa*), which I am, and set you a bad example, I am not setting any of them down here." [A new chapter begins here.] "So, when it is the Lord's will to draw the soul back to Himself, He occasionally brings it to a state of contemplation, even when it has not these virtues, though rarely and for but a short time, etc."

[13] *Lit.*: "and tenderness."

[14] T.: "and for a short space of time."

to enjoy this favour.[15] When the Lord does this and we ourselves leave nothing undone either, I think it is certain that He never ceases from giving until He has brought us to a very high degree of prayer. If we do not give ourselves to His Majesty as resolutely as He gives Himself to us, He will be doing more than enough for us if He leaves us in mental prayer and from time to time visits us as He would visit servants in His vineyard. But these others are His beloved children, whom He would never want to banish from His side; and, as they have no desire to leave Him, He never does so. He seats them at His table, and feeds them with His own food,[16] almost taking the food from His mouth in order to give it them.

Oh, what blessed care of us is this, my daughters! How happy shall we be if by leaving these few, petty[17] things we can arrive at so high an estate! Even if the whole world should blame you, *and deafen you with its cries*, what matter so long as you are in the arms of God? He is powerful enough to free you from everything; for only once did He command the world to be made and it was done;[18] with Him, to will is to do. Do not be afraid, then, if He is pleased to speak with you, for He does this for the greater good of those who love Him.[19] His love for those to whom He is dear is by no means so weak: *He shows it in every way possible*.[20] Why, then, my sisters, do we not show Him love in so far as we can? Consider what a wonderful exchange it is if we give Him our love and receive His. Consider that He can do all things, and we can do nothing here below save as He enables us. And what is it that we do for Thee, O Lord, our Maker? We do hardly anything [at all]—just make some

---

[15] E. adds: "always."

[16] In T. the rest of this sentence is deleted.

[17] *Lit.*: "low", contrasting with "high" at the end of the sentence. E. has: "vain."

[18] E. omits: "He . . . everything" and continues: "For only once did the Lord command the world to be made, or think (of its being made), and it was done."

[19] E.: "for He does this for your greater good."

[20] The words italicized are struck out in E. but they seem to follow quite naturally on the preceding sentence.

poor weak resolution. And, if His Majesty is pleased that by doing a mere nothing we should win everything,[21] let us not be so foolish as to fail to do it.

O Lord! All our trouble comes to us from not having our eyes fixed upon Thee. If we only looked at the way along which we are walking, we should soon arrive; but we stumble and fall a thousand times and stray from the way because, as I say, we do not set our eyes on the true Way. One would think that no one had ever trodden it before, so new is it to us. It is indeed a pity that this should sometimes happen.[22] *I mean, it hardly seems that we are Christians at all or that we have ever in our lives read about the Passion. Lord help us—that we should be hurt about some small point of honour! And then, when someone tells us not to worry about it, we think he is no Christian. I used to laugh—or sometimes I used to be distressed—at the things I heard in the world, and sometimes, for my sins, in religious Orders.* We refuse to be thwarted over the very smallest matter of precedence:[23] apparently such a thing is quite intolerable. We cry out at once: "Well, I'm no saint"; *I used to say that myself.*

God deliver us, sisters, from saying "We are not angels", or "We are not saints", whenever we commit some imperfection. We may not be; but what a good thing it is for us to reflect that we can be if we will only try and if God gives us His hand![24] Do not be afraid that He will fail to do His part if we do not fail to do ours. And since we come here for no other reason, let us put our hands to the plough, as they say. Let there be nothing we know of which it would be a service to the Lord for us to do, and which, with His help, we would not venture to take in hand. I should like that kind of venturesomeness to be found in this house, as it always[25] in-

[21] Or "merit the All", as P. Silverio's text has it. T. has: "should buy Him Who is the All." Each text ends the sentence, literally: "let us not be foolish."
[22] E. omits: "that this should sometimes happen."
[23] E. ends the sentence here.
[24] E.: "to reflect that God will give us His hand so that we may be." In both E. and V., as often in idiomatic Spanish, "hand" is used in the sense of "strength", "power".
[25] E. omits: "always."

creases humility. We must have a holy boldness, for God helps the strong[26], being no respecter of persons;[27] *and He will give courage to you and to me.*

I have strayed far from the point. I want to return to what I was saying—that is,[28] to explain the nature of mental prayer and contemplation. It may seem irrelevant, but it is all done for your sakes; you may understand it better as expressed in my rough style than in other books which put it more elegantly.[29] May the Lord grant me His favour, so that this may be so. Amen.

CHAPTER 17

How not all souls are fitted for contemplation and how some take long to attain it. True humility will walk happily along the road by which the Lord leads it.

I seem now to be beginning my treatment of prayer, but there still remains a little for me to say, which is of great importance because it has to do with humility, and in this house that is necessary. For humility is the principal virtue which must be practised by those who pray,[1] and, as I have said, it is very fitting that you should try to learn how to practise it often:[2] that is one of the chief things to remember about it and it is very necessary that it should be known by all who practise prayer. How can anyone who is truly humble think herself as good as those who become contemplatives?[3] God,

26 E. reads: "We must always have courage, which God gives to the strong."
27 Acts x, 34.
28 E.: "which, I believe, was."
29 E. ends the chapter here.
1 E.: "For you have all to engage, and do engage, in prayer."
2 E.: "in every way."
3 E.: "who reach this state."

it is true, by His goodness and mercy, can make her so;[4] but my advice is that she should always sit down in the lowest place, for that is what the Lord instructed us to do and taught us by His own example.[5] Let such a one make herself ready for God to lead her by this road if He so wills; if He does not, the whole point of *true* humility is that she should consider herself happy in serving the servants of the Lord[6] and in praising Him. For she deserves to be a slave of the devils in hell;[7] yet His Majesty has brought her here to live among His servants.[8]

I do not say this without good reason, for, as I have said, it is very important for us to realize that God does not lead us all by the same road, and perhaps she who believes herself to be going along the lowest of roads is the highest in the Lord's eyes. So it does not follow that, because all of us in this house practise prayer,[9] we are all *perforce* to be contemplatives. That is impossible; and[10] those of us who are not would be greatly discouraged if we did not grasp the truth that contemplation is something given by God, and, as it is not necessary for salvation and God does not ask it of us before He gives us our reward,[11] we must not suppose that anyone else will require it of us. We shall not fail to attain perfection if we do what has been said here; we may, in fact, gain much more merit, because what we do will cost us more labour; the Lord will be treating us like those who are strong and will be laying up for us all that we cannot enjoy in this life. Let us not be discouraged, then, and give up prayer or cease doing what the rest do; for the Lord sometimes tarries long,

---

[4] E.: "God, it is true, through the merits of Christ, can make her good enough to merit this."
[5] St. Luke xiv, 10. E. omits: "for . . . example."
[6] E.: "in being the servant of the servants of the Lord." Both E. and V. use the feminine form, for servant(s), *sierva(s)*, which I sometimes translate "handmaidens".
[7] T. omits: "in hell."
[8] This is an amplification of E.: "and in praising Him for bringing her here to live among His servants when she deserved to be in hell."
[9] E.: "that because, in this house, is (observed) the custom and practice of prayer."
[10] In T.: "That is impossible; and" is deleted.
[11] T. deletes: "before . . . reward."

and gives us as great rewards all at once as He has been giving to others over many years.[12]

I myself spent over[13] fourteen years without ever being able to meditate except while reading. There must be many people like this, and others who cannot meditate[14] even after reading, but can only recite vocal prayers, in which they chiefly occupy themselves *and take a certain pleasure*. Some find their thoughts wandering so much that they cannot concentrate upon the same thing, but are always restless, to such an extent that, if they try to fix their thoughts upon God, they are attacked by a thousand foolish ideas[15] and scruples and doubts *concerning the Faith*. I know a very old woman,[16] leading a most excellent life—*I wish mine were like hers*— a penitent[17] and a great servant of God, who for many years has been spending hours and hours in vocal prayer, but from mental prayer can get no help at all; the most she can do is to dwell upon each of her vocal prayers as she says them.[18] There are a great many other people *just* like this; if they are humble, they will not, I think, be any the worse off in the end,[19] but very much in the same state as those who enjoy numerous consolations. In one way they may feel safer, for we cannot tell if[20] consolations come from God or are sent by the devil. If they are not of God, they are the more dangerous; for the chief object of the devil's work on earth is to fill us with pride. If they are of God, there is no reason for fear, for they bring humility with them, as I explained in my other book at great length.[21]

---

12 In T.: "to others" is deleted.
13 E. omits: "over."
14 T.: "contemplate."
15 E.: "a thousand vanities."
16 E. has "nun", omits "leading a most excellent life" and inserts "holy woman and" before "penitent".
17 E. continues: "—altogether a great nun, much and habitually given to vocal prayer, but from mental prayer unable to get any help at all."
18 E.: "upon each of her Avemarias and Paternosters, as she says them, which is a very holy practice."
19 E.: "at the end of the year."
20 E.: "For how do we know if . . . ?"
21 E.: "there is no reason for fear, as I wrote in my other book." The reference is to the *Life*, Chapters XVII, XIX, XXVIII.

Others[22] walk in humility, and *always* suspect that if they fail to receive consolations the fault is theirs, and are always most anxious to make progress. They never see a person shedding a tear without thinking themselves very backward in God's service unless they are doing the same, whereas they may perhaps be much more advanced.[23] For tears, though good, are not invariably signs of perfection; there is always greater safety[24] in humility, mortification, detachment and other virtues. There is no reason for fear, and you must not be afraid[25] that you will fail to attain the perfection of the greatest contemplatives.

Saint Martha was holy, but we are not told that she was a contemplative. What more do you want than to be able to grow to be like that blessed woman, who was worthy to receive Christ our Lord so often in her house, and to prepare meals for Him, and to serve Him and *perhaps* to eat at table with Him?[26] If she[27] had been absorbed in devotion [all the time], as the Magdalen was, there would have been no one to prepare a meal for this Divine Guest.[28] Now remember that this *little* community is Saint Martha's house and that there must be people of all kinds here. Nuns who are called to the active life must not murmur at others who are very much absorbed in contemplation,[29] for contemplatives know that, though they themselves may be silent, the Lord will speak for them, and this, as a rule, makes them forget themselves and everything else.[30]

Remember that there must be someone to cook the meals and count yourselves happy in being able to serve like

---

[22] *Lit.*: "These others." T. has: "These others who do not receive consolations."

[23] E. omits: "perhaps."

[24] E.: "they are always safe."

[25] In T. "and you must not be afraid" is deleted.

[26] E. adds: "and even from His plate."

[27] Both E. and V. have "they" here and E. adds "both". T. prefers the singular.

[28] E.: "for the Heavenly Guest."

[29] E.: "in prayer."

[30] E. is shorter: "for this, as a rule, makes them forget themselves and everything else."

Martha.[31] Reflect that true humility[32] consists to a great extent in being ready for what the Lord desires to do with you and happy that He should do it, and in always considering yourselves unworthy to be called His servants. If contemplation and mental and vocal prayer and tending the sick and serving in the house and working at[33] even the lowliest tasks are of service to the Guest who comes to stay with us and to eat and take His recreation with us, what should it matter to us if we do one of these things rather than another?

I do not mean that it is for us to say what we shall do, but that we must do our best in everything, for the choice is not ours but the Lord's. If after many years He is pleased to give each of us her office, it will be a curious kind of humility for you to wish to choose; let the Lord of the house do that, for He is wise and powerful and knows what is fitting for you and for Himself as well. Be sure that, if you do what lies in your power and prepare yourself for *high* contemplation with the perfection aforementioned, then, if He does not grant it you (and I think He will not fail to do so if you have true detachment and humility),[34] it will be because He has laid up this joy for you so as to give it you in Heaven,[35] and because, as I have said elsewhere, He is pleased to treat you like people who are strong and give you a cross to bear on earth like that which His Majesty Himself always bore.

What better sign of friendship is there than for Him to give you what He gave Himself? It might well be that you would not have had so great a reward from contemplation. His judgments are His own; we must not meddle in them. It is indeed a good thing that the choice is not ours; for, if it were, we should think it the more restful life and all become great contemplatives. Oh, how much we gain if we have no desire to gain what seems to us best and so have no fear of

31 E.: "Remember that, if they are silent, the Lord will answer for them, and let them count themselves happy to be going and preparing His meal."
32 E. adds: "I really believe."
33 E. adds: "desiring"—perhaps a slip for "and desiring".
34 The words "and humility" are not found in E.
35 The words "so as . . . Heaven" are not found in E.

losing, since God never permits a truly mortified person to lose anything except when such loss will bring him greater gain![36]

CHAPTER 18

Continues the same subject and shows how much greater are the trials of contemplatives than those of actives. This chapter offers great consolation to actives.

I tell you, then, daughters—those of you whom God is not leading by this road [of contemplation]—that, as I know from what I have seen and been told by those who are following this road, they are not bearing[1] a lighter cross than you; you would be amazed at all the ways and manners in which God sends them crosses. I know about both types of life and I am well aware that the trials given by God to contemplatives are intolerable; and they are of such a kind that, were He not to feed them with consolations, they could not be borne. It is clear that, since God leads those whom He most loves by the way of trials, the more He loves them, the greater will be their trials; and there is no reason to suppose that He hates contemplatives, since with His own mouth He praises them and calls them friends.[2]

To suppose that He would admit to His close friendship pleasure-loving people who are free from all trials is ridiculous. I feel quite sure that God gives them much greater trials; and that He leads them by a hard and rugged road, so that they sometimes think they are lost and will have to go back and begin again.[3] Then His Majesty is obliged to give

---

[36] E. omits this last sentence.
[1] E.: "that those who are following this road are not bearing."
[2] E.: "and they are also friends."
[3] E.: "will have to begin again from the place they started from."

them sustenance—not water, but wine, so that they may become inebriated by it and not realize what they are going through and what they are capable of bearing. Thus I find few true contemplatives who are not courageous and resolute in suffering;[4] for, if they are weak, the first thing the Lord does is to give them courage so that they may fear no trials *that may come to them.*

I think, when those who lead an active life occasionally see contemplatives receiving consolations, they suppose that they never experience anything else. But I can assure you that you might not be able to endure their sufferings for as long as a day. The point is that the Lord knows everyone as he really is and gives each his work to do—according to what He sees to be most fitting for his soul, and for His own Self, and for the good of his neighbour. Unless you have omitted to prepare yourselves for your work you need have no fear that it will be lost. Note that I say we must all strive to do this, for we are here for no other purpose; and we must not strive merely for a year, or for two years or ten years,[5] or it will look as if we are abandoning our work like cowards. It is well that the Lord should see we are not leaving anything undone. We are like soldiers who, however long they have served, must always be ready for their captain to send them away on any duty which he wants to entrust to them, since it is he who is paying them.[6] And how much better is the payment given by our King than by people on this earth! *For the unfortunate soldiers die, and God knows who pays them after that!*

When their captain sees they are all present, and anxious for service,[7] he assigns duties to them according to their fit-

---

[4] E. omits: "and resolute in suffering." T. omits: "true."

[5] E.: "not merely for one year, or for ten." In this sentence E. also has the second person plural when V. has the first. T. follows E. in the first respect but V. in the second.

[6] E. has some slight verbal variations in this sentence, which ends: "is giving them their wages very well paid." It continues thus: "And how much better paid is (our soldier) than are those who serve the King!"

[7] E.: "When none of them is absent, and their captain sees they are desirous of serving." V. has "he" for "their captain", which I supply from E. In T., "present and" is deleted.

ness, *though not so well as our Heavenly Captain*. But if they were not present, He would give them neither pay[8] nor service orders. So practise mental prayer, sisters; or, if any of you cannot do that, vocal prayer, reading and colloquies with God, as I shall explain to you later. Do not neglect the hours of prayer which are observed by all the nuns;[9] you never know when the Spouse will call you (do not let what happened to the foolish virgins happen to you)[10] and if He will give you fresh trials under the disguise of consolations. If He does not,[11] you may be sure that you are not fit for them and that what you are doing is suitable for you. That is where both merit and humility come in,[12] when you really think that you are not fit for what you are doing.

Go cheerfully about whatever services you are ordered to do, as I have said; if such a servant is truly humble she will be blessed in her active life and will never make any complaint save of herself. *I would much rather be like her than like some contemplatives.* Leave others to wage their own conflicts, which are not light ones.[13] The standard-bearer is not a combatant, yet none the less he is exposed to great danger, and, inwardly, must suffer more than anyone, for he cannot defend himself, as he is carrying the standard, which he must

---

[8] *Lit.*: "would give them nothing", but the reference seems to be to payment. T. has "anxious" for "present".

[9] In T., "which . . . nuns" is deleted.

[10] This parenthetical sentence is not found in E., which also reads "Captain" for "Spouse".

[11] E. adds "call you", but the following sentence seems rather to refer to "give you fresh trials".

[12] E.: "That is where true humility comes in."

[13] E. continues: "Do you not know that in battles the standard-bearers and captains have the greatest obligations to fight? A poor soldier plods on step by step; and, if he sometimes hides, so as not to get into a place where he sees the mêlée to be thickest, no one observes him, and he loses neither his honour nor his life. (But) the standard-bearer is carrying the standard, which he must not allow to leave his hands even if he is cut to pieces: the eyes of all are upon him. Do you think those to whom the King gives these duties are being given a light task? In exchange for a little more honour they bind themselves to endure much more suffering; and, if they betray the slightest weakness, all is lost. So, friends, etc."

not allow to leave his hands, even if he is cut to pieces. Just so contemplatives have to bear aloft the standard of humility and must suffer all the blows which are aimed at them without striking any themselves. Their duty is to suffer as Christ did, to raise the Cross on high, not to allow it to leave their hands, whatever the perils in which they find themselves, and not to let themselves be found backward in suffering. It is for this reason that they are given such an honourable duty. Let the contemplative consider what he is doing; for, if he lets the standard fall, the battle will be lost. Great harm, I think, is done to those who are not so far advanced if those whom they consider as captains and friends of God let them see them acting in a way unbefitting to their office.

The other soldiers do as best they can; at times they will withdraw from some position of extreme danger, and, as no one observes them, they suffer no loss of honour. But these others have all eyes fixed on them and cannot move. Their office, then, is a noble one, and the King confers great honour and favour upon anyone to whom He gives it, and who, in receiving it, accepts no light obligation. So, sisters,[14] as we *do not understand ourselves and* know not what we ask, let us leave everything to the Lord, *Who knows us better than we know ourselves. True humility consists in our being satisfied with what is given us.* There are some people who seem to want to ask favours from God as a right. A pretty kind of humility that is! He Who knows us all does well in seldom[15] giving things to such persons; He sees clearly that they are unable to drink of His chalice.

If you want to know whether you have made progress or not, sisters, you may be sure that you have if each of you thinks herself the worst of all and shows that she thinks this by acting for the profit and benefit of the rest. Progress has nothing to do with enjoying the greatest number of consolations in prayer, or with raptures, visions or favours [often] given by the Lord,[16] the value of which we cannot estimate

---

14 E. (see preceding note) continues here, beginning: "So, friends (*fem.*)."
15 E. has: "rarely." V. adds: "I think."
16 E.: "or things of that kind."

until we reach the world to come. The other things I have been describing are current coin, an unfailing source of revenue and a perpetual inheritance—not payments liable at any time to cease, like those favours which are given us and then come to an end. I am referring to the great virtues of humility, mortification and an obedience so *extremely* strict that we never go an inch[17] beyond the superior's orders, knowing that these orders come from God since she is in His place.[18] It is to this duty of obedience that you must attach the greatest importance. It seems to me that anyone who does not have it is not a nun at all, and so I am saying no more about it, as I am speaking to nuns whom I believe to be good, or, at least, desirous of being so. So well known is the matter, and so important,[19] that a single word will suffice[20] to prevent you from forgetting it.

I mean that, if anyone is under a vow of obedience and goes astray through not taking the greatest care to observe these vows with the highest degree of perfection, I do not know why she is in the convent. I can assure her, in any case, that, for so long as she fails in this respect, she will never succeed in leading the contemplative life, or even in leading a good active life: of that I am absolutely certain.[21] And even a person who has not this obligation, but who wishes or tries to achieve contemplation, must, if she would walk safely, be fully resolved to surrender her will to a confessor who is himself a contemplative[22] *and will understand her.* It is a well-known fact that she will make more progress in this way in a year than in a great many years if she acts otherwise.[23]

---

[17] V. has, literally, "a point"; E.: "a tittle."

[18] T. interpolates a sentence here which is not found elsewhere: "(One who is obedient?) has the great and certain prize, the worth of which is clear." This looks like a reflection of the copyist.

[19] E.: "So important is the matter."

[20] T. ends the sentence here.

[21] *Lit.*: "very, very certain"—a typically Teresan repetition. T. has only one "very"; E. has both.

[22] *Lit.*: "who is such."

[23] In E. this sentence reads: "This is very well known and many have written about it."

As this does not affect you, however, I will say no more about it.

I conclude, my daughters, [by saying] that these are the virtues which I desire you to possess and to strive to obtain, and of which you should cherish a holy envy.[24] Do not be troubled because you have no experience of those other kinds of devotion:[25] they are very unreliable. It may be that to some people they come from God,[26] and yet that if they came to you it might be because His Majesty had permitted you to be deceived and deluded by the devil, as He has permitted others:[27] *there is danger in this for women.* Why do you want to serve the Lord in so doubtful a way when there are so many ways of [serving Him in] safety?[28] Who wants to plunge you into these perils? I have said a great deal about this, because I am sure it will be useful, for this nature of ours is weak, though His Majesty will strengthen those on whom He wishes to bestow contemplation.[29] With regard to the rest, I am glad to have given them this advice, which will teach contemplatives humility also. *If you say you have no need of it, daughters, some of you may perhaps find it pleasant reading.* May the Lord, for His own sake,[30] give us light to follow His will in all things and we shall have no cause for fear.

---

24 T. omits: "and of which . . . envy."
25 E., more succinctly: "Those other kinds of devotion—not in the least."
26 E. has, literally: "Perhaps in another (person) it will be God."
27 E.: "many" (*fem.*).
28 E.: "If you can serve the Lord so well in ways which are safe, who wants to plunge you into these perils?"
29 T. deletes part of the next sentence and substitutes: "These counsels are also (meant) to teach contemplatives humility."
30 T. omits: "for His own sake."

CHAPTER 19

Begins to treat of prayer. Addresses souls who cannot reason with the understanding.

It is a long time[1] since I wrote the last chapter and I have had no chance of returning to my writing, so that, without reading through what I have written, I cannot remember what I said. However, I must not spend too much time at this, so it will be best if I go right on[2] without troubling about the connection.[3] For those with orderly minds, and for souls who practise prayer and can be a great deal in their own company, many books have been written, and these are so good and are the work of such competent people that you would be making a mistake if you paid heed to anything about prayer that you learned from me. There are books, as I say, in which the mysteries of the life of the Lord and of His *sacred* Passion[4] are described in short passages, one for each day of the week; there are also meditations on the Judgment, on hell, on our own nothingness and on all that we owe to God,[5] and these books are excellent both as to their teaching and as to the way in which they plan the beginning and the end of the time of prayer.[6] There is no need to tell anyone who is capable of practising prayer in this way, and has already formed the habit of doing so, that by this good road the Lord will bring her to the harbour of light. If she begins so well, her end will be good also; and all who can walk along this road will walk restfully and securely, for one always walks

---

[1] *Lit.*: "so many days." But on St. Teresa's indefinite use of the word "days" see p. 35, n. 8, above.
[2] *Lit.*: "it will have to go as it comes out."
[3] "It is necessary to point out this," adds T.
[4] E.: "in which the scenes (*pasos*) of the sacred Passion."
[5] E.: "and on the favours of God."
[6] St. Teresa is probably referring to the treatises of Luis de Granada and St. Peter of Alcántara (S.S.M., I, 40–52, II, 106–20). Cf. *Constitutions* (Vol. III, p. 236, below).

restfully when the understanding is kept in restraint.[7] It is something else that I wish to treat of and help you about if the Lord is pleased to enable me to do so; if not, you will at least realize that there are many souls who suffer this trial, and you will not be so much distressed at undergoing it yourselves at first, *but will find some comfort in it.*

There are some souls, and some minds, as unruly as horses not yet broken in. No one can stop them: now they go this way, now that way; they are never still. *Although a skilled rider mounted on such a horse may not always be in danger, he will be so sometimes; and, even if he is not concerned about his life, there will always be the risk of his stumbling,*[8] *so that he has to ride with great care.* Some people are either like this by nature or God permits them to become so. I am very sorry for them; they seem to me like people who are very thirsty and see water a long way off, yet, when they try to go to it, find someone who all the time is barring their path[9]— at the beginning of their journey, in the middle and at the end. And when, after all their labour—and the labour is tremendous—they have conquered the first of their enemies, they allow themselves to be conquered by the second, and they prefer to die of thirst rather than drink water which is going to cost them so much trouble. Their strength has come to an end; their courage has failed them; and, though some of them are strong enough to conquer their second enemies as well as their first, when they meet the third group their strength comes to an end, though perhaps they are only a couple of steps from the fountain of living water, of which the Lord said to the Samaritan woman that whosoever drinks of it shall not thirst again.[10] How right and *how very* true is that which comes from the lips of Truth Himself! In this

[7] "So I am not speaking to such now," adds T.
[8] *Lit.:* "of his doing something on (the horse) which is not graceful."
[9] In E. and T. this sentence is in the singular, as it was originally in V. But the correction to the plural in V. seems to be in the Saint's own hand.
[10] St. John iv, 13.

life the soul will never thirst for anything more,[11] although its thirst for things in the life to come will exceed any natural thirst that we can imagine here below. How the soul thirsts to experience this thirst! For it knows how very precious it is, and, grievous though it be and exhausting, it creates the very satisfaction by which this thirst is allayed. It is therefore a thirst which quenches nothing but desire for earthly things, and, when God slakes it, satisfies in such a way that one of the greatest favours[12] He can bestow on the soul is to leave it with this longing, so that it has an even greater desire to drink of[13] this water again.

Water has three properties—three relevant properties which I can remember, that is to say, for it must have many more. One of them is that of cooling things; however hot we are, water[14] tempers the heat, and it will even put out a large fire, except when there is tar in the fire, in which case, *they say*, it only burns the more. God help me! What a marvellous thing it is that, when this fire is strong and fierce and subject to none of the elements, water should make it grow fiercer, and, though its contrary element, should not quench it but only cause it to burn the more! It would be very useful to be able to discuss this with someone who understands philosophy; if I knew the properties of things I could explain it myself;[15] but, though I love thinking about it, I cannot explain it[16]—perhaps I do not even understand it.

You will be glad, sisters, if God grants you to drink of this water, as are those who drink of it now, and you will understand how a genuine love of God, if it is really strong, and completely free from earthly things, and able to rise above

[11] "In such a way as to lose God," interpolates T., "that is to say, by His taking His hand away from it; and so it must always walk with fear." In the next sentence, T. omits the words "natural thirst".
[12] E.: "that the greatest favour." This was also the original reading of V. and T., but in each of these it has been corrected by the author to read as in the text.
[13] E.: "to ask for."
[14] E.: "however hot one is, entering a river."
[15] E.: "How useful it would be if I were a philosopher and knew the properties of things and could explain myself!"
[16] E.: "I cannot express what I understand."

them, is master of all the elements and of the whole world.[17] And, as water proceeds from the earth, there is no fear of its quenching this fire, which is the love of God;[18] though the two elements are contraries, it has no power over it. The fire is absolute master, and subject to nothing. You will not be surprised, then, sisters, at the way I have insisted in this book that you should strive to obtain this freedom. Is it not a funny thing that a poor *little* nun of Saint Joseph's should attain mastery over the whole earth and all the elements? What wonder that the saints did as they pleased with them by the help of God? Fire and water obeyed Saint Martin; even birds and fishes[19] were obedient to Saint Francis; and similarly with many other saints.[20] *Helped as they were by God, and themselves doing all that was in their power, they could almost have claimed this as a right.*[21] It was clear that they were masters over everything in the world, because they had striven so hard to despise it and subjected themselves to the Lord of the world with all their might. So, as I say, the water, which springs from the earth, has no power over this fire.[22]

---

17 "And how," adds T., "there is no need to be afraid, (if we are) trusting in the mercy of God." T. continues: "that the water, which proceeds from the earth, will quench this fire, etc."

18 E. omits: "which is the love of God."

19 E. omits: "birds and", and ends the sentence at "Francis".

20 T.: "with other saints, who are masters, etc."

21 The following passage is inserted here in E. but is lightly crossed out in the manuscript, probably by St. Teresa herself, and, as it does not occur in V., it would seem that she intended to omit it. "What do you suppose the Psalmist (means when he) says that all things are subjected to man and placed under his feet [the reference is to Psalm viii, 8]. Do you suppose (that means the feet) of all men? No fear of that! What I see is men subjected to them [i.e., the things of the world] and under *their* feet. I knew a man who was killed while he was arguing about a half-*real* [a small coin]: think what a wretched price he was paid for so subjecting himself. There are many things which you will see daily and which will tell you that I am speaking the truth. Indeed, the Psalmist could not lie, for his words are those of the Holy Spirit. I believe (though I may not understand it or I may be mistaken about having read it) that the perfect are said to be rulers over all the things of earth." E. then continues: "If it is water from Heaven, etc." (see n. 9.)

22 V. ends the sentence at "power" but "over it" is found in the margin. The reading in the text is from T.

Its flames rise high and its source is in nothing so base as the earth. There are other fires of love for God—small ones, which may be quenched by the least little thing. But this fire will most certainly not be so quenched.[23] Even should a whole sea of temptations assail it, they will not keep it from burning or prevent it from gaining the mastery over them.

Water which comes down as rain from Heaven will quench the flames even less,[24] for in that case the fire and the water are not contraries, but have the same origin. Do not fear that the one element may harm the other; each helps the other and they produce the same effect.[25] For the water of genuine tears—that is, tears which come from true prayer—is a good gift[26] from the King of Heaven; it fans the flames and keeps them alight, while the fire helps to cool the water.[27] God bless me! What a beautiful and wonderful thing it is that fire should cool water! But it does; and it even freezes all worldly affections,[28] when it is combined with the living water which comes from Heaven, the source of the above-mentioned tears, which are given us, and not acquired by our diligence.[29] Certainly, then, nothing worldly has warmth enough left in it to induce us to cling to it unless it is something which increases this fire, the nature of which is not to be easily satisfied, but, if possible, to enkindle the entire world.

[23] *Lit.*: "But this one—no, no."

[24] E.: "If it is water from Heaven, do not fear that it will quench this fire, any more than that that other (water) will revive it."

[25] Deletions are made here in T. and the following is substituted: "Thus the one will not harm the other, but they will help (each other)."

[26] T. (?by an error) reads *vienen* (come) for *bien* (well, good): "is (*lit.*, comes) given by."

[27] E.: "For the water keeps the fire alight and helps to feed it, while the fire helps to cool the water."

[28] E. ends the paragraph with the words: "affections. When with it is combined the living water which comes from Heaven, have no fear that it will give the slightest heat to anyone."

[29] Another hand than St. Teresa's has deleted the words "and not acquired by our diligence" in T. and substituted, after "given us", "by the King of Heaven". "Thus" is also substituted for "Certainly, then", in the following sentence.

The second property of water is that it cleanses things that are not clean already. What would become of the world if there were no water for washing? Do you know what cleansing properties there are in this living water, this heavenly water, this clear water,[30] when it is unclouded, and free from mud, and comes down from Heaven?[31] Once the soul has drunk of it I am convinced[32] that it makes it pure and clean of all its sins; for, as I have written, God does not allow us to drink of this water *of perfect contemplation* whenever we like: the choice is not ours; this Divine union is something quite supernatural, given that it may cleanse the soul and leave it pure and free from the mud and misery in which it has been plunged because of its sins. Other consolations, excellent as they may be, which come through the intermediacy of the understanding, are like water running all over the ground. This cannot be drunk directly from the source; and its course is never free from clogging impurities, so that it is neither so pure nor so clean as the other.[33] I should not say that this prayer I have been describing, which comes from reasoning with the intellect, is living water—I mean so far as my understanding of it goes. For, despite our efforts, there is always something clinging to the soul, through the influence of the body and of the baseness of our nature, which we should prefer not to be there.

I will explain myself further. We are meditating on the nature of the world, and on the way in which everything will come to an end, so that we may learn to despise it, when, almost without noticing it, we find ourselves ruminating on things in the world that we love. We try to banish these thoughts, but we cannot help being slightly distracted by thinking of things that have happened, or will happen, of things we have done and of things we are going to do. Then we begin to think of how we can get rid of these thoughts;

30 T. ends the sentence here.
31 E.: "and is taken from the same source?"
32 T.: "I think."
33 E. ends the paragraph: "I should not say that this was living water—I mean as far as my understanding of it goes," and omits the whole of the paragraph following.

and that sometimes plunges us once again into the same danger. It is not that we ought to omit such meditations; but we need to retain our misgivings about them and not to grow careless. In contemplation the Lord Himself relieves us of this care, for He will not trust us to look after ourselves. So dearly does He love our souls that He prevents them from rushing into things which may do them harm just at this time when He is anxious to help them. So He calls them to His side at once, and in a single moment reveals more truths to them and gives them a clearer insight into the nature of everything than they could otherwise gain in many years. For our sight is poor and the dust which we meet on the road blinds us; but in contemplation the Lord brings us to the end of the day's journey without our understanding how.

The third property of water is that it satisfies and quenches thirst. Thirst, I think, means the desire for something which is very necessary for us—so necessary that if we have none of it we shall die. It is a strange thing that if we have no water we die, and that we can also lose our lives through having too much of it, as happens to many people who get drowned. Oh, my Lord, if only one could be plunged so deeply into this living water that one's life would end! Can that be? Yes:[34] this love and desire for God[35] can increase so much that human nature is unable to bear it, and so there have been persons who have died of it. I knew one person[36] who had this living water in such great abundance that she would almost have been drawn out of herself by raptures if God had not quickly succoured her.[37] *She had such a thirst, and her*

---

[34] T., here and elsewhere, has *Sé* (I know) for *Sí* (yes). As this substitution is probably a slip, it is not normally recorded, though it sometimes changes the sense considerably.

[35] E.: "Oh, my Lord, if only one could be drowned by being plunged into this living water! But that is impossible. Still, the desire for it, this love and desire for God."

[36] The author probably refers to herself: Cf. *Life*, Chapter XX, and *Relations, passim.*

[37] V. and T. (the latter substituting "a great suspension" for "raptures") read: "who, if God had not quickly succoured her with this living water, in such great abundance that she would almost have been drawn out of herself." This leaves "who" without a verb and

desire grew so greatly, that she realized clearly that she might quite possibly die of thirst if something were not done for her.[38] I say that she would almost have been drawn out of herself because in this state the soul is in repose. So intolerable does such a soul find the world that it seems to be overwhelmed,[39] but it comes to life again in God; and in this way His Majesty enables it to enjoy experiences which, if it had remained within itself, would perforce have cost it its life.

Let it be understood from this that, as there can be nothing in our supreme Good which is not perfect, all that He gives is for our welfare; and, however abundant this water which He gives may be,[40] in nothing that He gives can there be superfluity. For, if His gift is abundant, He also bestows on the soul, as I have said, an abundant capacity for drinking; just as a glassmaker moulds his vessels to the size[41] he thinks necessary, so that there is room for what he wishes to pour into them. As our desires for this water come from ourselves, they are never free from fault; any good that there may be in them comes from the help of the Lord. But we are so indiscreet that, as the pain is sweet and pleasant, we think we can never[42] have too much of it. We have an immeasurable longing for it,[43] and, so far as is possible on earth, we stimulate this longing: sometimes this goes so far as to cause death. How happy is such a death! And yet by living one might per-

---

makes incomplete sense. St. Teresa's first editor, by substituting *era* for *con*, restored the sense and is followed in the text above. E., by means of the sentence given in italics, which combines with the preceding sentence, makes the substitution unnecessary, but at the cost of an unnatural word-sequence which St. Teresa was presumably trying to eliminate when she recast the passage in V.

38 E. ends the paragraph: "Blessed be He Who invites us to come and drink in His Gospel!"

39 *Lit.*: "drowned."

40 E. begins the paragraph: "And, as in our Good and Lord there can be nothing which is not perfect, and He alone gives us this water which we need, however much of it there may be."

41 T.: "in the way."

42 T.: "we never allow ourselves to."

43 *Lit.*: "We eat it without measure."

haps have helped others to die of the desire for it. I believe the devil has something to do with this: knowing how much harm we can do him by living, he tempts us to be indiscreet in our penances and so to ruin our health, which is a matter of no small moment to him.

I advise anyone who attains to an experience of this fierce thirst to watch herself carefully, for I think she will have to contend with this temptation. She may not die of her thirst, but her health will be ruined,[44] and she will involuntarily give her feelings outward expression, which ought at all costs to be avoided. Sometimes, however, all our diligence in this respect is unavailing and we are unable to hide our emotions as much as we should like. Whenever we are assailed by these strong impulses stimulating the increase of our desire, let us take great care not to add to them ourselves but to check them gently[45] by thinking of something else. For our *own* nature may be playing as great a part in producing these feelings as our love. There are some people *of this type* who have keen desires for all kinds of things, even for bad things,[46] but I do not think such people can have achieved great mortification, for mortification is always profitable. It seems foolish to check so good a thing[47] as this desire, but it is not. I am not saying that the desire should be uprooted—only checked; one may be able to do this by stimulating some other desire which is equally praiseworthy.

In order to explain myself better I will give an illustration. A man has a great desire to be with God, as Saint Paul had, and to be loosed from this prison.[48] This causes him pain which yet is in itself a great joy, and no small degree of mortification will be needed if he is to check it—in fact, he will not

---

[44] The next few lines are not found in E., which continues: "And when this increase of desire is very great let her try not to add to them, but check them gently, etc."

[45] *Lit.*: "to cut the thread." E. adds: "of the impulse."

[46] E. ends the sentence here.

[47] E.: "such a thing."

[48] Presumably a reminiscence of Romans vii, 24 or Philippians i, 23. E. continues: "and impetuous persons, without being conscious of it, will come to show outward signs (of their desire), which, as far as possible, should be avoided. Let us modify our desire, etc."

always be able to do so. But when he finds it oppressing him so much he may almost lose his reason. I saw this happen to someone not long ago; she was[49] of an impetuous nature, but so accustomed to curbing her own will that, from what I had seen at other times, I thought her will was completely annihilated; yet, when I saw her for a moment, the great stress and strain caused by her efforts to hide her feelings had all but destroyed her reason.[50] In such an extreme case, I think, even did the desire come from the Spirit of God, it would be true humility to be afraid; for we must not imagine that we have sufficient charity to bring us to such a state of oppression.

I shall not think it at all wrong[51] (if it be possible, I mean, for it may not always be so) for us to change our desire by reflecting that, if we live, we have more chance of serving God, and that we might do this by giving light to some soul which otherwise would be lost;[52] as well as that, if we serve Him more, we shall deserve to enjoy Him more, and grieve that we have served Him so little. These are consolations appropriate to such great trials: they will allay our pain and we shall gain a great deal by them if in order to serve the Lord Himself we are willing to spend a long time here below and to live with our grief. It is as if a person were suffering a

---

[49] T. inserts "not", perhaps in error, as another "not" precedes it, and the context suggests the affirmative sense. T. continues: "but accustomed, etc.", and the phrase "that, from . . . annihilated" is deleted.

[50] This, too, is generally taken as referring to St. Teresa herself.

[51] T.: "And so it will not be considered wrong."

[52] E. ends the sentence here and continues: "This is a consolation appropriate to so great a trial, which will allay our pain, and we shall gain by acquiring such great charity that, in order to serve the Lord Himself, we shall be willing to suffer here below for one day. It is as if a person were suffering a great trial or a grievous affliction and we consoled him by telling him to have patience. And if the devil had anything to do with such a strong desire, as he must have had in the case of one whom he persuaded to throw himself down a well so that he might go and see God, it would be a sign that (the person concerned) was not far from obtaining the increase of that desire, for, if it were from the Lord, it would do him no harm: it is impossible (that it should), for such desires bring with them, etc."

great trial or a grievous affliction and we consoled him by telling him to have patience and leave himself in God's hands so that His will might be fulfilled in him: it is always best to leave ourselves in God's hands.

And what if the devil had anything to do with these strong desires? This might be possible, as I think is suggested in Cassian's story of a hermit, leading the austerest of lives, who was persuaded by the devil to throw himself down a well so that he might see God the sooner.[53] I do not think this hermit can have served God either humbly or efficiently, for the Lord is faithful and His Majesty would never allow a servant of His to be blinded in a matter in which the truth was so clear. But, of course, if the desire had come from God, it would have done the hermit no harm; for such desires bring with them illumination, moderation and discretion. This is fitting, but our enemy and adversary seeks to harm us wherever he can; and, as he is not unwatchful, we must not be so either. This is an important matter in many respects:[54] for example, we must shorten our time of prayer, however much joy it gives us, if we see our bodily strength waning or find that our head aches: discretion is most necessary in everything.

Why do you suppose, daughters, that I have tried, *as people say*, to describe the end of the battle before it has begun and to point to its reward by telling you about the blessing which comes from drinking of the heavenly source of[55] this living water? I have done this so that you may not be distressed at[56] the trials and annoyances of the road, and may tread it with courage and not grow weary; for, as I have said, it may be that, when you have arrived, and have only to stoop and drink of the spring,[57] you may fail to do so and lose this blessing, thinking that you have not the strength to attain it and that it is not for you.

[53] Cassian: *Conferences*, II. v.
[54] E. ends the paragraph: "and sometimes it is very necessary that we should not forget it."
[55] E.: "of this heavenly source and of."
[56] T.: "may not complain of."
[57] E. omits: "have arrived, and" and "of the spring".

Remember, the Lord invites us all; and, since He is Truth Itself, we cannot doubt Him. If His invitation were not a general one, He would not have said: "I will give you to drink." He might have said: "Come, all of you, for after all you will lose nothing by coming; and I will give drink to those whom I think fit for it." But, as He said we were all to come, without making this condition, I feel sure that none will fail to receive this living water unless they cannot keep to the path.[58] May the Lord, Who promises it, give us grace, for His Majesty's own sake, to seek it as it must be sought.

CHAPTER 20

Describes how, in one way or another, we never lack consolation on the road of prayer. Counsels the sisters to include this subject continually in their conversation.

In this last chapter I seem to have been contradicting what I had previously said,[1] as, in consoling those who had not reached the contemplative state, I told them that the Lord had different roads by which they might come to Him, just as He also had many mansions.[2] I now repeat this: His Majesty, being Who He is and understanding our weakness, has provided for us. But He did not say: "Some must come by this way and others by that." His mercy is so great that He has forbidden none to strive to come and drink of this fountain of life. Blessed be He for ever! What good reasons there would have been for His forbidding me!

58 E. ends the chapter here. This final paragraph appears to be based upon St. John vii, 37.
1 E.: "I seem to be contradicting myself."
2 E.: "that God, our Good, had different roads, and that they might come to Him by different roads, and that thus He had [literally, both here and in the text above: "there were"] many mansions (*moradas*)." There is a reference here to St. John xiv, 2.

But as He did not order me to cease from drinking when I had begun to do so,[3] but caused me to be plunged into the depths of the water, it is certain that He will forbid no one to come: indeed, He calls us publicly, and in a loud voice, to do so.[4] Yet, as He is so good, He does not force us to drink, but enables those who wish to follow Him to drink in many ways so that none may lack comfort or die of thirst. For from this rich spring flow many streams—some large, others small, and also little pools for children, which they find quite large enough, for the sight of a great deal of water would frighten them: by children, I mean those who are in the early stages.[5] Therefore, sisters, have no fear that you will die of thirst on this road; you will never lack so much of the water of comfort that your thirst will be intolerable;[6] so take my advice and do not tarry on the way, but strive like strong men until you die in the attempt, for you are here for nothing else than to strive. If you always pursue this determination to die rather than fail to reach the end of the road,[7] the Lord may bring you through this life with a certain degree of thirst, but in the life which never ends He will give you great abundance to drink and you will have no fear of its failing you. May the Lord grant us never to fail Him. Amen.[8]

Now, in order to set out upon this aforementioned road so that we do not go astray at the very start, let us consider for a moment how the first stage of our journey is to be begun, for that is the most important thing—or rather, every part of the journey is of importance to the whole. I do not mean to say that no one who has not the resolution that I am going to describe should set out upon the road, for the Lord will

[3] E. continues: "and He did not plunge me"—perhaps a slip (*sino que* for *no* would give the same sense as in V.).
[4] St. John vii, 37.
[5] *Lit.*: "these are they who are, etc." E. is shorter: "which those who are in a very early stage of virtue find quite large enough."
[6] T.: "you will never lack the water of comfort."
[7] E.: "to reach this spring."
[8] E.: "the Lord may bring you through this life without reaching it, but in the next life He will give it you with great abundance, and you will drink without fear of its failing you through your own fault. May the Lord grant that His mercy may not fail us. Amen."

gradually bring her nearer to perfection. And even if she did no more than take one step, this alone[9] has such virtue that there is no fear of her losing it or of failing to be very well rewarded.[10] We might compare her to someone who has a rosary with a bead specially indulgenced:[11] one prayer in itself will bring her something, and the more she uses the bead the more she will gain; but if she left it in a box and never took it out it would be better for her not to have it. So, although she may never go any farther along the same road, the short distance she has progressed will give her light and thus help her to go along other roads, and the farther she goes the more light she will gain. In fact, she may be sure that she will do herself no kind of harm through having started on the road, even if she leaves it, for good never leads to evil.[12] So, daughters, whenever you meet people and find them well-disposed and even attracted to the life of prayer, try to remove from them all fear of beginning a course which may bring them such great blessings.[13] For the love of God, I beg you always to see to it that your conversation is benefiting those with whom you speak. For your prayers must be for the profit of their souls; and, since you must always pray to the Lord for them, sisters, you would seem to be doing ill if you did not strive to benefit them in every possible way.

If you would be a good kinswoman, this is true friendship; if you would be a good friend, you may be sure that this is the only possible way. Let the truth be in your hearts, as it will be if you practise meditation, and you will see clearly what love we are bound to have for our neighbours. This is no time for child's play, sisters, and these worldly friendships, good though they may be, seem no more than that. Neither

[9] E.: "the road alone."
[10] V.: "paid." E.: "guerdoned." E. adds: "It contains within itself many pardons (*perdones*), both great and small." Note, in the next sentence, that the Spanish phrase repeats *perdones*.
[11] *Cuenta de perdones*: a bead larger in size than the remainder in the rosary and carrying special indulgences for the souls in purgatory.
[12] T. deletes: "for good . . . evil."
[13] *Lit.*: "of beginning so great a good." T. amplifies: "of beginning to search for this hidden treasure."

with your relatives[14] nor with anyone else must you use such phrases as "If you love me", or "Don't you love me?" unless you have in view some noble end and the profit of the person to whom you are speaking. It may be necessary, in order to get a relative—a brother or some such person—to listen to the truth and accept it, to prepare him for it by using such phrases and showing him signs of love, which are always pleasing to sense. He may possibly be more affected, and influenced, by one kind word, as such phrases are called, than by a great deal which you might say about God,[15] and then there would be plenty of opportunities for you to talk to him about God afterwards. I do not forbid such phrases, therefore, provided you use them in order to bring someone profit. But for no other reason can there be any good in them and they may even do harm without your being aware of it. Everybody knows that you are nuns and that your business is prayer. Do not say to yourselves: "I have no wish to be considered good," for what people see in you is bound to bring them either profit or harm. People like nuns,[16] on whom is laid the obligation to speak of nothing save in the spirit of God,[17] act very wrongly if they dissemble in this way, except occasionally[18] for the purpose of doing greater good. Your intercourse and conversation must be like this: let any who wish to talk to you learn your language; and, if they will not, be careful never to learn theirs: it might lead you to hell.

It matters little if you are considered ill-bred and still less if you are taken for hypocrites: indeed, you will gain by this, because only those who understand your language will come to see you. If one knows no Arabic, one has no desire to talk a great deal[19] with a person who knows no other language.

---

[14] E.: "with a brother."
[15] T. omits: "and influenced" and goes on: "but he would get to know about this afterwards and it would give him pleasure", ending the sentence here.
[16] E. omits: "like nuns."
[17] *Lit.*: "save in God"—i.e., save as those whose life is centred in God: not necessarily, I think, only *of* God.
[18] E. omits: "occasionally."
[19] E.: "to have a great deal to do."

So worldly people will neither weary you nor do you harm —and it would do you no small harm to have to begin to *learn and* talk a new language; you would spend all your time learning it. You cannot know as well as I do, for I have found it out by experience, how very bad this is for the soul;[20] no sooner does it learn one thing than it has to forget another and it never has any rest. This you must at all costs avoid; for peace and quiet in the soul are of great importance on the road which we are about to tread.

If those with whom you converse wish[21] to learn your language, it is not for you to teach it to them, but you can tell them[22] what wealth they will gain by learning it.[23] Never grow tried of this, but do it piously, lovingly and prayerfully, with a view to helping them; they will then realize what great gain *it brings,* and will go and seek a master to teach it them. Our Lord would be doing you no light favour if through your agency He were to arouse some soul to obtain this blessing. When once one begins to describe this road, what a large number of things there are to be said about it,[24] even by those who have trodden it as unsuccessfully as I have! *I only wish I could write with both hands, so as not to forget one thing while I am saying another.* May it please the Lord, sisters, that you may be enabled to speak of it better than I have done.

20 E.: "what great labour this gives the soul."
21 E.: "If those who come (to see you) wish."
22 E.: "but it will be for you to tell them."
23 E.: "by trying to learn it."
24 E. ends the sentence here and ends the chapter with the italicized sentence ("I only wish . . . another!"), which follows directly upon it.

CHAPTER 21

Describes the great importance of setting out upon the practice of prayer with firm resolution and of heeding no difficulties put in the way by the devil.

Do not be dismayed, daughters,[1] at the number of things which you have to consider before setting out on this Divine journey, which is the royal road to Heaven.[2] By taking this road we gain such precious treasures that it is no wonder if the cost seems to us a high one. The time will come when we shall realize that all we have paid has been nothing at all by comparison with the greatness of our prize.

Let us now return to those who wish to travel on this road, and will not halt until they reach their goal, which is the place where they can drink of this water of life.[3] *Although in some book or other—in several, in fact—I have read what a good thing it is to begin in this way, I do not think anything will be lost if I speak of it here.* As I say, it is most important —all-important, indeed—that they should begin well by making an earnest and most determined resolve[4] not to halt until they reach their goal, whatever may come, whatever may happen to them, however hard they may have to labour, whoever may complain of them, whether they reach their goal or die on the road or have no heart[5] to confront the trials which they meet, whether the very world dissolves before them. Yet again and again people will say to us: "It is dangerous", "So-

---

[1] T.: "Do not marvel, sisters."
[2] E.: "Do not be surprised, daughters, for this is the royal road (*camino real*) to Heaven." A more idiomatic translation of *camino real* would be "king's highway": cf. the use of the phrase on p. 152, below.
[3] E.: "Let us now return to those who wish to drink of this water of life and wish to journey till they arrive at the spring itself."
[4] *Lit.*: "determined determination": this doubling of words is not uncommon in St. Teresa. Cf. n. 10, below.
[5] T.: "have not the devotion."

and-so was lost through doing this", "Someone else got into wrong ways",[6] "Some other person, who was always praying, fell just the same", "It is bad for virtue", "It is not meant for women; it may lead them into delusions",[7] "They would do better to stick to their spinning", "These subtleties are of no use to them", "It is quite enough for them to say their Paternoster and Ave Maria."

With this last remark, sisters, I quite agree. Of course it is enough! It is always a great thing to base your prayer on prayers which were uttered by the very lips of the Lord.[8] People are quite right to say this, and, were it not for our great weakness and the lukewarmness of our devotion, there would be no need for any other systems of prayer or for any other books at all.[9] I am speaking to souls who are unable to recollect themselves by meditating upon other mysteries, and who think they need special methods of prayer; some people have such ingenious minds[10] that nothing is good enough for them! So I think I will start to lay down some rules for each part of our prayer—beginning, middle and end —although I shall not spend long on the higher stages.[11] They cannot take books from you,[12] and, if you are studious and humble, you need nothing more.

I have always been fond of the words of the Gospels[13] and have found more recollection in them than in the most carefully planned books—especially books of which the authors were not fully approved,[14] and which I never wanted to read. If I keep close to this Master of wisdom,[15] He may per-

[6] E. omits this sentence.
[7] E.: "for women, who get delusions."
[8] E.: "by such lips."
[9] E. adds: "nor would other (kinds of) prayer be necessary."
[10] Lit.: "are such ingenious geniuses."
[11] E.: "although I shall only touch on the higher stages, for, as I say, I have already written about them."
[12] E. adds: "so that such a good book does not remain to you."
[13] E. adds: "which came from those most sacred lips just as He spoke them."
[14] V.: muy aprobado. E. is stronger: muy muy aprobado.
[15] E.: "of all wisdom." T.: "to this Lord and Master of wisdom."

haps give me some thoughts[16] which will help you. I do not
say that I will explain these Divine prayers, for that I should
not presume to do, and there are a great many explanations
of them already. Even were there none,[17] it would be ridiculous for me to attempt any. But I will write down a few
thoughts on the words of the Paternoster;[18] for sometimes,
when we are most anxious to nurture our devotion, consulting
a great many books will kill it. When a master is himself
giving a lesson, he treats his pupil kindly and likes him[19] to
enjoy being taught and does his utmost to help him learn.
Just so will this heavenly Master do with us.

Pay no heed, then,[20] to anyone who tries to frighten you
or depicts to you the perils of the way. What a strange idea
that one could ever expect to travel on a road infested by
thieves, for the purpose of gaining some great treasure, without running into danger! Worldly people like to take life
peaceably; but they will deny themselves sleep, *perhaps* for
nights on end, in order to gain a farthing's profit, and they
will leave you no peace either of body or of soul. If, when
you are on the way to gaining this treasure, or to taking it by
force (as the Lord says the violent do)[21] and are travelling
by this royal road—this safe road trodden by our King[22] and
by His elect and His saints—if even then they tell you it is
full of danger and make you so afraid, what will be the dangers encountered by those who think they will be able to gain
this treasure and yet are not on the road to it?

[16] V.: *alguna consideración*: the use of the singular form in a plural
sense, with the shade of meaning which might be conveyed by "some
occasional thoughts," is common in Spanish. E. uses one of St.
Teresa's characteristic diminutives (see Vol. 1, p. xxi) *alguna con-
sideracioncita*—"some (occasional) trifling thoughts."
[17] E. omits: "Even were there none."
[18] E.: "on some of the words of them."
[19] T. has "and seeks for him"; but this (*busca* for *gusta*) might be
an error, and the construction suggests to me that it is.
[20] E. begins a new chapter here with the words: "Returning to what
I was saying, pay no heed."
[21] The original has *robar* (steal), which is perhaps nearer the A.V.
of St. Matthew xi, 12 than the D.V. "bear it away".
[22] E.: "by Christ our Emperor."

Oh, my daughters, how incomparably greater must be the risks they run! And yet they have no idea of this until they fall headlong into some real danger. Having *perhaps* no one to help them, they lose this water altogether, and drink neither much nor little of it, either from a pool or from a stream. How do you suppose they can do without a drop of this water and yet travel along a road on which there are so many adversaries to fight? Of course, sooner or later, they will die of thirst; for we must all journey to this fountain, my daughters, whether we will or no, though we may not all do so in the same way. Take my advice, then, and let none mislead you by showing you any other road than that of prayer.

I am not now discussing whether or no everyone must practise mental or vocal prayer; but I do say that you yourselves require both.[23] For prayer is the duty of religious. If anyone tells you it is dangerous, look upon that person himself as your principal danger and flee from his company. Do not forget this, for it is advice that you may possibly need. It will be dangerous for you if you do not possess humility and the other virtues; but God forbid that the way of prayer should be a way of danger! This fear seems to have been invented by the devil, who has apparently been very clever in bringing about the fall of some who practise prayer.[24]

See how blind the world is![25] It never thinks of all the thousands who have fallen into heresies and other great evils through yielding to distractions and not practising prayer.[26] As against these multitudes there are a few[27] who did practise prayer and whom the devil has been successful enough at his own trade to cause to fall: in doing this he has also

---

[23] E. is more concise: "but I do say—for you, both."

[24] E. and T. omit: "apparently." E. ends: "of some who were following this road." T. adds, after "practise prayer": "and in frightening some with regard to matters of virtue."

[25] E. reads: "See what great blindness!" and, instead of "all the (*muchos*) thousands", uses a hyperbolical expression then current: "the world of thousands, as they say." T. omits: "See how . . . virtuous practices."

[26] E. reads: "evils, and not practising prayer, or knowing what it is —a condition very much to be feared."

[27] "A very small number," adds E.

caused some to be very much afraid of virtuous practices. Let those who make use of this pretext[28] to absolve themselves from such practices take heed, for in order to save themselves from evil they are fleeing from good. I have never heard of such a wicked invention; it must indeed come from the devil. Oh, my Lord, defend Thyself. See how Thy words are being misunderstood. Permit no such weakness in Thy servants.[29]

There is one great blessing—you will always find a few people ready to help you. For it is a characteristic of the true servant of God, to whom His Majesty has given light to follow the true path, that, when beset by these fears, his desire not to stop only increases. He sees clearly[30] whence the devil's blows are coming, but he parries each blow and breaks his adversary's head. The anger which this arouses in the devil is greater than all the satisfaction which he receives from the pleasures[31] given him by others. When, in troublous times, he has sown his tares, and seems to be leading men everywhere in his train, half-blinded, and [deceiving them into] believing themselves to be zealous for the right,[32] God raises up someone to open their eyes and bid them look at the fog with which the devil has obscured their path. (How great God is! To think that just one man, or perhaps two,[33] can do more by telling the truth than can a great many men all together!) And then they gradually begin to see the path again and God gives them courage. If people say there is danger in prayer,[34] this servant of God, by his deeds if not by his words, tries to make them realize what a good thing it is.

---

[28] E. has "who have these remedies and take (them) in order to absolve themselves, etc.", and a different construction, though the same sense, in the clause following.

[29] E. adds: "It is well, daughters: they will not take the Paternoster and the Ave María from you" (cf. p. 151, n. 12, above), but these words, which constitute a somewhat violent transition, have been crossed out in the manuscript, nor do they appear in V. E. then continues: "You will always find many people ready to help you."

[30] T. deletes: "clearly".

[31] E.: "than all the pleasures."

[32] E.: "to be great Christians."

[33] E.: "one man, or perhaps ten."

[34] E.: "there must be no prayer."

If they say that frequent communion is[35] inadvisable, he only practises it[36] the more. So, because just one or two are fearlessly following the better path, the Lord gradually regains what He had lost.[37]

Cease troubling about these fears, then, sisters; and never pay heed to such matters of popular opinion. This is no time for believing everyone; believe only those whom you see modelling their lives on the life[38] of Christ. Endeavour always to have a good conscience; practise humility; despise all worldly things; and believe firmly in the teaching of our Holy Mother [the Roman][39] Church. You may then be quite sure that you are on a [very] good road. Cease, as I have said, to have fear where no fear is; if any one attempts to frighten you, point out the road[40] to him in all humility. Tell him that you have a Rule which commands you, as it does, to pray without ceasing, and that that rule you must keep. If they tell you that you should practise only vocal prayer, ask whether your mind and heart ought not to be in what you say. If they answer "Yes"—and they cannot do otherwise—you see they are admitting that you are bound to practise mental prayer, and even contemplation, if God should grant it you. [Blessed be He for ever.]

---

35 E.: "that so many communions are."
36 E.: "he approaches the Most Holy Sacrament."
37 E.: "If there is just one with courage, another comes at once, and the Lord regains what He had lost."
38 T.: "the law."
39 The interpolation in T. is in St. Teresa's own hand.
40 T. deletes "road" and substitutes "truth".

CHAPTER 22

Explains the meaning of mental prayer.

You must know, daughters, that[1] whether or no you are practising mental prayer has nothing to do with keeping the
lips closed. If, while I am speaking with God,[2] I have a clear
realization and full consciousness that I am doing so, and if
this is more real to me than the words I am uttering, then I
am combining mental and vocal prayer. When people tell
you that you are speaking with God by reciting the Paternoster[3] and thinking of worldly things—well, words fail me.
When you speak, as it is right for you to do, with so great a
Lord, it is well that you should think of Who it is that you
are addressing, and what you yourself are, if only that you
may speak to Him with proper respect. How can you address
a king[4] with the deference due to him, or how can you know
what ceremonies have to be used when speaking to a grandee,
unless you are clearly conscious of the nature of his position
and of yours? It is because of this, and because it is the custom to do so, that you must behave respectfully to him,[5]
and must learn *what the custom is, and not be careless about
such things*, or you will be dismissed as a simpleton and obtain none of the things you desire. *And furthermore, unless
you are quite conversant with it, you must get all necessary
information, and have what you are going to say written down
for you. It once happened to me, when I was not accustomed
to addressing aristocrats, that I had to go on a matter of ur-
gent business to see a lady who had to be addressed as "Your*

---

[1] E. begins the chapter: "Yes, whether or no, etc."
[2] T. adds: "and praying vocally."
[3] E. has: "reciting the Ave Maria." On revising her work the Saint
evidently reflected that the recitation of the Paternoster would provide a more suitable illustration of "speaking with God".
[4] E.: "a prince."
[5] E. omits: "respectfully."

Ladyship".[6] *I was shown that word in writing; but I am stupid, and had never used such a term before; so when I arrived I got it wrong. So I decided to tell her about it and she laughed heartily and told me to be good enough to use the ordinary form of polite address,*[7] *which I did.*

How is it, my Lord, how is it, my Emperor, that Thou canst suffer this, *Prince of all Creation?* For Thou, my God, art a King without end, and Thine is no borrowed Kingdom, *but Thine own, and it will never pass away.* When the Creed says "Whose Kingdom shall have no end" the phrase nearly always makes me feel particularly happy. I praise Thee, Lord, and bless Thee, *and all things praise Thee* for ever—for Thy Kingdom will endure for ever. Do Thou never allow it to be thought right, Lord, for those who *praise Thee and* come to speak with Thee to do so with their lips alone. What do you mean, Christians, when you say that mental prayer is unnecessary?[8] Do you understand what you are saying? I really do not think you can. And so you want us all to go wrong: you cannot know what mental prayer is,[9] or how vocal prayers should be said, or what is meant by contemplation. For, if you knew this, you would not condemn on the one hand what you praise on the other.

Whenever I remember to do so, I shall always speak of mental and vocal prayer together, daughters, so that you may

---

[6] This is generally taken as referring to St. Teresa's visit to Doña Luisa de la Cerda in 1562 (Vol. I, pp. 232, ff., above).

[7] *Lit.:* "to call her 'Honour'." The point of this delightfully unaffected reminiscence, omitted in V. and inserted here rather for its attractiveness than for its artistic appropriateness, is that "Your Honour" (*Vuestra Merced:* now abbreviated to Vd. and used as the third personal pronoun of ordinary polite address) was an expression merely of respect and not of rank: the Saint often uses it, for example, in addressing her confessors. It was as though a peer of the realm were to say "Just call me 'Sir'."

[8] E.: "What do you mean, Christians? Though only what I am, I should like to cry aloud and dispute with those who say that mental prayer is unnecessary."

[9] E.: "I am sure you do not, nor can you, know what mental prayer is."

not be alarmed. I know what such fears lead to,[10] for I have suffered a certain number of trials in this respect,[11] and so I should be sorry if anyone were to unsettle you, for it is very bad for you to have misgivings[12] while you are walking on this path. It is most important that you should realize you are making progress; for if a traveller is told[13] that he has taken the wrong road, and has lost his way, he begins to wander to and fro and the constant search for the right road tires him, wastes his time and delays his arrival. Who can say that it is wrong if, before we begin reciting the Hours or the Rosary, we think Whom we are going to address,[14] and who we are that are addressing Him, so that we may do so in the way we should? I assure you, sisters, that if you gave all due attention to a consideration of these two points before beginning the vocal prayers which you are about to say[15] you would be engaging in mental prayer for a very long time. For we cannot approach a prince and address him in the same careless way that we should adopt in speaking to a peasant[16] or to some poor woman like ourselves, whom we may address however we like.[17]

The reason we sometimes do so is to be found in the humility[18] of this King, Who, unskilled though I am in speaking with Him, does not refuse to hear me[19] or forbid me to approach Him, or command His guards to throw me out. For

[10] For "fears" the original has "things"; but that seems to be the meaning.
[11] This clause is not in E., which continues: "and I should be sorry if anyone were to deceive you, for it is very bad, etc."
[12] In T. a hand, not the author's, has crossed out "have misgivings" and written "be unsettled".
[13] E.: "if one is told."
[14] T.: "we are addressing."
[15] E.: "before beginning vocal prayer, which consists in the recitation of Hours and Rosary."
[16] E. has: "to a little peasant-boy" (*labradorcito*, the familiar diminutive: cf. p. 152, n. 16, above).
[17] E.: "whom it matters not if we call *tú* or *vos*." *Tú* was the familiar form; *vos*, the polite form, eventually superseded by Vd. (cf. p. 157, n. 7, above).
[18] T.: "benignity."
[19] E.: "does not think any the less of me."

the angels in His presence know well that their King is such that He prefers the unskilled language of a humble peasant boy, knowing that he would say more if he had more to say, to the speech of the wisest and most learned men, however elegant may be their arguments, if these are not accompanied by humility.[20] But we must not be unmannerly because He is good. If only to show our gratitude to Him for enduring our foul odour and[21] allowing such a one as myself to come near Him, it is well that we should try to realize His purity and His nature.[22] It is true that we recognize this at once when we approach Him, just as we do when we visit the lords of the earth. Once we are told about their fathers' names and their incomes and dignities, there is no more for us to know about them; for on earth one makes account of persons, and honours them,[23] not because of their merits but because of their possessions.

O miserable world! Give hearty praise to God, daughters, that you have left so wretched a place,[24] where people are honoured, not for their own selves, but for what they get from their tenants and vassals:[25] if these fail them, they have no honour left.[26] It is a curious thing, and when you go out to recreation together you should laugh about it, for it is a good way of spending your time to reflect how blindly people in the world spend theirs.

O Thou our Emperor! Supreme Power, Supreme Goodness, Wisdom Itself, without beginning, without end and without measure in Thy works:[27] infinite are these and incomprehensible, a fathomless ocean of wonders, O Beauty[28]

---

20 E.: "to that of the most systematic theologies (sic) if they are not accompanied by great humility."

21 T. omits: "enduring our foul odour and".

22 E.: "for enduring the foul odour when He endures us, it is well that we should see Who He is." There is deeper self-abasement, and also greater clarity, in V.

23 "And honours them" does not occur in E.

24 Lit.: "a thing".

25 In E. the sentence ends here.

26 T.: "The world ceases to do them honour."

27 T. deletes "works" and writes "perfections."

28 Lit.: "a Beauty . . . . itself", as though referring to obras: "works."

containing within Thyself all beauties. O Very Strength! God help me! Would that I could command all the eloquence of mortals and all wisdom, so as to understand, as far as is possible here below, that to know nothing is everything, and thus to describe some of the many things on which we may meditate in order to learn something of the nature of this our Lord and Good.[29]

When you approach God, then, try[30] to think and realize Whom you are about to address and continue to do so while you are addressing Him. If we[31] had a thousand lives, we should never fully understand how this Lord merits that we behave toward Him, before Whom[32] even the angels tremble. He orders all things and He can do all things:[33] with Him to will is to perform. It will be right, then, daughters, for us to endeavour to rejoice in these wondrous qualities[34] of our Spouse and to know Whom we have wedded and what our lives should be. Why, God save us, when a woman in this world is about to marry, she knows beforehand whom she is to marry, what sort of a person he is and what property he possesses. Shall not we, then, who are already betrothed,[35] think about our Spouse,[36] before we are wedded to Him and He takes us home to be with Him? If these thoughts are not forbidden to those who are betrothed to men on earth, how can we be forbidden to discover Who this Man is, Who is

[29] V. has expanded this paragraph, which reads in E.: "O King of glory, Lord of lords, Emperor of emperors, Holy of the holy, Power above all powers, Knowledge above all knowledge, Wisdom Itself: Thou, Lord, art Truth Itself, Riches Itself, and Thou shalt reign without fail for ever."

[30] Lit.: "Yes, approach God, and, in approaching, try." T. begins: "There is nothing more, when you approach God, but to think, etc."

[31] E. continues in the second person.

[32] T.: "before Whose presence."

[33] E. omits: "and He can do all things."

[34] E.: "to endeavour to comprehend at least something of these wondrous qualities."

[35] E. adds: "and all souls, through baptism."

[36] The words "think about our Spouse" appear in no manuscript but were added by Luis de León.

His Father, what is the country to which He[37] will take me, what are the riches with which He promises to endow me,[38] what is His rank, how I can best make Him happy, what I can do that will give Him pleasure, and how I can bring my rank into line with His. If a woman is to be happy in her marriage, it is just those things that she is advised to see about,[39] even though her husband be a man of very low station.

Shall less respect be paid to Thee, then, my Spouse, than to men? If they think it unfitting to do Thee honour, let them at least leave Thee Thy brides, who are to spend their lives with Thee. A woman is indeed fortunate in her life if her husband is so jealous that he will allow her to speak with no one but himself;[40] it would be a pretty pass if she could not resolve to give him this pleasure, for it is reasonable enough that she should put up with this and not wish to converse with anyone else, since in him she has all that she can desire. To understand these truths, my daughters, is to practise mental prayer. If you wish to learn to understand them, and at the same time to practise vocal prayer, well and good. But do not, I beg you, address God while you are thinking of other things, for to do that is the result of not understanding what mental prayer is. I think I have made this clear. May the Lord grant us to learn how to put it into practice.[41] Amen.

---

37 T.: "they".
38 This clause is not in E., which has some other, but quite slight, divergences in this sentence.
39 E. "to study."
40 E.: "that he will not allow his wife to leave home or to speak with anyone other than himself."
41 E., instead of the last sentence, has: "I think it has been shown that no one should alarm you with these fears. Praise God, Who is more powerful than all men, and they cannot take Him from you. If any one of you cannot say her vocal prayers with this attentiveness, she should know that she is not fulfilling her obligation, and that, if she wishes to say them perfectly, the obligation is upon her to strive after this (mental prayer) with all her might, under pain of not doing her duty as the bride of so great a King. Beseech Him, daughters, to give me grace to do as I admonish you, which I am very far from doing. May His Majesty supply this, for His own sake."

CHAPTER 23

Describes the importance of not turning back when one has set out upon the way of prayer. Repeats how necessary it is to be resolute.

Now,[1] as I have said, it is most important that from the first we should be very resolute, and for this there are so many reasons that if I were to give them all I should have to write at great length. *Some of them are given in other books.* I will tell you just two or three of them, sisters. One is that when we decide to give anything—such as this slight effort of recollection[2]—to Him Who has given us so much, and Who is continually giving, it would be wrong for us not to be entirely resolute in doing so and to act like a person who lends something and expects to get it back again. (Not that we do not receive interest: on the contrary, we gain a great deal.) I do not call this "giving". Anyone who has been lent something always feels slightly displeased when the lender wants it back again, especially if he is using it himself and has come to look upon it as his own. If the two are friends[3] and the lender is indebted to the recipient for many things of which he has made him free gifts, he will think it meanness and a great lack of affection[4] if he will leave not even the smallest thing[5] in his possession, merely as a sign of love.

What wife is there who, after receiving many valuable jewels from her husband, will not give him so much as a ring—

[1] V. substitutes "now" for the exclamation with which the chapter begins in E.: "How I do let myself wander!"
[2] *Este cuidadito*: lit., "this little attentiveness"—another characteristic diminutive (not used in T., which has *cuidado*). In "to give anything", V. simplifies the reading in E.: "to serve (in any way) or to give anything."
[3] E. omits: "he is. . . . If" and begins a new sentence at: "He will think. . . ."
[4] E.: "of good-will."
[5] The diminutive *cosita*: T. has *cosa*.

which he wants, not because of its value, for all she has is his, but as *a sign of love and* a token that she will be his until she dies? Does the Lord deserve less than this that we should mock Him by taking away the worthless gift[6] which we have given Him? Since we have resolved to devote to Him this very brief period of time—only a small part of what we spend upon ourselves and upon people who are not particularly grateful to us for it—let us give it Him freely, with our minds unoccupied by other things[7] and entirely resolved never to take it back again, whatever we may suffer through trials, annoyances or aridities. Let me realize that this time is being lent me and is not my own, and feel that I can rightly be called to account for it if I am not prepared to devote it wholly to God.

I say "wholly", but we must not be considered as taking it back if we should fail to give it Him for a day, or for a few days, because of legitimate occupations[8] or through some indisposition. Provided the intention remains firm,[9] my God is not in the least meticulous;[10] He does not look at trivial details; and, if you are trying to please Him in any way, He will assuredly accept that as your gift. The other way is suitable for ungenerous souls, so mean that they are not large-hearted enough to give but find it as much as they can do to lend. Still, let them make some effort, for this Lord of ours[11] will reckon everything we do to our credit and accept everything we want to give Him.[12] In drawing up our reckoning, He is not in the least exacting, but generous; however large the amount we may owe Him, it is a small thing for Him to forgive us.[13] And, as to paying us, He is so careful about this

---

[6] *Lit.*: "a nothing at all" (*una nonada*).
[7] T. omits: "by other things."
[8] E. ends this sentence here.
[9] T. joins this phrase to the preceding sentence and continues: "That is a gift. The other way, etc."
[10] *No es nada delicado mi Dios.* "Fastidious" might be nearer to the characteristically bold adjective of the original.
[11] E.: "this Emperor."
[12] T. continues: "He is generous; however large, etc."
[13] T.: "for Him to forgive us in order to gain us: He is so grateful that, if we only raise our eyes to Heaven and remember Him, He will not leave (us) without a reward."

that you need have no fear He will leave us without our reward[14] if only we raise our eyes to Heaven and remember Him.

A second reason why we should be resolute is that this[15] will give the devil less opportunity to tempt us. He is very much afraid of resolute souls, knowing by experience that they inflict great injury upon him, and, when he plans to do them harm, he only profits them and others and is himself the loser. We must not become unwatchful, or count upon this, for we have to do with treacherous folk, who are great cowards and dare not attack the wary, but, if they see we are careless, will work us great harm. And if they know anyone to be changeable, and not resolute in *doing* what is good and firmly determined to persevere, they will not leave him alone either by night or by day and will suggest to him endless misgivings and difficulties. This I know very well by experience and so I have been able to tell you about it: I am sure that none of us realize its great importance.

Another reason, very much to the point, is that a resolute person fights more courageously.[16] He knows that, come what may, he must not retreat. He is like a soldier in battle who is aware that if he is vanquished his life will not be spared and that if he escapes death in battle he must die afterwards. *It has been proved, I think, that* such a man will fight more resolutely and will try, as they say, to sell his life dearly, fearing the enemy's blows[17] the less because he understands the importance of victory[18] and knows that his very life depends upon his gaining it. We must also be *firmly* convinced from the start that, if we *fight courageously and* do not allow ourselves to be beaten, we shall get what we want,[19] and there is no doubt that, however small our gains may be, they will

---

[14] E.: "without our payment."
[15] T. begins the paragraph: "And this."
[16] E.: "fights courageously." T. omits: "very much to the point."
[17] E.: "will fight much more courageously and will fear the enemy's blows." T. omits: "as they say."
[18] E. ends the sentence here.
[19] E. continues: "and without fail. However small your gains may be, He calls you to drink of this spring."

make us very rich. Do not be afraid that the Lord Who has called us to drink of this spring will allow you[20] to die of thirst. This I have already said and I should like to repeat it; for people are often timid when they have not learned by experience[21] of the Lord's goodness, even though they know of it[22] by faith. It is a great thing to have experienced what friendship and joy He gives to those who walk on this road[23] and how He takes almost the whole cost of it upon Himself.

I am not surprised that those who have never made this test should want to be sure that they will receive some interest on their outlay. But you already know that even in this life we shall receive a hundredfold, and that the Lord says: "Ask and it shall be given you."[24] If you do not believe His Majesty in those passages of His Gospel where He gives us this assurance, it will be of little help to you, sisters, for me to weary my brains by telling you of it. Still, I will say to anyone who is in doubt that she will lose little by putting the matter to the test;[25] for this journey has the advantage[26] of giving us *very much* more than we ask or shall even get so far as to desire.[27] This is a never-failing truth: I know it; *though, if you do not find it so, do not believe any of the things I tell you.* I can call as witnesses those of you who, by God's goodness, know it from experience.[28]

20 T.: "very rich. For the Lord . . . spring, will not allow you, etc."
21 E.: "learned to know by experience."
22 T.: "they confess it."
23 E. ends the sentence here.
24 St. Luke xi, 9. E.: "says we are to ask and He will give us."
25 E.: "in doubt: 'Put it to the test. What is lost (by your doing so)?' "
26 *Lit.*: "the good." E.: "the excellence."
27 E.: "as to ask."
28 In E. this sentence reads: "You, sisters, already know it by experience, and I can call you as witnesses, by God's goodness." E. then adds: "This which has been said is good for those who are coming (after us)."

CHAPTER 24

Describes how vocal prayer may be practised with perfection and how closely allied it is to mental prayer.

Let us now return to speak of those souls I have mentioned who cannot[1] practise recollection or tie down their minds to mental prayer or make a meditation. We must not talk to them of either of those two things—they will not hear of them; as a matter of fact, there are a great many people who seem terrified at the very name[2] of contemplation or mental prayer.[3]

In case any such person should come to this house (for, as I have said, not all are led by the same path), I want to advise you, or, I might even say, to teach you (for, as your mother, and by the office of prioress which I hold, I have the right to do so)[4] how you must practise vocal prayer, for it is right that you should understand what you are saying. Anyone unable to think of God may find herself wearied by long prayers, and so I will not begin to discuss these, but will speak simply of prayers which, as[5] Christians, we must perforce recite—namely, the Paternoster and the Ave Maria[6]—and then no one will be able to say of us that we are repeating words without understanding what we are saying. We may, of course, consider it enough to say our prayers as a mere habit, repeating the words and thinking that this will suffice.[7]

---

[1] E.: "I have already said that I am dealing with souls who cannot."
[2] E. ends the sentence here.
[3] T.: "consideration" (i.e., meditation, and so translated in the text below).
[4] E.: "for, as your mother, I now have this duty."
[5] E.: "which, if we are."
[6] E. continues: "It is clear that we must consider what we are saying, as I have said. No one must be able to say of us, etc."
[7] E.: "You may, of course, say that this [i.e., understanding] is unnecessary, that you say your prayers as a habit, that it suffices to re-

Whether it suffices or no I will not now discuss.[8] Learned men must decide:[9] *they will instruct people to whom God gives light to consult them, and I will not discuss the position of those who have not made a profession like our own.* But what I should like, daughters, is for us not to be satisfied with that alone: when I say the Creed, it seems to me right, *and indeed obligatory,* that I should understand and[10] know what it is that I believe; and, when I repeat the "Our Father", my love should make me want to understand Who this Father of ours is and Who the Master is that taught us this prayer.[11]

If you assert that you know Who He is already, and so there is no need for you to think about Him, you are not right; there is a great deal of difference[12] between one master and another, and it would be very wrong of us not to think about those who teach us, even on earth; if they are holy men and[13] spiritual masters, and we are good pupils, it is impossible for us *not to have great love for them, and indeed to hold them in honour and often to talk about them.*[14] And when it comes to the Master Who taught us this prayer, and Who loves us so much and is so anxious for us to profit by it, may God forbid that we should fail to think[15] of Him

---

peat the words." T.: "repeating the words, which I will not now discuss. Learned men will say if it suffices or no. But what I should like, etc."

[8] The word rendered "discuss", both here and below, is a strong one, *entrometerse,* to intermeddle.

[9] E.: "It is a matter for learned men."

[10] "Understand and" is not found in E.

[11] E.: "and when I say 'Father', it should, I think, be a matter of love for me to understand Who this Father is. It will be well, too, for us to see Who the Master is that teaches us this prayer."

[12] E.: "If we assert that it is sufficient to know once and for all Who the Master is, without thinking of Him again, you might equally well say that it is sufficient to recite the prayer once in a lifetime. Yes, but there is a great deal of difference."

[13] E. omits: "holy men and."

[14] Thus E., which I prefer here: V. has: "it is impossible for us not to do so."

[15] T.: "fail to profit by thinking."

often when we repeat it, although our own weakness may prevent us from doing so every time.

Now, in the first place, you know that His Majesty[16] teaches that this prayer must be made when we are alone, just as He was often alone when He prayed,[17] not because this was necessary for Him, but for our edification. It has already been said that it is impossible to speak to God and to the world at the same time; yet this is just what we are trying to do when we are saying our prayers and at the same time listening to the conversation of others or letting our thoughts wander on any matter that occurs to us,[18] without making an effort to control them.[19] There are occasions when one cannot help doing this: times of ill-health (especially in persons who suffer from melancholia); or times when our heads are tired, and, however hard we try, we cannot concentrate; or times when, for their own good, God allows His servants for days on end to go through great storms. And, although they are distressed and strive to calm themselves, they are unable to do so and incapable of attending to what they are saying, however hard they try, nor can they fix their understanding on anything: they seem to be in a frenzy, so distraught are they.

The very suffering of anyone in this state will show her that she is not to blame, and she must not worry, for that only makes matters worse, nor must she weary herself by trying to put sense into something—namely, her mind—which for the moment is without any. She should pray as best she can: indeed, she need not pray at all, but may try to rest her spirit as though she were ill and busy herself with some other virtuous action. These directions are meant for persons who keep careful guard over themselves and know that they must

16 E.: "that this heavenly Master."
17 V. has "always" for "often". T. reads: "Now, in the first place, it is best to be alone, just as His Majesty was often alone" and omits: "when He prayed." The adverbial correction of T. is clearly justified.
18 E.: "or thinking of anything we like."
19 E. continues: "This, we know quite well, is not good: we must try to be alone—and please God we may realize in Whose presence we are, etc." Cf. p. 169, n. 20, below.

not speak to God and to the world at the same time. What we can do ourselves is to try to be alone—and God grant that this may suffice, as I say, to make us realize in Whose presence we are[20] and how the Lord answers our petitions. Do you suppose[21] that, because we cannot hear Him, He is silent? He speaks clearly to the heart when we beg Him from our hearts to do so. It would be a good idea for us to imagine[22] that He has taught this prayer to each one of us individually, and that He is continually expounding it to us. The Master is never so far away that the disciple needs to raise his voice in order to be heard: He is always right at his side. I want you to understand that, if you are to recite the Paternoster well, one thing is needful: you must not leave the side of the Master Who has taught it you.

You will say *at once* that this is meditation, and that you are not capable of it, and do not even wish to practise it, but are content with vocal prayer.[23] For there are impatient people who dislike giving themselves trouble, and it is troublesome at first to practise recollection of the mind when one has not made it a habit. So, in order not to make themselves the least bit tired, they say they are incapable of anything but vocal prayer and do not know how to do anything further. You are right to say that what we have described is mental prayer; but I assure you that I cannot distinguish it from vocal prayer faithfully recited with a realization of Who it is that we are addressing. Further, we are under the obligation of trying to pray attentively: may God grant that, by using these means, we may learn to say the Paternoster well and not find ourselves thinking of something irrelevant. I have sometimes experienced this myself, and the best remedy I have found for it is to try to fix my mind on the Person by

20 This phrase ends the interpolation in V. referred to in the last note.
21 T. has: "Do not suppose . . ."
22 More literally: "consider", "reflect". E. begins: "With this presupposition, that we must be alone, we shall do well, etc."
23 E. continues: "and to some extent you are right. But I assure you etc."

Whom the words were first spoken. Have patience, then, and try to make this necessary practice into a habit,[24] *for necessary it is, in my opinion, for those who would be nuns, and indeed for all who would pray like good Christians.*

CHAPTER 25

Describes the great gain which comes to a soul when it practises vocal prayer perfectly. Shows how God may raise it thence to things supernatural.

In case you should think there is little gain to be derived from practising vocal prayer perfectly, I must tell you that, while you are repeating the Paternoster or some other vocal prayer, it is quite possible for the Lord to grant you perfect contemplation.[1] In this way His Majesty shows that He is listening to the person who is addressing Him, and that, in His greatness, He is addressing her,[2] by suspending the understanding, putting a stop to all thought, and, as we say, taking the words out of her mouth, so that even if she wishes to speak she cannot do so, or at any rate not without great difficulty.

Such a person understands that, without any sound of words,[3] she is being taught by this Divine Master, Who is suspending her faculties, which, if they were to work, would be causing her harm rather than profit. The faculties rejoice

---

[24] The phrase "and try . . . habit" is not found in E.

[1] E. begins "It will be possible that, while you are repeating the Paternoster, the Lord may grant you perfect contemplation, if you repeat it well."

[2] *Lit.*: "and that His greatness is addressing her." E. has "His Majesty": the change may not have quite the full significance implied in the English version.

[3] E. continues, and ends the paragraph, thus: "her Master is working in her soul, and that her own faculties are not working, so far as she understands. This is perfect contemplation."

without knowing how they rejoice; the soul is enkindled in love without understanding how it loves; it knows that it is rejoicing in the object of its love,[4] yet it does not know how it is rejoicing in it. It is well aware that this is not a joy which can be attained by the understanding; the will embraces it, without understanding how; but, in so far as it can understand anything, it perceives that this is a blessing which could not be gained by the merits of all the trials suffered on earth put together. It is a gift of the Lord of earth and Heaven, Who gives it like the God He is. This, daughters, is perfect contemplation.

You will now understand how different it is from mental prayer, which I have already described, and which consists in thinking of what we are saying, understanding it, and realizing Whom we are addressing, and who we are that are daring to address so great a Lord. To think of this and other similar things, such as how little we have served Him and how great is our obligation to serve Him, is mental prayer. Do not think of it as one more thing with an outlandish name[5] and do not let the name frighten you. To recite the Paternoster and the Ave Maria,[6] or any other petition you like, is vocal prayer. But think how harsh your music will be without what must come first; sometimes even the words will get into the wrong order. In these two kinds of prayer, with God's help, we may accomplish something ourselves. In the contemplation which I have just described we can do nothing.[7] It is His Majesty Who does everything; the work is His alone and far transcends human nature.

I described this as well as I was able in the relation which I made of it, as I have said,[8] so that my confessors should

---

[4] T. omits: "it knows . . . its love."

[5] *algarabía. Lit.*: "Arabic" (as in p. 148, l. 29, above: cf. p. 206, n. 36, below) and hence "gibberish," "jargon."

[6] E. omits: "and the Ave Maria." Cf. p. 156, n. 3, above.

[7] "Except," adds P. Báñez in the margin, "prepare ourselves with prayer."

[8] P. Silverio has "Relation" and takes the reference to be to the first six *Relations* as well as to the *Life*. But the context and the apparent allusion to the Prologue to this book (pp. 34–5, above) sug-

see it when they read the account of my life which they had ordered me to write. As I have explained all this about contemplation at such length, therefore, I shall not repeat myself here and I am doing no more than touch upon it. If those of you who have experienced the happiness of being called by the Lord to this state of contemplation can get this book, you will find in it points and counsels which the Lord was pleased to enable me to set down. These should bring you great comfort and profit—in my opinion, at least, and in the opinion of several people who have seen it[9] and who keep it at hand in order to make frequent use of it. I am ashamed to tell you that anything of mine is made such use of and the Lord knows with what confusion I write a great deal that I do. Blessed be He for thus bearing with me. Those of you who, as I say, have experience of supernatural prayer should procure the book after my death;[10] those who have not have no need to do so but they should try to carry out what has been said in this one.[11] Let them leave everything to the Lord, to Whom it belongs to grant this gift, and He will not deny it you if you do not tarry on the road but press forward so as to reach the end of your journey.

---

gests that what the author has in mind is only the *Life*. I therefore read "relation".

[9] T. ends the sentence here.

[10] E. abbreviates: "As I have explained all the best part of this in the book which, as I say, I have written, there is no need for me to treat it in such great detail here, for I said all that I knew about it there. Any one of you who has reached such a point that God has brought her to this state of contemplation (and, as I said, some of you are in it) should procure it, for it will be of great importance to you when I die."

[11] About profiting in as many ways as is possible," adds E., ending the chapter thus: "and to be diligent, for if they entreat the Lord and do what they can for themselves, He will grant them this gift. For the rest, it is for the Lord Himself to grant it, and He denies it to no one who fights on till he reaches the end of the road, as has been said."

CHAPTER 26

Continues the description of a method for recollecting the thoughts. Describes means of doing this. This chapter is very profitable for those who are beginning prayer.

Let us now return to our vocal prayer, so that we may learn to pray in such a way that, without our understanding how, God may give us everything at once:[1] if we do this, as I have said, we shall pray as we ought. As you know, the first things must be examination of conscience, confession of sin and the signing of yourself with the Cross. Then, daughter, as you are alone, you must look for a companion—and who could be a better Companion than the very Master Who taught you the prayer that you are about to say? Imagine that this Lord Himself is at your side and see how lovingly and how humbly He is teaching you—and, believe me, you should stay with so good a Friend for as long as you can before you leave Him. If you become accustomed to having Him at your side, and if He sees that you love Him to be there and are always trying to please Him, you will never be able, as we put it, to send Him away, nor will He ever fail you. He will help you in all your trials and you will have Him everywhere. Do you think it is a small thing to have[2] such a Friend as that beside you?

O sisters, those of you whose minds cannot[3] reason for long or whose thoughts cannot dwell *upon God* but are *constantly* wandering must at all costs form this habit.[4] I know quite well that you are capable of it—for many years I endured this

---

[1] T. continues: "and, as you know, (if we are) to pray as we ought, the first things must be, etc."
[2] T.: "See what a great thing it is to have."
[3] E.: "O souls, whose minds cannot."
[4] The original (both in E. and in V.) has, after "wandering": "get used (to this)! get used (to this)!" The repetition is typically Teresan.

trial of being unable to concentrate on one subject, and a very sore trial it is. But I know the Lord does not leave us so devoid of help that if we approach Him humbly and ask Him to be with us He will not grant our request. If a whole year passes without our obtaining what we ask, let us be prepared to try for longer.[5] Let us never grudge time so well spent. Who, after all, is hurrying us? I am sure we can form this habit and strive to walk at the side of this true Master.

I am not asking you now to think of Him, or to form numerous conceptions of Him, or to make long and subtle meditations with your understanding. I am asking you only to look at Him. For who can prevent you from turning the eyes of your soul (just for a moment, if you can do no more) upon this Lord? You are capable of looking at very ugly *and loathsome* things: can you not, then, look at the most beautiful thing imaginable?[6] Your Spouse never takes His eyes off you, daughters. He has borne with thousands of foul and abominable sins which you have committed against Him, yet even they have not been enough to make Him cease looking upon you. Is it such a great matter, then, for you to avert the eyes *of your soul* from outward things and sometimes to look at Him? See, He is only waiting for us to look at Him, as He says to the Bride.[7] If you want Him[8] you will find Him. He longs so much for us to look at Him once more that it will not be for lack of effort on His part if we fail to do so.

A wife, they say, must be like this if she is to have a happy married life with her husband. If he is sad, she must show signs of sadness; if he is merry, even though she may not in fact be so, she must appear merry too. See what slavery you have escaped from, sisters![9] Yet this, without any pretence,

[5] E. ends the paragraph: "I mean that it is possible to form the habit of walking at the side of this true Master."
[6] E. adds, parenthetically: "If you do not think Him so, I give you leave to stop looking at Him."
[7] A vague reminiscence of some phrase from Canticles: perhaps ii, 14, 16, v, 2, or vi, 12.
[8] Or "love Him". The verb in the Spanish can have either meaning.
[9] This sentence does not appear in E.; the idea evidently came to St. Teresa's mind as she was rewriting the chapter.

is really how we are treated by the Lord. He becomes subject to us and is pleased to let you be the mistress and to conform to your will. If you are happy, look upon your risen Lord, and the very thought of how He rose from the sepulchre will gladden you. How bright and how beautiful was He then! How majestic![10] How victorious! How joyful! He was like one emerging from a battle in which He had gained a great kingdom, all of which He desires you to have[11]—and with it Himself. Is it such a great thing that you should turn your eyes but once and look upon Him Who has made you such great gifts?

If you are suffering trials, or are sad, look upon Him[12] on His way to the Garden. What sore distress He must have borne in His soul, to describe His own suffering as He did and to complain of it! Or look upon Him bound to the Column, full of pain, His flesh all torn to pieces by His great love for you. How much He suffered, persecuted by some, spat upon by others, denied by His friends, and even deserted by them,[13] with none to take His part, frozen with the cold and left so completely alone that you may well comfort each other! Or look upon Him bending under the weight of the Cross[14] and not even allowed to take breath: He will look upon you with His lovely and compassionate eyes, full of tears, and in comforting your grief will forget His own because you are bearing Him company in order to comfort Him and turning your head to look upon Him.

"O Lord of the world, my true Spouse!" you may say to Him, if seeing Him in such a plight has filled your heart with such tenderness that you not only desire to look upon Him but love to speak to Him, not using forms of prayer, but

---

10 *Lit.*: "With what majesty!" E. reads: "With what dominion!" In T., "How victorious!" comes between "How bright!" and "how beautiful!"

11 T. ends the sentence here.

12 This first picture does not appear in E., which continues: "at the Column, full of pain, etc."

13 The phrases "How much He suffered", "and even deserted by them", are not found in E.

14 E.: "Or look upon Him in the Garden, or on the Cross, or bending under its weight."

words issuing from the compassion of your heart, which means so much to Him: "Art Thou so needy, my Lord and my Good, that Thou wilt accept poor companionship like mine? Do I read in Thy face that Thou hast found comfort, even in me?[15] How can it be possible, Lord, that the angels are leaving Thee alone and that Thy Father is not comforting Thee?

"If Thou, Lord, art willing to suffer all this for me, what am I suffering for Thee?[16] What have I to complain of? I am ashamed, Lord,[17] when I see Thee in such a plight, and if in any way I can imitate Thee[18] I will suffer all trials that come to me and count them as a great blessing. Let us go[19] both together, Lord: whither Thou goest,[20] I must go; through whatsoever Thou passest, I must pass." Take up this cross, sisters: never mind if the Jews trample upon you provided you can save Him some of His trials.[21] Take no heed of what they say to you; be deaf to all detraction; stumble and fall with your Spouse, but do not draw back from your cross or give it up.[22] Think often of the weariness of His journey and of how much harder His trials were than those which you have to suffer.[23] However hard you may imagine yours to be, and however much affliction they may cause you, they will be a source of comfort to you, for you will see that they are matters for scorn compared with the trials endured by the Lord.

You will ask me, sisters, how you can possibly do all this, and say that, if you had seen His Majesty with your bodily eyes at the time when He lived in the world, you would have done it willingly and gazed at Him for ever. Do not believe it: anyone who will not make the slight effort necessary for

---

[15] E., omits "like mine" in the previous sentence, and, for "that . . . in me", reads: "that Thou hast forgotten Thy griefs for mine?" [lit.: "with me"].
[16] E. omits: "for Thee."
[17] E.: "my Good."
[18] E.: "can resemble Thee."
[19] E.: "We are going."
[20] E.: "whither Thou wentest."
[21] "Provided . . . trials" is not found in E.
[22] "Or give it up" is not found in E.
[23] E.: "than yours."

recollection in order to gaze upon this Lord present within her, which she can do without danger and with only the minimum of trouble, would have been far less likely to stand at the foot of the Cross with the Magdalen, who looked death (*as they say*) straight in the face.[24] What the glorious Virgin and this blessed saint must have suffered! What threats, what malicious words, what shocks,[25] what insults! For the people they were dealing with were not exactly polite to them. No, indeed; theirs was the kind of courtesy you might meet in hell, for they were the ministers of the devil himself. Yet, terrible as the sufferings of these women must have been, they would not have noticed them[26] in the presence of pain so much greater.

So do not suppose, sisters, that you would have been prepared to endure such great trials then, if you are not ready for such trifling ones now.[27] Practise enduring these and you may be given others which are greater. *Believe that I am telling the truth when I say that you can do this, for I am speaking from experience.* You will find it very helpful if you can get an image or a picture of this Lord—one that you like[28]— not to wear round your neck and never look at but to use regularly whenever you talk to Him, and He will tell you what to say. If words do not fail you when you talk to people *on earth*, why should they do so when you talk to God?[29] Do not imagine that they will—I shall certainly not believe that they have done so if you once form the habit.[30] For when you never have intercourse with a person he soon becomes a stranger to you, and you forget how to talk to him; and before long, even if he is a kinsman, you feel as if you do not know

24 T. weakens this vivid phrase to "who saw death present".

25 "What shocks" is not in E.

26 T.: "they did not notice them."

27 E.: "endure the one . . . ready for the other."

28 This parenthesis, not in E., is a characteristic later addition.

29 "More than to others", interpolates T., redundantly.

30 "If you once form the habit" is not in E., which also ends the paragraph at "done so". The Spanish is exceedingly condensed here and other interpretations are possible.

him, for both kinship and friendship lose their influence when communication ceases.

It is also a great help to have a good book, written in the vernacular, simply as an aid to recollection. With this aid you will learn to say your vocal prayers well, *I mean, as they ought to be said*—and little by little, persuasively and methodically, you will get your soul used to this, so that it will no longer be afraid of it. Remember that many years have passed since it went away from[31] its Spouse, and it needs very careful handling before it will return home. We sinners are like that: we have accustomed our souls and minds to go after their own pleasures (or pains, it would be more correct to say) until the unfortunate soul no longer knows what it is doing. When that has happened, a good deal of skill is necessary before it can be inspired with enough love to make it stay at home; but unless we can gradually do that we shall accomplish nothing.[32] Once again I assure you that, if you are careful to form habits of the kind I have mentioned, you will derive[33] such great profit from them that I could not describe it even if I wished.[34] Keep at the side of this good Master,[35] then, and be most firmly resolved to learn what He teaches you; His Majesty will then ensure your not failing to be good disciples, and He will never leave you unless you leave Him. Consider the words uttered by those Divine lips: the very first of them will show you at once what love He has for you, and it is no small blessing and joy for the pupil to see that his Master loves Him.

[31] E.: "went away, having fled from."
[32] E.: "a good deal of skill is necessary to make it conceive fresh love for its Spouse [*lit*.: "Husband"] and become accustomed to staying at home: this has to be done gradually and by means of love—otherwise we shall accomplish nothing."
[33] E. begins the sentence: "And be quite sure that if you accustom yourselves carefully to the idea that you have this Lord with you, and speak to Him frequently, you will derive."
[34] E.: "that, even if I want to describe it to you, you will perhaps not believe me."
[35] E.: "of your Master."

CHAPTER 27

Describes the great love shown us by the Lord in
the first words of the Paternoster and the great importance of our making no account of good birth if
we truly desire to be the daughters of God.

"Our Father, which art in the Heavens." O my Lord, how
Thou dost reveal Thyself as the Father of such a Son, while
Thy Son reveals Himself as the Son of such a Father! Blessed
be Thou for ever and ever. Ought not so great a favour as
this, Lord, to have come at the end of the prayer? Here, at
the very beginning, Thou dost fill our hands and grant us so
great a favour that it would be a very great blessing if our
understanding could be filled with it so that the will would
be occupied and we should be unable to say another word.
Oh, how appropriate, daughters, would perfect contemplation be here! Oh, how right would the soul be to enter within
itself, so as to be the better able to rise above itself, that this
holy Son might show it the nature of the place where He says
His Father dwells—namely, the Heavens! Let us leave earth,
my daughters, for it is not right that a favour like this should
be prized so little, and that, after we have realized how great
this favour is, we should remain on earth any more.

O Son of God and my Lord! How is it that Thou canst
give us so much with Thy first word? It is so wonderful that
Thou shouldst descend to such a degree of humility as to
join with us when we pray and make Thyself the Brother of
creatures so miserable and lowly! How can it be that, in the
name of Thy Father, Thou shouldst give us all that there is
to be given, by willing Him to have us as His children—and
Thy word cannot fail?[1] [It seems that] Thou dost oblige Him
to fulfil Thy word, a charge by no means light, since, being
our Father, He must bear with us, however great our of-

[1] E. adds: "but must be fulfilled."

fences.[2] If we return to Him, He must pardon us, as He pardoned the prodigal son,[3] must comfort us in our trials, and must sustain us,[4] as such a Father is bound to do, for He must needs be better than any earthly father, since nothing good can fail to have its perfection in Him. *He must cherish us; He must sustain us;*[5] and at the last He must make us participants and fellow-heirs with Thee.

Behold, my Lord, with the love that Thou hast for us and with Thy humility, nothing can be an obstacle to Thee. And then, Lord, Thou hast been upon earth and by taking our nature upon Thee hast clothed Thyself with humanity: Thou hast therefore some reason to care for our advantage.[6] But behold, Thy Father is in Heaven, as Thou hast told us, and it is right that Thou shouldst consider His honour. Since Thou hast offered Thyself to be dishonoured by us, leave Thy Father free. Oblige Him not to do so much for people as wicked as I, who will make Him such poor acknowledgment.[7]

O good Jesus! How clearly hast Thou shown that Thou art One with Him and that Thy will is His and His is Thine! How open a confession is this, my Lord! What is this love that Thou hast for us? Thou didst deceive the devil, and conceal from him that Thou art the Son of God, but Thy great desire for our welfare overcomes all obstacles to Thy granting us this greatest of favours. Who but Thou could do this, Lord? I cannot think how the devil failed to understand from

[2] T. deletes: "a charge by no means light" and has here: "He must bear with our offences, however great they be."

[3] E.: "If we return to Him, as did the prodigal son, He must pardon us."

[4] E. omits: "and must sustain us."

[5] E. adds: "for He has the wherewithal," which spoils the rhythm of the sentence and is not explicit enough to be a valuable addition.

[6] E.: "and the part Thou dost play seems to oblige Thee to do us good." Originally this read: "and after the part Thou playest with us I do not know how Thou canst have so much humility." The alteration is in St. Teresa's hand.

[7] E. adds: "and there are also others who do not make Him good [acknowledgment]."

that word of Thine Who Thou wert, beyond any doubt.[8] I, at least, my Jesus, see clearly that Thou didst speak as a dearly beloved son both for Thyself and for us,[9] and Thou hast such power that what Thou sayest in Heaven shall be done on earth. Blessed be Thou for ever, my Lord, Who lovest so much to give[10] that no obstacle can stay Thee.

Do you not think, daughters, that this is a good Master, since He begins by granting us this great favour so as to make us love to learn what He teaches us? Do you think it would be right for us,[11] while we are repeating this prayer with our lips, to stop trying to think of what we are saying, lest picturing such love[12] should tear our hearts to pieces? No one who realized His greatness could possibly say it would be. What son is there in the world who would not try to learn who his father was if he had one as good, and of as great majesty[13] and dominion, as ours? Were God not all this, it would not surprise me if we had no desire to be known as His children;[14] for the world is such that, if the father is of lower rank than his son, the son feels no honour in recognizing him as his father.[15] This does not apply here: God forbid that such a thing should ever happen in this house—it would turn the place into hell. Let the sister who is of the highest birth speak of her father least; we must all be equals.

O College of Christ, in which the Lord was pleased that Saint Peter, who was a fisherman, should have more authority than Saint Bartholomew, who was the son of a king![16]

---

[8] T. omits this sentence.

[9] E.: "and for all."

[10] T. ends the sentence here, deleting the words which follow.

[11] E., more bluntly: "Would it be right for us . . . ?" T. deletes the reading in the text and substitutes: "It would be right for us."

[12] E. reads: "lest so great a favour."

[13] E.: "goodness, majesty."

[14] E.: "daughters."

[15] E.: "than his son, in two words he will not recognize him as his father." In the next sentence, T. has "affect us" for "apply".

[16] "I do not know where she found this," observes P. García de Toledo (not P. Báñez, as the Paris Carmelites say) in the margin of V. There seems, in fact, to be no foundation for the assertion in the text. T. inserts "they say".

His Majesty knew what a fuss would be made in the world[17] about who was fashioned from the finer clay—which is like discussing whether clay is better for bricks or for walls.[18] Dear Lord, what a trouble we make about it![19] God deliver you, sisters, from such contentions,[20] even if they be carried on only in jest; I hope that His Majesty will indeed deliver you. If anything like this should be going on among you, apply the remedy immediately, and let the sister concerned fear lest she be a Judas among the Apostles.[21] Do *what you can to get rid of such a bad companion. If you cannot,* give her penances *heavier than for anything else* until she realizes that she has not deserved to be even the basest clay. You have a good Father, given you by the good Jesus:[22] let no other father be known or referred to here.[23] Strive, my daughters, to be such that you deserve to find comfort in Him and to throw yourselves into His arms. You know that, if you are good children, He will never[24] send you away. And who would not do anything rather than lose such a Father?

Oh, thank God, what cause for comfort there is here! Rather than write more about it I will leave it for you to think about; for, however much your thoughts may wander, between such a Son and such a Father there must needs be the Holy Spirit.[25] May He enkindle[26] your will and bind you

---

[17] E. omits: "in the world."
[18] E.: "for mud or for bricks."
[19] E.: "what great blindness!" T.: "what great nonsense!"
[20] E.: "from such conversations."
[21] E.: "among you, do not allow it in the house, for it is (like having a) Judas among the Apostles."
[22] E.: "The good Jesus gives you a good Father."
[23] E. continues, repeating what has just been said: "save Him Whom your Spouse gives you."
[24] E.: "He has the obligation never to." T. deletes much of this and the last sentence and substitutes: "deserve to imitate Him in something; for, if you are good children, He will never."
[25] In T. this reading is altered to the following: "for, your thoughts being between such a Son and such a Father, the Holy Spirit will come (to you)."
[26] E.: "May He work in."

to Himself with the most fervent love, since even the great advantage you gain will not suffice to do so.[27]

CHAPTER 28

Describes the nature of the Prayer of Recollection and sets down some of the means by which we can make it a habit.

Consider now what your Master says next: "Who art in the Heavens."[1] Do you suppose it matters little what Heaven is and where you must seek your most holy Father? I assure you that for minds which wander it is of great importance not only to have a right belief about this but to try to learn it by experience,[2] for it is one of the best ways of concentrating the mind[3] and effecting recollection in the soul.

You know[4] that God is everywhere; and *this is a great truth, for,* of course, wherever the king is, or so they say, the court is too: that is to say, wherever God is, there is Heaven. No doubt you can believe that, in any place where His Majesty is, there is fulness of glory.[5] Remember how Saint Augustine tells us[6] about his seeking God in many places and eventually finding Him within himself. Do you suppose[7] it is

27 E.: "with the strongest love, supposing that the advantage you will gain does not bind you (to Him)."

1 E.: "in Heaven."

2 E.: "but to think about it a great deal."

3 E.: "the very best ways of concentrating the thoughts."

4 E.: "You will have heard."

5 T. deletes "wherever the king. . . . God is" and substitutes: "You know that God is everywhere, for, of course, wherever His Majesty is, there is Heaven. No doubt you can believe that, and fulness of glory." The deletion of "in any . . . there is" is quite in keeping with St. Teresa's elliptical style.

6 E. adds: "in the book of his Meditations, I believe." The actual reference is *Confessions*, Bk. X., Chap. XXVII.

7 T. deletes: "Do you suppose" and turns the sentence into an affirmation with "Believe that it is of great importance, etc."

of little importance that a soul which is often distracted should come to understand this truth and to find that, in order to speak to its Eternal Father and to take its delight in Him, it has no need to go to Heaven or to speak[8] in a loud voice? However quietly we speak, He is so near that[9] He will hear us: we need no wings to go in search of Him but have only to find a place where we can be alone and look upon Him present within us. Nor need we feel strange in the presence of so kind a Guest; we must talk to Him very humbly, as we should to our father,[10] ask Him for things as we should ask a father, tell Him our troubles, beg Him to put them right, and yet realize that we are not worthy to be called His children.

Avoid being bashful with God, as some people are, in the belief that they are being humble. It would not be humility on your part if the King were to do you a favour and you refused to accept it; but you would be showing humility by taking it, and being pleased with it, yet realizing how far you are from deserving it. A fine humility it would be if I had the Emperor of Heaven and earth in my house, coming to it to do me a favour and to delight in my company, and I were so humble that I would not answer His questions, nor remain with Him, nor accept what He gave me,[11] but left Him alone. Or if He were to speak to me and beg me[12] to ask for what I wanted, and I were so humble that I preferred to remain poor and even let Him go away, so that He would see I had not sufficient resolution.

Have nothing to do with that kind of humility, daughters, but speak with Him as with a Father, a Brother, a Lord and a Spouse—and, sometimes in one way and sometimes in another, He will teach you what you must do to please Him. Do not be foolish; ask Him to let you speak to Him, and, as He is your Spouse, to treat you as His brides. *Remember*

---

[8] E.: "to pray."

[9] E. and T. omit: "He is so near that."

[10] E. continues, and ends the paragraph thus: "seek comfort in Him as in a father, yet realize that we are not worthy for Him to be so."

[11] "Nor accept what He gave me" is not found in E.

[12] E.: "Or if He were to tell me."

*how important it is for you to have understood this truth—
that the Lord is within us and that we should be there with
Him.*

If one prays in this way, the prayer may be only vocal, but
the mind will be recollected much sooner; and this is a prayer
which brings with it many blessings.[13] It is called recollection because the soul collects together all the faculties and
enters within itself to be with its God. Its Divine Master
comes more speedily to teach it, and to grant it the Prayer
of Quiet, than in any other way. For, hidden there within
itself, it can think about[14] the Passion, and picture the Son,
and offer Him to the Father, without wearying the mind by
going to seek Him on Mount Calvary, or in the Garden, or
at the Column.

Those who are able to shut themselves up in this way
within this little Heaven of the soul, wherein dwells the
Maker of Heaven and earth,[15] and who have formed the
habit of looking at nothing and staying in no place which
will distract these outward senses,[16] may be sure that they
are walking on an excellent road, and will come without fail
to drink of the water of the fountain, for they will journey a
long way in a short time. They are like one who travels in a
ship, and, if he has a little good wind, reaches the end of his
voyage in a few days, while those who go by land take *much*
longer.[17]

These souls have already, as we may say, put out to sea;
though they have not sailed quite out of sight of land, they

13 E.: "a thousand blessings."
14 E.: "about all."
15 This is the reading of E. V. has: "the Maker of it, and of the
earth."
16 E.: "where it hears anything to destroy it." But "destroy"
(*destruya*) looks like a slip of the pen for "distract" (*destraya*:
mod. *distraiga*—the form used in V.).
    T. omits: "looking at nothing and", and, just below, reads: "on
a good road, and, with the favour of God, will come, etc."
17 E. continues: "This is the road to Heaven. I say 'to Heaven'
because there they are hidden in the King's palace, and are not on
earth, and are more secure from many occasions of sin." (Cf. p. 187,
l. 16).

do what they can to get away from it, in the time at their disposal, by recollecting their senses. If their recollection is genuine, the fact becomes very evident, for it produces certain effects which I do not know how to explain but which anyone will recognize who has experience of them. It is as if the soul were rising from play, for it sees that worldly things are nothing but toys;[18] so in due course it rises above them, like a person entering a strong castle, in order that it may have nothing more to fear from its enemies. It withdraws the senses from all outward things and spurns them so completely that, without its understanding how, its eyes close and it cannot see them and the soul's spiritual sight becomes clear. Those who walk along this path almost invariably close their eyes when they say their prayers; this, for many reasons, is an admirable custom, since it means that they are making an effort not to look at things of the world. The effort has to be made only at the beginning; later it becomes unnecessary: eventually, in fact, it would cost a greater effort to open the eyes during prayer than to close them. The soul seems to gather up its strength and to master itself at the expense of the body, which it leaves weakened and alone: in this way it becomes stronger for the fight against it.

This may not be evident at first, if the recollection is not very profound—for at this stage it is sometimes more so and sometimes less. At first it may cause a good deal of trouble, for the body insists on its rights, not understanding that if it refuses to admit defeat it is, as it were, cutting off its own head. But if we cultivate the habit, make the necessary effort and practise the exercises for several days,[19] the benefits will reveal themselves, and when we begin to pray we shall realize that the bees are coming to the hive and entering it to make the honey, and all without any effort of ours. For it is the Lord's will that, in return for the time which their efforts have cost them, the soul and the will should be given this power over the senses. They will only have to make a

---

[18] T. deletes part of this and substitutes: "rising from worldly things with the fire that it feels within itself."
[19] T. omits: "if we . . . several days."

sign to show that they wish to enter into recollection and the senses will obey and allow themselves to be recollected. Later they may come out again, but it is a great thing that they should ever have surrendered, for if they come out it is as captives and slaves and they do none of the harm that they might have done before. When the will calls them afresh they respond more quickly, until, after they have entered the soul many times, the Lord is pleased that they should remain there altogether in perfect contemplation.

What has been said should be noted with great care, for, though it seems obscure, it will be understood by anyone desirous of putting it into practice. The sea-voyage, then, can be made; and, as it is very important that we should not travel too slowly, let us just consider how we can get accustomed to these good habits. Souls who do so are more secure from many occasions of sin,[20] and the fire of Divine love is the more readily enkindled in them; for they are so near that fire that, however little the blaze has been fanned with the understanding, any small spark that flies out at them will cause them to burst into flame. When no hindrance comes to it from outside, the soul remains alone with its God and is thoroughly prepared to become enkindled.[21]

And now let us imagine that we have within us a palace of priceless worth,[22] built entirely of gold and precious stones— a palace, in short, fit for so great a Lord. Imagine that it is partly your doing that this palace should be what it is[23]—and this is really true, for there is no building so beautiful as a soul that is pure and full of virtues, and, the greater these virtues are, the more brilliantly do the stones shine. Imagine

---

20 Everything between p. 185, l. 24 and this point is an interpolation of V. E. takes up the argument here.
21 E. reads: "to understand itself (*entenderse*)." But I feel sure that the author intended to write *encenderse* ("become enkindled") as she does in V. E. rounds off the paragraph with the somewhat redundant sentence: "I should like you to have a very good grasp of (*que entendiésedes muy bien*) this method of prayer, which, as I have said, is called recollection," and with the metaphor of the palace begins a new chapter.
22 E.: "Imagine that you have within you a palace."
23 E.: "should be so precious."

that within the palace dwells this great King, Who has vouch-safed to become your Father, and Who is seated upon a throne of supreme price—namely, your heart.

At first you will think this irrelevant—I mean the use of this figure to explain my point—but it may prove very useful, especially to persons like yourselves. For, as we women are not learned *or fine-witted*, we need all these things to help us realize that we actually have something within us incomparably more precious than anything we see outside. Do not let us suppose that the interior of the soul is empty;[24] God grant that only women may be so thoughtless as to suppose that. If we took care always to remember what a Guest we have within us, I think it would be impossible for us to abandon ourselves to *vanities and* things of the world, for we should see how worthless they are by comparison with those which we have within us. What does an animal do beyond satisfying his hunger by seizing whatever attracts him when he sees it? There should surely be a great difference between the brute beasts and ourselves, *as we have such a Father*.

Perhaps you will laugh at me and say that this is obvious enough; and you will be right, though it was some time before I came to see it. I knew perfectly well that I had a soul, but I did not understand what that soul merited, or Who dwelt within it, until[25] I closed my eyes to the vanities of this world in order to see it. I think, if I had understood then,[26] as I do now, how this great King *really* dwells within this little palace of my soul, I should not have left Him alone so often, but should have stayed with Him and never have allowed His dwelling-place to get so dirty. How wonderful it is that He Whose greatness could fill a thousand worlds, and very many more,[27] should confine Himself within so small a space, *just as He was pleased to dwell within the womb of His most holy Mother!* Being the Lord, He has, of

---

[24] E. adds: "which is very important."
[25] In T., the copyist, apparently misunderstanding the sense, altered "until" to "because".
[26] The words "I had understood then" were added to the text by Luis de León in order to complete the sense.
[27] "And very many more" is not in E.

course, perfect freedom, and, as He loves us, He fashions Himself to our measure.

When a soul sets out upon this path, He does not reveal Himself to it, lest it should feel dismayed at seeing that its littleness can contain such greatness; but gradually He enlarges it to the extent requisite for what He has to set within it. It is for this reason that I say He has perfect freedom, since He has power to make the whole of this palace great.[28] The important point is that we should be absolutely resolved to give it to Him for His own and should empty it so that He may take out and put in just what He likes, as He would with something of His own. His Majesty is right in demanding this; let us not deny it to Him.[29] And, as He refuses to force our will, He takes what we give Him but does not give Himself wholly until *He sees that* we are giving ourselves wholly to Him. This is certain, and, as it is of such importance,[30] I often remind you of it. Nor does He work within the soul as He does when it is wholly His and keeps nothing back. I do not see how He can do so, since He likes everything to be done in order. If we fill the palace with vulgar people and all kinds of junk, how can the Lord and His Court occupy it? When such a crowd is there it would be a great thing if He were to remain for even a short time.

Do you suppose, daughters, that He is alone when He comes to us? Do you not see[31] that His *most holy* Son says: "Who art in the Heavens"? Surely such a King would not be abandoned by His courtiers. They stay with Him and pray to Him on our behalf and for our welfare, for they are full of charity. Do not imagine that Heaven is like this earth, where, if a lord or prelate shows anyone favours, whether for some

---

28 The passage in the text from "How wonderful" (in the preceding paragraph) down to this point was crossed out by St. Teresa in V., and does not appear in T. nor in the Évora edition. Luis de León, however, published it, and it is also found in E.

29 E. adds here a charmingly natural phrase which, however, somewhat interrupts the trend of thought: "Even in this world, it worries us to have visitors in the house when we cannot tell them to go."

30 E.: "and for that reason."

31 T.: "know."

particular reason or simply because he likes him, people at once become envious, and, though the poor man has done nothing to them, he is maliciously treated, *so that his favours cost him dear.*

CHAPTER 29

Continues to describe methods for achieving this Prayer of Recollection. Says what little account we should make of being favoured by our superiors.

For the love of God, daughters, avoid making any account of these favours.[1] You should each do your duty; and, if this is not appreciated by your superior, you may be sure that it will be appreciated and rewarded by the Lord. We did not come here to seek rewards in this life, *but only in the life to come.* Let our thoughts always be fixed upon what[2] endures, and not trouble themselves with earthly things which do not endure even for a lifetime. For to-day some other sister will be in your superior's good books; whereas to-morrow, if she sees you exhibiting some additional virtue, it is with you that she will be better pleased—and if she is not it is of little consequence. Never give way to these thoughts, which sometimes begin in a small way but may cost you a great deal of unrest.[3] Check them by remembering that your kingdom is not of this world, and that everything comes quickly to an end, *and that there is nothing in this life that goes on unchangingly.*

But even that is a poor remedy and anything but a perfect

[1] E.: "avoid such things." That is, such partiality shown to one by persons in authority, as is described at the end of the last chapter. E. does better than V. here by not beginning a new chapter till after the end of this paragraph. T. attempts to clarify the sense by adding, after "favours", "of superiors".
[2] T.: "upon the little, which".
[3] E.: "Never give way to these first movements."

one; it is best that this state of things should continue, and that you should be humbled and out of favour, and should wish to be so for the sake of the Lord Who dwells in you.[4] Turn your eyes upon yourself and look at yourself inwardly, as I have said. You will find your Master;[5] He will not fail you: indeed, the less outward comfort you have, the [much] greater the joy He will give you. He is full of compassion and never fails those who are afflicted and out of favour[6] if they trust in Him alone. Thus David tells us that *he never saw the just forsaken*[7], *and again, that* the Lord is with the afflicted.[8] Either you believe this or you do not: if you do, *as you should*, why do you wear yourselves to death with worry?[9]

O my Lord, if we had a real knowledge of Thee, we should make not the slightest account of anything,[10] since Thou givest so much to those who will set their whole trust on Thee.[11] Believe me, friends, it is a great thing to realize the truth of this so that we may see how deceptive are earthly *things and* favours when they deflect the soul in any way from its course and hinder it from entering within itself.[12] God help me! If only someone could make you[13] realize this! I myself, *Lord*, certainly cannot; I know that [in truth] I owe *Thee* more than anyone else but I cannot realize this myself as well as I should.

Returning to what I was saying, I should like to be able to explain[14] the nature of this holy companionship with our

4 E.: "of Him Who dwells in you." *Lit.*, in both E. and V., "with you."
5 E. omits "as I have said" and has "your Spouse" for "your Master".
6 "And out of favour" is not found in E.
7 Psalm xxxvi (A.V., xxxvii, 25).
8 Psalm xxxiii, 20-1 (A.V., xxxiv, 19-20).
9 The original, both in E. and V., has: "With what do you kill yourselves?"
10 E.: "of anyone."
11 E.: "will truly give themselves to Thee."
12 *Lit.*: "when they deflect the soul in any way from going within itself." E.: "deflect in any way from this truth."
13 E.: "make mortals."
14 E. begins: "Oh, if only one could explain."

great Companion,[15] the Holiest of the holy, in which there is nothing to hinder the soul and her Spouse from remaining alone together, when the soul desires to enter within herself, to shut the door behind her so as to keep out all that is worldly and to dwell in that Paradise with her God.[16] I say "desires", because you must understand[17] that this is not a supernatural state but depends upon our <u>volition</u>, and that, by God's favour, we can enter it of our own accord: *this condition must be understood of everything that we say in this book can be done,*[18] for without it nothing can be accomplished and we have not the power to think a single good thought. For this is not a silence of the faculties: it is a shutting-up of the faculties within itself by the soul.[19]

There are many ways in which we can gradually acquire this habit, as various books[20] tell us. We must cast aside everything else, they say, in order to approach God inwardly and we must retire within ourselves even during our ordinary occupations. If I can recall the companionship which I have within my soul for as much as a moment, that is of great utility.[21] *But as I am speaking only about the way to recite vocal prayers well, there is no need for me to say as much as this. All I want is that we should know[22] and abide with the Person with Whom we are speaking, and not turn our backs upon Him; for that, it seems to me, is what we are doing when we talk to God and yet think of all kinds of vanity. The whole mischief comes from our not really grasping the fact that He is near us, and imagining Him far away*

---

[15] E.: "with the Companion of souls."

[16] T. omits: "with her God."

[17] E. begins the sentence with the imperative: "Understand . . ." and omits: "but depends upon our volition."

[18] E. ends the sentence by adding: "and without it absolutely nothing [*nada, nada*] can be done."

[19] In T., St. Teresa corrects this to: "of the faculties within themselves."

[20] E. substitutes the ordinary for the continuous form of the present tense of "acquire", which is rendered in our text by the adverb "gradually", and adds: "(by) those who write on mental prayer."

[21] "And we must . . . utility" is not found in E.

[22] *Lit.:* "see."

act or power of willing

—so far, that we shall have to go to Heaven in order to find Him. How is it, Lord, that we do not look at Thy face, when it is so near us? We do not think people are listening to us when we are speaking to them unless we see them looking at us. And do we close our eyes so as not to see that Thou art looking at us? How can we know if Thou hast heard what we say to Thee?

The great thing I should like to teach you is that, in order to accustom ourselves gradually to giving our minds confidence, so that we may readily understand what we are saying, and with Whom we are speaking, we must recollect our outward senses, take charge of them ourselves and give them something which will occupy them. It is in this way that we have Heaven within ourselves since the Lord of Heaven is there. If once we accustom ourselves to being glad[23] that there is no need to raise our voices in order to speak to Him, since His Majesty will make us conscious that He is there, we shall be able to say the Paternoster and whatever other prayers we like with great peace of mind, and the Lord Himself will help us not to grow tired.[24] Soon after we have begun to force ourselves to remain near the Lord, He will give us indications by which we may understand that, though we have had to say the Paternoster many times, He heard us the first time.[25] For He loves to save us worry; and, even though we may take a whole hour over saying it once, if we can realize that we are with Him, and what it is we are asking Him, and how willing He is, *like any father*, to grant it to us, and how He loves to be with us, *and comfort us*, He

---

[23] *Lit.*: "once we begin to be glad."
[24] This sentence is from E., which in the context gives the better reading. V. has: "In brief, we must gradually accustom ourselves to being glad that there is no need to raise our voices in order to speak to Him, since His Majesty will make us conscious that He is there. We shall then be able to say our vocal prayers with great peace of mind, and this will save us much worry."
[25] T. deletes: "He will . . . first time" and substitutes: "it will (come to) be very easy for us." In the next sentence T. has "the Paternoster" for "it".

has no wish for us to tire our brains by a great deal of talking.[26]

For love of the Lord, then, sisters, accustom yourselves to saying the Paternoster in this recollected way, and before long you will see how you gain by doing so. It is a method of prayer which establishes habits that prevent the soul from going astray and the faculties from becoming restless. This you will find out in time: I only beg you to test it, even at the cost of a little trouble, which always results when we try to form a new habit. I assure you, however, that before long you will have the great comfort of finding it unnecessary to tire yourselves with seeking this holy Father to Whom you pray, for you will discover Him within you.

May the Lord teach this to those of you who do not know it: for my own part I must confess that, until the Lord taught me this method, I never knew what it was to get satisfaction and comfort out of prayer, and it is because I have always gained such great benefits from this custom of interior recollection[27] that I have written about it at such length. *Perhaps you all know this, but some sister may come to you who will not know it, so you must not be vexed at my having spoken about it here.*[28]

I conclude by advising anyone who wishes to acquire it (since, as I say, it is in our power to do so) not to grow weary of trying to get used to the method which has been described, for it is equivalent to a gradual gaining of the mastery over herself and is not vain labour. To conquer oneself for one's own good is to make use of the senses in the service of the interior life. If she is speaking she must try to remember that there is One within her to Whom she can speak; if she is listening, let her remember that she can listen to Him Who is nearer to her than anyone else. Briefly, let her realize that, if she likes, she need never[29] withdraw from this good companionship, and let her grieve when she has left her Father alone for so long though her need of Him is so sore.

---

[26] E. ends the sentence at "brains".
[27] Lit.: "of recollection within me." T. omits: "within me."
[28] E. continues: "We must now come, etc." (Cf. p. 195, n. 2).
[29] T.: "need not."

If she can, let her practise recollection many times daily; if not, let her do so occasionally. As she grows accustomed to it, she will feel its benefits, either sooner or later. Once the Lord has granted it to her, she would not exchange it for any treasure.

Nothing, sisters, can be learned without a little trouble, so do, for the love of God, look upon any care which you take about this as well spent. I know that, with God's help, if you practise it for a year, or perhaps for only six months, you will be successful in attaining it. Think what a short time that is for acquiring so great a benefit, for you will be laying a good foundation, so that, if the Lord desires to raise you up to achieve great things, He will find you ready, because you will be close to Himself. May His Majesty never allow us to withdraw ourselves from His presence. Amen.

CHAPTER 30

Describes the importance of understanding what we ask for in prayer. Treats of these words in the Paternoster: "Sanctificetur nomen tuum, adveniat regnum tuum."[1] Applies them to the Prayer of Quiet, and begins the explanation of them.

We must now come to consider the next petition in our good Master's prayer, in which He begins to entreat His holy Father on our behalf, and see what it is that He entreats, as it is well that we should know this.[2]

What person, however careless, who had to address someone of importance, would not spend time in thinking how to approach him so as to please him and not be considered

---

[1] "Hallowed be Thy name. Thy kingdom come."
[2] In E. this paragraph comes at the end of the preceding chapter. The context seems to place it more naturally here, or as a subtitle to Chapter XXX.

tedious? He would also think what he was going to ask for and what use he would make of it, especially if his petition were for some particular thing, as our good Jesus tells us our petitions must be. This point seems to me *very* important. Couldst Thou not, my Lord, have ended this prayer in a single sentence, by saying: "Give us, Father, whatever is good for us"? For, in addressing One Who knows everything, there would seem to be no need to say any more.

This would have sufficed, O Eternal Wisdom,[3] as between Thee and Thy Father. It was thus that Thou didst address Him in the Garden, telling Him of Thy will and Thy fear, but leaving Thyself in His hands.[4] But Thou knowest us, my Lord, and Thou knowest that we are not as resigned as wert Thou to the will of Thy Father; we needed, therefore, to[5] be taught to ask for particular things so that we should stop *for a moment* to think if what we ask of Thee is good for us, and if it is not, should not ask for it. For, being what we are and having our free will, if we do not receive what we ask for, we shall not accept what the Lord gives us. The gift might be the best one possible—but we never think we are rich unless we actually see money in our hands.

Oh, God help me! What is it that sends our faith to sleep, so that we cannot realize how certain we are, on the one hand, to be punished, and, on the other, to be rewarded? It is for this reason, daughters, that it is good for you to know what you are asking for in the Paternoster, so that, if the Eternal Father gives it you, you shall not cast it back in His face. You must think carefully if what you are about to ask for will be good for you; if it will not, do not ask for it, but[6] ask His Majesty to give you light. For we are blind[7] and often we have such a loathing for life-giving food that we

---

[3] E.: "O Wisdom of the angels!"
[4] T. deletes this sentence.
[5] T. deletes "we . . . to" and writes "we would rather".
[6] T. interpolates: "remembering that (your prayer) must be in conformity with the will of God, as we say in this prayer, ask, etc."
[7] T.: "For you (*fem.*) are blind."

cannot eat it but prefer what will cause us death—and what a death: so terrible and eternal!

Now the good Jesus bids us say these words, in which we pray that this Kingdom may come in us:[8] "Hallowed be Thy Name, Thy Kingdom come in us." Consider now, daughters, how great is our Master's[9] wisdom. I am thinking here of what we are asking in praying for this kingdom, and it is well that we should realize this. His Majesty, knowing of how little we are capable, saw that, unless He provided for us by giving us His Kingdom here on earth, we could neither hallow nor praise nor magnify nor glorify *nor exalt* this holy name of the Eternal Father in a way befitting it. The good Jesus, therefore, places these two petitions next to each other. Let us understand this thing that we are asking for, daughters, and how important it is that we should pray for it without ceasing[10] and do all we can to please Him Who will give it us: it is for that reason that I want to tell you what I know about the matter now. If you do not like the subject, think out some other meditations for yourselves, for our Master will allow us to do this, provided we submit in all things to the teaching of the [Holy Roman] Church, as I do here.[11] *In any case I shall not give you this book to read until persons who understand these matters have seen it: so, if there is anything wrong with it, the reason will be, not wickedness, but my imperfect knowledge.*

To me, then, it seems that, of the many joys[12] to be found in the kingdom of Heaven, the chief is that we shall have no more to do with the things of earth; for in Heaven we shall have an intrinsic tranquillity and glory, a joy in the rejoicings of all, a perpetual peace, and a great interior satisfaction which will come to us when we see that all are hallowing and praising the Lord, and are blessing His name, and that none is offending Him. For all love Him there and the soul's one concern is loving Him, nor can it cease from loving Him

---

[8] E.: "Now the good Jesus says."
[9] E.: "our Spouse's."
[10] E.: "that we should ask for it."
[11] E.: "as I always do."
[12] E. begins: "Of the many joys."

because it knows Him. And this is how we should love Him on earth, though we cannot do so[13] with the same perfection nor yet all the time; still, if we knew Him, we should love Him very differently from the way we do now.

It looks as though I were going to say that we must be angels to make this petition and to say our vocal prayers well. This would indeed be our Divine Master's wish, since He bids us make so sublime a petition. You may be quite sure[14] that He never tells us to ask for impossibilities, so it must be possible, with God's help, for a soul living in that state of exile to reach such a point, though not as perfectly as those who have been freed from this prison, for we are making a sea-voyage and are still on the journey. But there are times when we are wearied with travelling and the Lord grants our faculties tranquillity and our soul quiet, and while they are in that state He gives us a clear[15] understanding of the nature of the gifts He bestows upon those whom He brings to His Kingdom. Those to whom, while they are still on earth, He grants what we are asking Him for receive pledges which will give them a great hope of eventually attaining to a perpetual enjoyment of what on earth He only allows them to taste.

If it were not that you would tell me I am treating of contemplation, it would be appropriate, in writing of this petition, to say a little about the beginning of pure contemplation, which those who experience it call the Prayer of Quiet; but, as I have said, I am discussing vocal prayer here, and anyone ignorant of[16] the subject might think that the two had nothing to do with one another, though I know this is *certainly* not true. Forgive my wanting to speak of it, for I know there are many people who practise vocal prayer in the manner already described and are raised[17] by God to the higher kind of contemplation without *having had any hand in this themselves or even* knowing how it has happened.

---

[13] T. interpolates: "in the same way and."
[14] T.: "It is clear."
[15] T.: "gives us an."
[16] T.: "anyone who did not like."
[17] E.: "prayer and are raised."

For this reason, daughters, I attach great importance to your saying your vocal prayers well. I know a nun[18] who could never practise anything but vocal prayer[19] but who kept to this and found she had everything else; yet if she omitted saying her prayers her mind wandered so much that she could not endure it. May we all practise such mental prayer as that.[20] She would say a number of Paternosters, corresponding to the number of times Our Lord shed His blood, and on nothing more than these and a few other prayers she would spend two or three[21] hours. She came to me once in great distress, saying that she did not know how to practise mental prayer,[22] and that she could not contemplate but could only say vocal prayers. *She was quite an old woman and had lived an extremely good and religious life.* I asked her what prayers she said, and *from her reply* I saw that, though keeping to the Paternoster, she was experiencing pure contemplation, and the Lord was raising her to be with Him in union.[23] She spent her life so well, too, that her actions made it clear she was receiving great favours.[24] So I praised the Lord and envied her her vocal prayer. If this story is true —and it is—none[25] of you who have had a bad opinion of contemplatives can suppose that you will be free from the risk of becoming like them if you say your vocal prayers as they should be said and keep a pure conscience.[26] *I shall have to say still more about this. Anyone not wishing to hear it may pass it over.*

18 So E. V. has "a person".
19 T.: "practise mental prayer."
20 T.: "such as that."
21 So E. V. has "several".
22 E. makes the anecdote still more striking by omitting "mental".
23 E.: "I saw that, while she was keeping to the Paternoster, the Lord was raising her to experience union."
24 E. omits this sentence. T. ends it at "clear".
25 E. begins the sentence: "So none."
26 T. turns this sentence into a question (". . . can any of you suppose . . . ?") and closes the chapter with the words: "You (*pl.*) are mistaken."

CHAPTER 31

Continues the same subject. Explains what is
meant by the Prayer of Quiet. Gives several counsels to those who experience it. This chapter is very
noteworthy.[1]

Now, daughters, I still want to describe this Prayer of Quiet
to you, in the way I have heard it talked about, and as the
Lord has been pleased to teach it to me, perhaps in order
that I might describe it to you. It is in this kind of prayer,
as I have said, that the Lord seems to me to begin to show
us that He is hearing our petition: He begins to give us His[2]
Kingdom on earth so that we may truly praise Him and
hallow His name and strive to make others do so likewise.[3]

This is a supernatural state, and, however hard we try, we
cannot reach it for ourselves;[4] for it is a state in which the
soul enters into peace, or rather in which the Lord gives it
peace through His presence, as He did to that just man
Simeon.[5] In this state all the faculties are stilled. The soul,
in a way which has nothing to do with the outward senses,
realizes that it is now very close to its God, and that, if it
were but a little closer, it would become one with Him
through union. This is not because it sees Him either with
its bodily or with its spiritual eyes. The just man Simeon

---

[1] In the Évora edition, the whole of this chapter is omitted.
[2] T. has *declarar* ("declare", "show forth") for *dar* ("give").
[3] E. begins: "This Prayer of Quiet (is that) in which, as I have
said, I believe the Lord begins to show us that He is hearing our
petition, and begins to give us His Kingdom here, so that we may
truly praise His name and strive that others may praise it. Though,
having written of this elsewhere, as I have said, I shall not describe
it at great length, I shall say something about it." T. has "praise
and hallow Him".
[4] "By our ability," adds P. Báñez, in the margin.
[5] The allusion is, of course, to St. Luke ii, 25 ("just and devout"),
29.

saw no more than the glorious Infant—a poor little Child, Who, to judge from the swaddling-clothes in which He was wrapped and from the small number of the people whom He had *as a retinue* to take Him up to the Temple, might well have been[6] the son of these poor people rather than the Son of his Heavenly Father. But the Child Himself revealed to him Who He was. Just so, though less clearly, does the soul know Who He is. It cannot understand how it knows Him, yet it sees that it is in the Kingdom[7] (or at least is near to the King Who will give it the Kingdom), and it feels such reverence that it dares to ask nothing. It is, as it were, in a swoon, both inwardly and outwardly, so that the outward man (let me call it the "body", and then you will understand me better)[8] does not wish to move, but rests, like one who has almost reached the end of his journey,[9] so that it may the better start again upon its way, with redoubled strength for its task.

The body experiences the greatest delight and the soul is conscious of a deep satisfaction. So glad is it merely to find itself near the fountain that, even before it has begun to drink, it has had its fill.[10] There seems nothing left for it to desire. The faculties are stilled and have no wish to move, for any movement they may make appears to hinder the soul from loving God.[11] They are not completely lost, however, since, two of them being free, they can realize in

---

[6] E. interpolates here, in apposition with "son", the word *romerito*: "a little pilgrim."

[7] E.: "it can only understand that it is in the Kingdom."

[8] "and then you will understand me better" is a softened (some might say a regrettably emasculated) version of the reading in E.: "or some little simpleton [*simplecita*] will come along not knowing what 'inward' and 'outward' mean." But as the revised version is the more suitable for the Saint's wider audience, my text respects her amendment.

[9] E. continues: "and experiences the greatest delight in the body and deep satisfaction." The word translated "deep" in both text and note is *grande*, "great".

[10] T. omits: "even . . . fill" and reads: "near the fountain that there seems, etc."

[11] The phrase "for any . . . loving God" does not appear in E.

Whose Presence they are.[12] It is the will that is in captivity now; and, if while in this state it is capable of experiencing any pain, the pain comes when it realizes that it will have to resume its liberty. The mind[13] tries to occupy itself with only one thing, and the memory has no desire to busy itself with more: they both see that this is the one thing needful and that anything else will unsettle them. Persons in this state prefer the body to remain motionless, for otherwise their peace would be destroyed: for this reason they dare not stir. Speaking is a distress to them: they will spend a whole hour on a single repetition of the Paternoster. They are so close to God that they know they can make themselves understood by signs.[14] They are in the palace, near to their King,[15] and they see that He is already beginning to give them His Kingdom on earth. *Sometimes tears come to their eyes, but they weep very gently and quite without distress: their whole desire is the hallowing of this name.* They seem not to be in the world, and have no wish to see or hear anything but their God; nothing distresses them, nor does it seem that anything can possibly do so.[16] In short, for as long as this state lasts, they are so overwhelmed and absorbed by the joy and delight which they experience that they can think of nothing else to wish for, and will gladly say with Saint Peter: "Lord, let us make here three mansions."[17]

[12] E. omits: "two of them being free", and adds, rather confusedly: "and (?what they) can (?do): it is a restful thought." The following sentences in V. are an enlargement of E., which continues: "(Persons in this state) prefer the body to remain motionless, lest it should cause them unrest. They think of one thing and not of many. Speaking is distress to them: they will spend a whole hour on a single repetition of the Paternoster, etc."

[13] "As before," adds P. Báñez, marginally.

[14] T. omits: "by signs."

[15] E. continues: "they are in His Kingdom, which the Lord is already beginning to give them on earth."

[16] E. ends the paragraph here. The next four paragraphs in the text above are omitted (cf. however, P. Silverio, III, 313, n. 1) and E. continues: "With respect to the Prayer of Quiet, I omitted to say this. It may come about, etc." (p. 204, n. 21)

[17] *Moradas.* Cf. p. 145, n. 2, above. The "three tabernacles" of St. Matthew xvii, 4.

Occasionally, during this Prayer of Quiet, God grants the soul another favour which is hard to understand if one has not had long experience of it. But any of you who have had this will at once recognize it and it will give you great comfort to know what it is. I believe God often grants this favour together with the other. When this quiet is felt in a high degree and lasts for a long time, I do not think that, if the will were not made fast to something, the peace could be of such long duration. Sometimes it goes on for a day, or for two days, and we find ourselves—I mean those who experience this state—full of this joy without understanding the reason. They see clearly that their whole self is not in what they are doing, but that the most important faculty is absent—namely, the will, which I think is united with its God—and that the other faculties are left free to busy themselves with His service. For this they have much more capacity at such a time, though when attending to worldly affairs they are dull and sometimes[18] stupid.

It is a great favour which the Lord grants to these souls, for it unites the active life with the contemplative. At such times they serve the Lord in both these ways at once; the will, while in contemplation, is working without knowing how it does so; the other two faculties are serving Him as Martha did. Thus Martha and Mary work together. I know someone to whom the Lord often granted this favour; she could not understand it and asked a great contemplative[19] about it; he told her that what she described was quite possible and had happened to himself. I think, therefore, that as the soul experiences such satisfaction in this Prayer of Quiet the will must be almost continuously united with Him Who alone can give it happiness.

[18] T. omits: "sometimes."
[19] In the margin of T. the author adds, in her own hand, that this contemplative was St. Francis Borgia, Duke of Gandía (cf. *Life*, Chapter XXIV: Vol. I, p. 154, above). No doubt, then, the other person referred to was St. Teresa herself. The addition reads: "who was a religious of the Company of Jesus, who had been Duke of Gandía," and to this are added some words, also in St. Teresa's hand, but partially scored out and partially cut by the binder, which seem to be: "who knew it well by experience."

I think it will be well, sisters, if I give some advice here to any of you whom the Lord, out of His goodness alone, has brought to this state, as I know that this has happened to some of you. First of all, when such persons experience this joy, without knowing whence it has come to them, but knowing at least that they could not have achieved it of themselves, they are tempted to imagine that they can prolong it and they may even try not to breathe. This is ridiculous: we can no more control this prayer than we can make the day break, or stop night from falling; it is supernatural and something we cannot acquire. The most we can do to prolong this favour is to realize that we can neither diminish nor add to it, but, being most unworthy and undeserving of it, can only receive it with thanksgiving. And we can best give thanks, not with many words, but by lifting up our eyes, like the publican.[20]

It is well to seek greater solitude so as to make room for the Lord and allow His Majesty to do His own work in us. The most we should do is occasionally, and quite gently, to utter a single word, like a person giving a little puff to a candle, when he sees it has almost gone out, so as to make it burn again; though, if it were fully alight, I suppose the only result of blowing it would be to put it out. I think the puff should be a gentle one because, if we begin to tax our brains by making up long speeches, the will may become active again.

Note carefully, friends, this piece of advice which I want to give you now. You will often find that these other two faculties are of no help to you. It may come about that the soul[21] is enjoying the highest degree of quiet, and that the understanding[22] has soared so far aloft that what is happening to it seems not to be going on in its own house at all; it

---

[20] St. Luke xviii, 13. St. Teresa apparently forgot that the publican "would not so much as lift his eyes towards heaven".

[21] E. here picks up the argument again, continuing: "is often enjoying true quiet."

[22] "Or thought," adds T. As will be seen, the author or the copyist seems to have been rather afraid of using the word "understanding" in this context, and to have tried to explain it.

really seems to be a guest in somebody else's house, looking for other lodgings, since its own lodging no longer satisfies it and it cannot remain there for long together. Perhaps this is only my own experience and other people[23] do not find it so. But, speaking for myself, I sometimes long to die because I cannot cure this wandering of the mind.[24] At other times the mind seems to be settled in its own abode and to be remaining there with the will as its companion. When all three faculties work together[25] it is wonderful. The harmony is like that between husband and wife: if they are happy and love each other, both desire the same thing; but if the husband is unhappy in his marriage he soon begins to make the wife restless. Just so, when the will finds itself in this state of quiet,[26] it must take no more notice of the understanding[27] than it would of a madman, for, if it tries to draw the understanding along with it, it is bound to grow preoccupied and restless, with the result that this state of prayer will be all effort and no gain and the soul will lose what God has been giving it without any effort of its own.

Pay great attention to the following comparison, which *the Lord suggested to me when I was in this state of prayer, and which* seems to me very appropriate.[28] The soul is like an infant still at its mother's breast: such is the mother's care for it that she gives it its milk without its having to ask for it so much as by moving its lips. That is what happens here. The will simply loves, and[29] no effort needs to be

23 E.: "Perhaps other people."
24 E. omits: "wandering of the mind."
25 E.: "If both work together."
26 "And this counsel should be carefully noted," adds E., "for it is important."
27 "Or thought, or imagination, for I do not know what it is," adds T.
28 "And explains it," adds T., which does not include the italicized phrase from E.
29 E. omits: "the will simply loves, and". After "understanding", E. continues: "for the Lord puts it into the soul, and His will is that it should realize He is there, and should swallow the milk that He gives it, and should realize all the time (*y esté entendiendo*) that He is giving it, and should love (*y[esté]amando*). If it begins to strive, so that the mind may be apprised, etc."

made by the understanding, for it is the Lord's pleasure that, without exercising its thought, the soul should realize that it is in His company, and should merely drink the milk which His Majesty puts into its mouth and enjoy its sweetness. The Lord desires it to know that it is He Who is granting it that favour and that in its enjoyment of it He too rejoices. But it is not His will that the soul should try to understand how it is enjoying it, or what it is enjoying; it should lose all thought of itself, and He Who is at its side will not fail to see what is best for it. If it begins to strive with its mind so that the mind may be apprised of what is happening and thus induced to share in it,[30] it will be quite unable to do so, and the soul will perforce lose the milk[31] and forgo that Divine sustenance.

This state of prayer is different from that in which the soul is wholly united with God,[32] for in the latter state it does not even swallow its nourishment:[33] the Lord places this within it, and it has no idea how. But in this state it *even* seems to be His will that the soul should work a little, though so quietly that it is hardly conscious of doing so.[34] What disturbs it is the understanding,[35] and this is not the case when there is union of all the three faculties, since He Who created them suspends them: He keeps them occupied with the enjoyment that He has given them, without their knowing, or being able to understand, the reason. *Anyone who has had experience of this kind of prayer will understand quite well what I am saying if, after reading this, she considers it carefully, and thinks out its meaning: otherwise it will be Greek*[36] *to her.*

Well, as I say, the soul is conscious of having reached this

---

[30] *Lit.*: "and drawn along with it"; the same phrase is found at the end of the preceding paragraph.
[31] *Lit.*: "let the milk fall out of its mouth."
[32] E.: "is different, in this and in other ways, from union."
[33] E. omits: "its nourishment" and substitutes that phrase for the following "this".
[34] E. continues: "Anyone who has, etc."
[35] "Or imagination," adds T.
[36] *Algarabía.* Cf. p. 171, n. 5 above.

state of prayer, which is a quiet, deep *and peaceful* happiness of the will, without being able to decide precisely what it is, although it can clearly see how it differs from the happiness of the world. To have dominion over the whole world, with all its happiness, would not suffice to bring the soul such inward satisfaction as it enjoys now in the depths of its will. For other kinds of happiness in life, it seems to me, touch only the outward part of the will, which we might describe as its rind.

When[37] one of you finds herself in this sublime state of prayer, which, as I have already said, is most markedly[38] supernatural, and the understanding (or, to put it more clearly, the thought)[39] wanders off after the most ridiculous things in the world, she should laugh at it and treat it as the silly thing it is, and remain in her state of quiet. For thoughts will come and go, but the will is mistress and all-powerful, and will recall them without your having to trouble about it.[40] But if you try to drag the understanding back by force, you lose your power over it, which comes from your taking and receiving that Divine sustenance, and neither will nor understanding will gain[41], but both will be losers. There is a saying that, if we try very hard to grasp all, we lose all;[42] and so I think it is here. Experience will show you the truth of this;[43] and I shall not be surprised if those of you who have none think this very obscure and unnecessary. But, as I have said, if you have only a little experience of it you will understand it and be able to profit by it, and you will praise the Lord for being pleased to enable me to explain it.

Let us now conclude by saying that, when the soul is

37 E.: "I mean that, when."
38 T. omits: "most markedly."
39 This parenthesis is not found in E.
40 E.: "without your doing anything."
41 *Lit.*: "neither the one nor the other will gain." E. continues: "But we might say that, if we try very hard, etc."
42 E. ends the sentence here.
43 E. ends the paragraph thus: "for we need much experience to understand it without having it explained to us, though we need little to practise it and to understand it after we have read about it."

brought to this state of prayer, it would seem that the Eternal Father has already granted its petition that He will give it His Kingdom on earth.[44] O blessed request, in which we ask for so great a good without knowing what we do! Blessed manner of asking! It is for this reason, sisters, that I want us to be careful how we say this prayer, the Paternoster, and all other vocal prayers,[45] *and what we ask for in them.* For *clearly,* when God has shown us this favour, we shall have to forget worldly things,[46] all of which the Lord of the world has come and cast out. I do not mean that everyone who experiences[47] the Prayer of Quiet must perforce be detached from everything in the world; but at least I should like all such persons to know what they lack and to humble themselves *and not to make so great a petition as though they were asking for nothing, and, if the Lord gives them what they ask for, to throw it back in His face.*[48] They must try to become more and more detached from everything, for otherwise they will only remain where they are. If God gives a soul such pledges, it is a sign that He has great things in store for it. It will be its own fault if it does not make great progress. But if He sees that, after He has brought the Kingdom of Heaven into its abode, it returns to earth, not only will He refrain from showing it the secrets of His Kingdom but He will grant it this other favour only for short periods and rarely.

I may be mistaken about this, but I have seen it and know that it happens, and, for my own part, I believe this is why spiritual people are not much more numerous. They do not

---

[44] E. begins the paragraph thus: "Finally, in view of the permanence of the satisfaction and delight that the soul experiences, it may rightly be said that it is in its kingdom, and that the Eternal Father has heard its petition for (the kingdom) to come to it."

[45] E.: "this heavenly prayer", with "it" for "them" to end the sentence.

[46] E.: "affairs." The author added "even against our will", but afterwards crossed these words out.

[47] E.: "who prays for."

[48] E. omits the rest of this paragraph and part of the next, continuing: "There are many—and I have been one of these—to whom the Lord gives tenderness, etc."

respond to so great a favour in a practical way: instead of preparing themselves to receive this favour again, they[49] take back from the Lord's hands the will which He considered His own and centre it upon base things. So He seeks out others who love Him in order to grant them His greater gifts, although He will not take away all that He has given from those who live in purity of conscience. But there are persons— and I have been one of them—to whom the Lord gives tenderness of devotion and holy inspirations and light on everything. He bestows this Kingdom on them and brings them to this Prayer of Quiet, and yet they deafen their ears to His voice. For they are so fond of talking and of repeating a large number of vocal prayers in a great hurry, as though they were anxious to finish their task[50] of repeating them daily, that when the Lord, as I say, puts His Kingdom into their very hands, *by giving them this Prayer of Quiet and this inward peace*, they do not accept it, but think that they will do better to go on reciting their prayers, which only distract them from their purpose.

Do not be like that, sisters, but be watchful[51] when the Lord grants you this favour. Think what a great treasure you may be losing and realize that you are doing much more by occasionally repeating a single petition of the Paternoster than by repeating the whole of it many times in a hurry *and not thinking what you are saying*. He to Whom you are praying is very near to you and will not[52] fail to hear you; and you may be sure that you are truly praising Him and hallowing His name, since you are glorifying the Lord as a member of His household and praising Him with increasing affection and desire so that it seems you can never forsake His service. So I *advise you to be very cautious about this, for it is of the greatest importance.*

---

49 T. adds: "rather."
50 E.: "in order to finish their task."
51 "But be watchful" is not found in E. The rest of this paragraph in T. is on a page which is missing from the copy.
52 E.: "and cannot."

CHAPTER 32

Expounds these words of the Paternoster: "Fiat voluntas tua sicut in coelo et in terra."[1] Describes how much is accomplished by those who repeat these words with full resolution and how well the Lord rewards them for it.[2]

Now that our good Master has asked on our behalf, and has taught us ourselves to ask, for a thing so precious that it includes all we can desire on earth, and has granted us the great favour of making us His brethren, let us see what He desires us to give to His Father, and what He offers Him on our behalf, and what He asks of us, for it is right that we should render Him some service in return for such great favours. O good Jesus! Since Thou givest so little (little, that is to say, on our behalf)[3] how canst Thou ask [so much] for us? What we give is in itself nothing at all by comparison with all that has been given us and with the greatness of Our Lord.[4] But in truth, my Lord, Thou dost not leave us with nothing to give and we give all that we can—I mean if we give in the spirit of these words: "Thy will be done; as in Heaven, so on earth."

Thou didst well, O our good Master,[5] to make this last petition, so that we may be able to accomplish what Thou dost promise in our name. For truly, Lord, hadst Thou not done this, I do not think it would have been possible *for us to accomplish it*. But, since Thy Father does what Thou

[1] "Thy will be done: as in Heaven, so on earth."
[2] The title of this chapter, the first two paragraphs and part of the third paragraph are not found in T. P. Silverio supplies the corresponding text of the Évora edition.
[3] Évora adds: "because of our weakness", but there is no means of telling if this is an addition made by St. Teresa or no.
[4] E.: "of (our) King."
[5] E.: "O good Master and Lord."

askest Him in granting us His Kingdom on earth, I know that I can truly fulfil Thy word by giving what Thou dost promise in our name. For since my earth has now become Heaven, it will be possible for Thy will to be done in me. Otherwise, on an earth so wretched as mine, and so barren of fruit, I know not, Lord, how it could be possible. It is a great thing that Thou dost offer.[6]

When I think of this, it amuses me that there should be people who dare not ask the Lord for trials,[7] thinking that His sending them to them depends upon their asking for them! I am not referring to those who omit to ask for them out of humility because they think themselves to be incapable of bearing them, though for my own part I believe that He who gives them love enough to ask for such a stern method of proving it will give them love enough to endure it. I should like to ask those who are afraid to pray for trials lest they should at once be given them what they mean when they beg the Lord to fulfil His will in them. Do they say this because everyone else says it and not because they want it to be done? That would not be right,[8] sisters. Remember that the good Jesus is our Ambassador here, and that His desire has been to mediate between us and His Father at no small cost to Himself: it would not be right for us to refuse to give what He *promises and* offers on our behalf[9] or to say nothing about it. Let me put it in another way. Consider, daughters, that, whether we wish it or no, God's will must be done,[10]

---

[6] "For that reason, daughters," adds E., "I should like you to understand this."

[7] E. reads: "who say that it is not well to ask the Lord for trials", and continues: "(saying) that this shows little humility. And I have found some persons so pusillanimous that, even without making this pretext of humility, they have not the courage to pray for trials, because they think that these would be given them at once. I should like to ask them what they understand this will to mean which they ask His Majesty to fulfil in them. Do they say, etc."

[8] E.: "That would be very wrong, daughters."

[9] T. ends the sentence here.

[10] E.: "See, sisters, and do as I suggest: it will have to be, whether you wish it or no."

and must be done both in Heaven and on earth. Believe me, then, do as I suggest and make[11] a virtue of necessity.

O my Lord, what a great comfort it is to me that Thou didst not entrust the fulfilment of Thy will to one so wretched as I! Blessed be Thou for ever and let all things praise Thee. May Thy name be for ever glorified. I should indeed have had to be good, Lord, if the fulfilment or non-fulfilment of Thy will [in Heaven and on earth] were in my hands. But as it is, though my will is not yet free from self-interest, I give it to Thee freely.[12] For I have proved, by long experience, how much I gain by leaving it freely in Thy hands. O friends,[13] what a great gain is this—and how much we lose through not fulfilling our promises to the Lord in the Paternoster, and giving Him what we offer Him!

Before I tell you in what this gain consists, I will explain to you how much you are offering, lest later you should exclaim that you had been deceived and had not understood what you were saying. Do not behave like some religious among us,[14] who do nothing but promise, and then excuse ourselves for not fulfilling our promises by saying that we had not understood what we were promising.[15] That may well be true,[16] *for it is easy to say things and hard to put them into practice, and anyone who thought that there was no more in the one than in the other certainly did not understand.*[17] It seems very easy to say that we will surrender our will to someone, until we try it and realize that it is the hardest thing we can do if we carry it out as we should. Our superiors do not always treat us strictly when they see we are weak; and sometimes they treat both weak and strong in the

---

[11] E.: "Believe me, then, and make."

[12] T. adds: "with Thy help."

[13] E.: "O daughters."

[14] E. reads "like some nuns" and continues in the third, not, like V., in the first person.

[15] E.: "and, when they fulfil nothing, say that, when they made their profession, they did not understand what they were promising."

[16] E.: "I quite believe it."

[17] E. continues: "Make those who profess here understand, by means of a long probation, that they must not only talk but act as well. So I want you to realize, etc."

same way. That is not so with the Lord; He knows what each of us can bear, and, when He sees that one of us is strong, He does not hesitate to fulfil His will in him.

So I want you to realize with Whom (as they say) you are dealing and what the good Jesus offers on your behalf to the Father, and what you are giving Him when you pray that His will may be done in you: it is nothing else than this that you are praying for.[18] Do not fear that He will give you riches or pleasures or *great* honours or any such earthly things; His love for you is not so poor as that. And He sets a very high value on what you give Him and desires to recompense you for it since He gives you His Kingdom while you are still alive. Would you like to see how He treats those who make this prayer from their hearts? Ask His glorious Son, Who made it thus in the Garden. Think with what resolution[19] and fullness of desire He prayed; and consider if the will of God was not perfectly fulfilled in Him through the trials, sufferings, insults and persecutions which He gave Him, until at last His life ended with death on a Cross.

So you see, daughters, what God gave to His best Beloved, and from that you can understand what His will is.[20] These, then, are His gifts in this world. He gives them in proportion to the love which He bears us. He gives more to those whom He loves most, and less to those He loves least; and He gives in accordance with the courage which He sees that each of us has and the love we bear to His Majesty. When He sees a soul who loves Him greatly, He knows that soul can suffer much for Him, whereas one who loves Him little will suffer little. For my own part, I believe that love is the measure of our ability to bear crosses, whether great or small. So if you have this love, sisters, try not to let the prayers you make to so great a Lord be words of mere politeness but brace yourselves to suffer what His Majesty desires. For if you give Him your will in any other way, you are just

---

18 V. abridges this passage to read: "I want to counsel you and remind you what His will is."
19 E.: "with what truth."
20 E. continues: "Consider what you are doing: try not to let the prayers, etc."

showing Him a jewel,[21] making as if to give it to Him and
begging Him to take it, and then, when He puts out His
hand to do so, taking it back and holding on to it tightly.

Such mockery is no fit treatment for One who endured so
much for us. If for no other reason than this, it would not be
right to mock Him so often—and it is by no means seldom
that we say these words to Him in the Paternoster. Let us
give Him once and for all the jewel which we have so often
undertaken to give Him. For the truth is that He gives it to
us first[22] so that we may give it back to Him. *Ah, my God!
How well Jesus knows us and how much He thinks of our
good! He did not say we must surrender our wills to the
Lord until we had been well paid for this small service. It
will be realized from this how much the Lord intends us to
gain by rendering it to Him: even in this life He begins to
reward us for this, as I shall presently explain.* Worldly people
will do a great deal if they sincerely resolve to fulfil the will of
God. But you, daughters, must both say and act, and give
Him both words and deeds, as I really think we religious do.
Yet sometimes not only do we undertake to give God the
jewel but we even put it into His hand[23] and then take it
back again. We are so generous all of a sudden, and then we
become so mean, that it would have been better if we had
stopped to think before giving.

The aim of all my advice to you in this book is that we
should surrender ourselves wholly to the Creator, place our
will in His hands and detach ourselves from the creatures.
As you will already have understood how important this is,
I will say no more about it, but I will tell you why our good
Master puts these words here. He knows how much we shall
gain by rendering this service to His Eternal Father. We are
preparing ourselves for the time, which will come very soon,

[21] E. continues: "and telling Him to take it, and then, etc."
[22] E. ends the sentence here. Both E. and V. have: "He does not
give to us first", a reading which may be thought to find some support in the following sentences of E., but in the context of V.
would be inexplicable. It seems to me likely that the negative was
inserted in error.
[23] E.: "Yet sometimes we put the jewel into the Lord's hand."

when we shall find ourselves at the end of our journey[24] and shall be drinking of living water from the fountain I have described. Unless we make a total surrender of our will[25] to the Lord, *and put ourselves in His hands* so that He may do in all things what is best for us in accordance with His will, He will never allow us to drink of it. This is the perfect contemplation of which you asked me to write to you.

In this matter, as I have already said, we can do nothing of ourselves, either by working hard or by making plans,[26] nor is it needful that we should. For everything else[27] hinders and prevents[28] us from saying [with real resolution], "Fiat voluntas tua": that is, may the Lord fulfil His will in me, in every way and manner which Thou, my Lord, desirest. If Thou wilt do this by means of trials, give me strength and let them come. If by means of persecutions and sickness and dishonour and need, here I am, my Father, I will not turn my face away from Thee nor have I the right to turn my back upon them. For Thy Son gave Thee this will of mine[29] in the name of us all and it is not right that I for my part should fail. Do Thou grant me the grace of bestowing on me Thy Kingdom so that I may do Thy will, since He has asked this of me. Dispose of me as of that which is Thine own, in accordance with Thy will.

Oh, my sisters, what power this gift has! If it be made with due resolution, it cannot fail to draw the Almighty to become one with our lowliness and to transform us into Himself[30] and to effect a union between the Creator[31] and the creature. Ask yourselves if that will not be a rich reward for

24 T. adds: "as can be seen here on earth."
25 E.: "of ourselves."
26 T. ends the sentence here.
27 "If by our own industry and skill we try to attain to Quiet," adds P. Báñez.
28 T. has a semi-colon after "hinders" and continues: "it suffices to say, with real, etc."
29 T.: "gave Thee my will."
30 T.: "to draw our lowliness to become one with the Almighty and to transform it into God."
31 E.: "the Maker." T.: "the creature and the Creator." Neither this emendation nor that of the last note is by St. Teresa.

you, and if you have not a good Master. For, knowing how the good will of His Father is to be gained, He teaches us how and by what means we must serve Him.

The more *resolute we are in soul and the more* we show Him by our actions that the words we use to Him are not words of mere politeness, the more and more does Our Lord draw us to Himself and raise us above all *petty* earthly things, and above ourselves, in order to prepare us to receive great favours *from Him*, for His rewards for our service will not end with this life. So much does He value this service of ours that we do not know for what more we can ask, while His Majesty never wearies of giving. Not content with having made this soul one with Himself, through uniting it to Himself,[32] He begins to cherish it, to reveal secrets to it, to rejoice in its understanding of what it has gained and in the knowledge which it has of all He has yet to give it. He causes it gradually to lose its exterior senses so that nothing may occupy it. This we call rapture. He begins to make such a friend of the soul that not only does He restore its will to it but He gives it His own also. For, now that He is making a friend of it, He is glad to allow it to rule with Him, as we say, turn and turn about. So He does what the soul asks of Him, just as the soul does what He commands, only in a much better way, since He is all-powerful and can do whatever He desires, and His desire never comes to an end.

But the poor soul, despite its desires, is *often* unable[33] to do all it would like, nor can it do anything at all unless it is given the power.[34] And so it grows richer and richer; and the more it serves, the greater becomes its debt; and often, growing weary of finding itself subjected to all the inconveniences and impediments and bonds[35] which it has to endure while

---

[32] E. reads: "through converting it to Himself", but the word "converting" was crossed through and "uniting" substituted by P. García de Toledo and the author incorporated the correction in the text of V.

[33] T.: "is unable always."

[34] *Lit.*: "given it." E. continues: "Its debt becomes greater all the time; and often, etc."

[35] E. omits: "and impediments and bonds."

it is in the prison of this body, it would gladly pay something of what it owes, for it is quite worn out. But even if we do all that is in us, how can we repay God, since, as I say, we have nothing to give save what we have first received? We can only learn to know ourselves and do what we can[36]—namely, surrender our will and fulfil God's will in us.[37] Anything else must be a hindrance to the soul which the Lord has brought to this state. It causes it, not profit, but harm, for nothing but humility is of any use here, and this is not acquired by the understanding but by a clear perception of the truth, which comprehends in one moment what could not be attained over a long period by the labour of the imagination—namely, that we are nothing and that God is infinitely great.

I will give you one piece of advice: do not suppose that you can reach this state by your own effort or diligence; that would be too much to expect. On the contrary, you would turn what devotion you had quite cold. You must practise simplicity and humility, for those are the virtues which achieve everything. You must say: "Fiat voluntas tua."

[36] T. adds: "with the favour of God."
[37] The rest of this paragraph is not found in E., which ends it on a more personal note: "Since, as I have said, the nature of this prayer has already been described elsewhere, together with the way in which the soul should behave at such a time, and since a great deal has been said about what the soul feels and how it knows this to be the work of God, I do no more here than touch on these details of (the life of) prayer so as to show you how to repeat this prayer, the Paternoster."

CHAPTER 33

Treats of our great need that the Lord should give us what we ask in these words of the Paternoster: "Panem nostrum quotidianum da nobis hodie."[1]

The good Jesus understands, as I have said, how difficult a thing He is offering on our behalf, for He knows our weakness,[2] and how often we show that we do not understand what the will of the Lord is, since we are weak[3] while He is so merciful. He knows that some means must be found[4] by which we shall not omit to give what He has given on our behalf, for if we did that it would be anything but good for us, since everything we gain comes from what we give. Yet He knows that it will be difficult for us to carry this out; for if anyone were to tell some wealthy, pampered person[5] that it is God's will for him to moderate his eating so that others, who are dying of hunger, shall have at least bread to eat, he will discover a thousand reasons for not understanding this but interpreting it in his own way. If one tells a person who speaks ill of others that it is God's will that he should love his neighbour as himself,[6] he will lose patience and no amount of reasoning will convince him.[7] If one tells a religious[8] who is accustomed to liberty and indulgence that he

---

[1] "Give us this day our daily bread."
[2] T.: "misery."
[3] T. ends the sentence here.
[4] In T. St. Teresa has deleted the following words and substituted: "for its fulfilment, so He begs the Eternal Father a remedy as sovereign as that of the Most Holy Sacrament, which gives strength and fortitude. For if anyone, etc."
[5] E. omits "pampered".
[6] *Lit.*: "should want as much *for himself as for his neighbour, and* for his neighbour as for himself." The italicized phrase is found in E. only.
[7] T.: "will make him want to do it even though he be convinced."
[8] V. has *relisioso* (masc.); E., *relisioso . . . u relisiosa.*

must be careful to set a good example and to remember that when he makes this petition it is his duty to keep what he has sworn and promised, and that not in word alone; that it is the will of God that he should fulfil his vows and see that he gives no occasion for scandal by acting contrarily to them, even though he may not actually break them; that he has taken the vow of poverty and must keep it without evasions, because that is the Lord's will—it would be impossible, in spite of all this, that some religious should not still want their own way. What would be the case, then, if the Lord had not done most of what was necessary by means of the remedy He has given us? There would have been very few who could have fulfilled this petition, which the Lord made to the Father on our behalf:[9] "Fiat voluntas tua."[10] Seeing our need, therefore, the good Jesus has sought[11] the admirable means whereby He has shown us the extreme love which He has for us, and in His own name and in that of His brethren He has made this petition: "Give us, Lord, this day our daily bread."

For the love of God, sisters, let us realize the meaning of our good Master's petition,[12] for our very life depends on our not disregarding it. Set very little store by what you have given, since there is so much that you will receive. It seems to me, in the absence of a better opinion, that the good Jesus knew what He had given for us and how important it was for us to give this to God, and yet how difficult it would be for us to do so, as has been said, because of our natural inclination to base things and our want of love and courage. He saw that, before we could be aroused, we needed His aid, not once but every day, and it must have been for this reason that He resolved to remain with us. As this was so weighty and important a matter, He wished it to come from the hand of the Eternal Father. Though both Father

[9] E.: "fulfilled His petition [*lit.:* "word," as also in V.], and what He offered to the Father."
[10] E. adds the reflection: "and may it please His Majesty that, as it is, there may be a great many."
[11] E.: "the Lord has thought of."
[12] E.: "of the good Jesus' petition."

and Son are one and the same, and He knew that whatever He did on earth God would do in Heaven, and would consider it good, since His will and the Father's will were one,[13] yet the humility of the good Jesus was such that He wanted, as it were, to ask leave of His Father, for He knew that He was His beloved Son and that He was well pleased with Him. He knew quite well that in this petition He was asking for more than He had asked for[14] in the others, but He already knew what death He was to suffer and what dishonours and affronts He would have to bear.

What father could there be, Lord, who, after giving us his son, and such a Son, would allow Him to remain among us[15] day by day to suffer as He had done already? None, Lord, in truth, but Thine: well dost Thou know of Whom Thou art asking this. God help me! What a great love is that of the Son and what a great love is that of the Father! I am not so much amazed at the good Jesus, because, as He had already said "Fiat voluntas tua", He was bound, being Who He is, to put what He had said into practice. Yes, for He is not like us; knowing that He was carrying out His words by loving us as He loves Himself, He went about seeking how He could carry out this commandment more perfectly, even at His own cost. But how, Eternal Father, couldst Thou[16] consent to this? How canst Thou see Thy Son every day in such wicked hands? Since first Thou didst permit it and consent to it, Thou seest how He has been treated. How can Thy Mercy, day by day and every day,[17] see Him affronted? And how many affronts are being offered to-day to this Most Holy Sacrament? How often must the Father see Him in the hands of His enemies? What desecrations these heretics commit!

O Eternal Lord! How canst Thou grant such a petition?

[13] E.: "on earth would be done in Heaven, and that His will and His Father's will were one for so great a thing."
[14] E.: "than He asks for."
[15] T. ends the sentence here.
[16] E.T.: "canst Thou."
[17] Lit.: "each day, each day."

How canst Thou consent to it? Consider not His love,[18] which, for the sake of fulfilling Thy will and of helping us, would allow Him to submit day by day to being cut to pieces. It is for Thee to see to this, my Lord, since Thy Son allows no obstacle to stand in His way. Why must all the blessings that we receive be at His cost? How is it that He is silent in face of all, and cannot speak for Himself, but only for us? Is there none who will speak for this most loving[19] Lamb? *Give me permission to speak for Him, Lord, since Thou hast been pleased to leave Him in our power, and let me beseech Thee on His behalf, since He gave Thee such full obedience and surrendered Himself to us with such great love.*

I have been reflecting how in this petition alone the same words are repeated: first of all the Lord speaks of "our daily bread" and asks Thee to give it,[20] and then He says: "Give it us to-day, Lord."[21] He lays the matter before His Father in this way: the Father gave us His Son once and for all to die for us, and thus He is our own;[22] yet He does not want the gift to be taken from us[23] until the end of the world but would have it left to be a help to us every day. Let this melt your hearts, my daughters, and make you love your Spouse, for there is no slave who would willingly call himself by that name, yet the good Jesus seems to think it an honour.

O Eternal Father, how great is the merit of this humility! With what a treasure are we purchasing Thy Son! How to sell Him we already know, for He was sold for thirty pieces of silver; but, if we would purchase Him, no price is suffi-

18 P. Báñez altered "His love" to "the love of your Spouse"; and, just below, "Thy will" to "the will of the Father". He also made the following sentence begin: "It was for Thee to care for Thy son, O Eternal Father; He allows, etc." These adulterations of the text are not found in T., nor were they adopted by Luis de León.

19 E.: "most meek."

20 T. deletes: "and asks Thee to give it," and, for "He lays . . . this way," has "As much as to say:"

21 This, as will be observed from the title to this chapter, is the order of the words in the Latin.

22 T. omits: "to die for us, and thus He is our own."

23 E. ends the sentence here and continues: "See, then, my sisters, and let this melt your hearts, and make you, etc."

cient.[24] Being made one with us through the portion of our nature which is His, and being Lord of His own will, He reminds His Father that, as our nature is His, He is able to give it to us, and thus He says "our bread".[25] He makes no difference between Himself and us, though we make one between ourselves and Him through not giving ourselves daily for His Majesty's sake.[26]

CHAPTER 34

Continues the same subject. This is very suitable for reading after the reception of the Most Holy Sacrament.

We have now reached the conclusion that the good Jesus, being ours, asks His Father to let us have Him daily—which appears[1] *to mean "for ever". While writing this I have been* wondering[2] *why, after saying "our 'daily' bread", the Lord repeated the idea in the words "Give us this day, Lord."*[3] *I will tell you my own foolish idea: if it really is foolish, well and good—in any case, it is quite bad enough that I should interfere in such a matter at all. Still, as we are trying to understand what we are praying for, let us think carefully what this means, so that we may pray rightly, and thank Him Who is taking such care about teaching us. This bread, then,*

[24] E.: "what price is sufficient?"
[25] E.: "and thus He calls Himself 'ours'."
[26] E.: "though we make one through not giving ourselves daily for His sake." T.: "so let us not make one: uniting our prayer with His, it will have merit before God and thus what we ask in it will be granted."
[1] So E. V. begins: "In this petition the word 'daily' appears, etc."
[2] E.: "I have had the desire to know."
[3] E.: "in the word 'to-day'." T. has "Our Lord" and continues: "I think myself that He said 'daily' because we have Him here on earth, etc."

is[4] ours daily, it seems to me, because we have Him here on earth, *since He has remained with us here and we receive Him*; and, if we profit by His company, we shall also have Him in Heaven, for the only reason He remains with us is to help and encourage and sustain us so that we shall do that will, which, as we have said, is to be fulfilled in us.

In using the words "this day" He seems to me to be *thinking of a day of the length of this life*.[5] And a day indeed it is! As for the unfortunate souls who *will* bring damnation upon themselves and will not have fruition of Him in the world to come, *they are His own creatures, and He did everything to help them on, and was with them, to strengthen them, throughout the "to-day" of this life*, so it is not His fault if they are vanquished.[6] They will have no excuse to make nor will they be able to complain of the Father for taking this bread from them at the time when they most needed it.[7] Therefore the Son prays the Father that,[8] since this life[9] lasts no more than a day, He will allow Him to spend it in our service.[10] As His Majesty has already given His Son to us, by sending Him, of His will alone,[11] into the world, so now, of that same will,[12] He is pleased not to abandon us, but to remain here with us for the greater glory of His friends and the discomfiture of His enemies.[13] He prays for nothing

---

[4] V.: "It is."
[5] Thus E., which seems preferable here. V. has: "to be indicating a period of time equivalent to the duration of the world."
[6] V. adds a shortened version of the passage it has omitted: "for He never fails to encourage them down to the very end of the battle."
[7] E. omits this sentence, though working the phrase "at . . . needed it" into the argument below.
[8] E.: "And, so that the Father may grant Him (His petition, the Son) puts it to Him that."
[9] E.: "the world"; V.: "it." But E. obviously means by "world" "life in the world."
[10] *Lit.*: "in service"—*en servidumbre*, a strong word, better rendered, perhaps, "servitude," and not far removed from "slavery." Luis de León softened the phrase to "spend it among His own."
[11] T. has "of His goodness alone," but these words are deleted.
[12] T. omits "of that same will."
[13] E.: "As (His Majesty) has given Him to us, it is unlikely that He will take Him when we most need Him, for all this evil treatment

more than this "to-day" since He has given us this most holy Bread.[14] He has given it to us for ever, as I have said, as the sustenance and manna of humanity. We can have it[15] whenever we please and we shall not die of hunger save through our own fault, for, in whatever way the soul desires to partake of food, it will find joy and comfort in the Most Holy Sacrament.[16] There is no need or trial or persecution that cannot be easily borne if we begin to *partake and* taste of[17] those which He Himself bore, *and to make them the subject of our meditations.*

With regard to other bread[18]—*the bread of bodily necessaries and sustenance—I neither like to think that the Lord is always being reminded of it nor would I have you remember it yourselves. Keep on the level of the highest contemplation, for anyone who dwells there no more remembers that he is in the world than if he had already left it—still less does he think about food. Would the Lord ever have insisted upon our asking for food, or taught us to do so by His own example? Not in my opinion. He teaches us to fix our desires upon heavenly things and to pray that we may begin to enjoy these things while here on earth: would He, then, have us trouble about so petty a matter as praying for food? As if He did not know that, once we begin to worry about the needs of the body, we shall forget the needs of the soul! Besides, are we such moderately minded people that we shall be satisfied with just a little and pray only for a little? No: the more food we*

---

which He is being offered undeservingly will last only for a day. Let Him consider how He is bound to help us in every possible way, since for our sakes He has made so great an offer (on our behalf) as the resignation of our wills to the will of God."

[14] E. continues: "It is certain that we have it for ever, this sustenance, etc." St. Teresa also interpolated, after "ever," and subsequently crossed out, the words: "and He gave it us without our asking for it."

[15] E. adds: "it seems." "Have it whenever" is, literally, "find it however".

[16] E.: "it will find in it joy and comfort and sustenance."

[17] E.: "and masticate."

[18] The whole of this paragraph is lightly crossed out in the manuscript.

are given, the less we shall get of the water from Heaven. Let those of you, daughters, who want more of the necessaries of life pray for this.

Join with the Lord, then, daughters, in begging the Father to let you have[19] your Spouse to-day, so that, *as long as you live,* you may never find yourself in this world without Him. Let it suffice to temper your great joy[20] that He should remain disguised beneath these accidents of bread and wine,[21] which is a real torture to those who have nothing else to love[22] and no other consolation. Entreat Him not to fail you but to prepare you to receive Him worthily.

As for that other bread, have no anxiety about it if you have truly resigned yourselves to God's will. I mean that at these hours of prayer you are dealing with more important matters and there is time enough for you to labour and earn your daily bread.[23] Try never at any time to let your thoughts dwell on this; work with your body, for it is good for you to try to support yourselves, but let your soul be at rest. Leave anxiety about this to your Spouse, as has been said at length already, and He will always bear it for you.[24] *Do not fear that He will fail you if you do not fail to do what you have promised and to resign yourselves to God's will. I assure you, daughters, that, if I myself were to fail in this, because of my wickedness, as I have often done in the past, I would not beg Him to give me that bread, or anything else to eat. Let Him leave me to die of hunger. Of what use is life to me if it leads me daily nearer to eternal death?*

If, then, you are really surrendering yourselves to God, as you say, cease to be anxious for yourselves, for He bears your anxiety, and will bear it always. It is as though a servant had

---

19 E. begins: "Beg Him to let you have."
20 E. omits: "to temper your great joy."
21 E. omits: "and wine."
22 E.: "who have no other love."
23 E.: "and there are other times when the person whose office it is to do so will see about what you have to eat—I mean, will give you what she has."
24 T.: "but let your soul be at rest, as has been said at length already. He is your Spouse and He will be with you."

gone into service and were anxious to please his master in everything. The master is bound to give him food for so long as he remains in his house, and in his service, unless he is so poor that he has food neither for his servant nor for himself. Here, however, the comparison breaks down, for God is, and will always be, rich and powerful. It would not be[25] right for the servant to go to his master *every day* and ask him for food when he knew that his master would see that it was given him and so he would be sure to receive it. *To do this would be a waste of words.* His master would quite properly tell him that he should look after his own business of serving and pleasing him, for, if he worried himself unnecessarily, he would not do his work as well as he should.[26] So, sisters, those who will may worry about asking for[27] earthly bread; let our own task be to beg the Eternal Father that we may merit our heavenly bread, so that,[28] although our bodily eyes cannot feast themselves on the sight of Him since He is thus hidden from us, He may reveal Himself to the eyes of the soul and may make Himself known to us as another kind of food, full of delight and joy, which sustains our life.[29]

Do you suppose that this most holy food[30] is not *ample* sustenance even for the body and a potent medicine for bodily ills? I am sure that it is. I know a person who was subject to serious illnesses and often suffered great pain; and

[25] E. omits "rich and", and makes the next sentence interrogative: "Now would it be . . . ?"
[26] This sentence is an expansion from E.
[27] E.: "those who will may ask for."
[28] E.: "let us beg Him Whose business it is and beseech the Father to give us grace to prepare ourselves to receive so great a gift and such heavenly sustenance, so that."
[29] E. interrupts the thread of thought thus: "We shall quite unconsciously come and desire or ask Him (for earthly bread) more often than we wish. There is no need to arouse ourselves to do this, for our miserable inclination toward base things will arouse us, as I say, more often than we wish. But let us not purposely take any trouble except about entreating the Lord for what I have described. If we have that, we shall have everything."
[30] E.: "this Most Holy Sacrament."

this pain was taken away from her in a flash[31] and she became quite well again. This often occurs, I believe; and cures are recorded from quite definite illnesses which could not be counterfeited. As the wondrous effects produced by this most holy bread in those who worthily receive it are very well known, I will not describe all the things that could be related about this person I mentioned,[32] though I have been enabled to learn about them and I know that they are not fabrications. The Lord had given this person[33] such a lively faith that, when she heard people[34] say they wished they had lived when Christ[35] walked on this earth, she would smile to herself, for she knew that we have Him as truly with us in the Most Holy Sacrament as people had Him then, and wonder what more they could possibly want.

I know, too, that for many years this person, though by no means perfect, always tried to strengthen her faith, when she communicated, by thinking that it was exactly as if she saw the Lord entering her house, with her own bodily eyes,[36] for she believed in very truth that this Lord was entering her poor abode, and she ceased, as far as she could, to think of outward things, and went into her abode with Him. She tried to recollect her senses so that they might all become aware of this great blessing, or rather, so that they should not hinder the soul from becoming conscious of it. She imagined herself at His feet and wept with the Magdalen exactly as if she had seen Him with her bodily eyes in the Pharisee's house. Even

---

[31] *Lit.*: "as if by (someone's) hand." St. Teresa is thought here to be referring to herself.
[32] E.: "As for the many other effects produced in this soul, there is no need to speak of them."
[33] E.: "This person had so much devotion and."
[34] E. adds: "at certain festivals."
[35] So E. V. adds: "our Good."
[36] E. continues: "for this made her believe that it was the same thing, and that she had Him in a house as poor as her own, and she ceased to think of outward things, and went into a corner, trying to recollect her senses so that she might be alone with her Lord, and imagined herself at His feet, and remained there, even if she felt no devotion, speaking with Him."

if she felt no devotion, faith told her that it was good for her to be there.[37]

For, unless we want to be foolish and to close our minds to facts, we cannot suppose that this is the work of the imagination, as it is when we think of the Lord on the Cross, or of other incidents of the Passion, and picture within ourselves[38] how these things happened. This is something which is happening now; it is absolutely true; and we have no need to go and seek Him somewhere a long way off.[39] For we know that, until the accidents of bread have been consumed by our natural heat, the good Jesus is with us and we should [not lose so good an opportunity but should] come to Him.[40] If, while He went about in the world, the sick were healed merely by touching His clothes, how can we doubt that He will work miracles when He is within us, if we have faith, or that He will give us what we ask of Him since He is in our house? His Majesty is not wont to offer us too little payment for His lodging if we treat Him well.[41]

If you grieve[42] at not seeing Him with the eyes of the body, remember that that would not be good for us,[43] for it is one thing to see Him glorified and quite another to see Him as He was when He lived in the world. So weak is our nature that nobody could endure the sight—in fact, there would be no one left to endure it, for no one would wish to remain in the world any longer. Once having seen this Eternal Truth, people would realize that all the things we prize here are mockery and falsehood.[44] And if such great Majesty could be

[37] T.: "faith told her that her Good was there."
[38] T. omits: "within ourselves."
[39] E.: "For, unless we want to be blind and foolish, and if we have faith, it is clear that He is within us. Why, then, do we need to go and seek Him a long way off, as has been said?"
[40] "And we should . . . come to Him" is not found in E. In the following sentence the singular of the first person is used, not the plural, as in the text. V. begins in the singular and continues in the plural.
[41] E. omits this sentence.
[42] E. is even stronger: "If it causes you anguish" (os congojáis).
[43] E.: "that it is good for us (that it should be so)."
[44] E. omits: "and falsehood", and continues: "Have no fear that,

seen, how could a miserable sinner like myself, after having so greatly offended Him, remain so near to Him? Beneath those accidents of bread,[45] we can approach Him; for, if the King disguises Himself, it would seem that we need not mind coming to Him without so much circumspection and ceremony: by disguising Himself, He has, as it were, obliged Himself to submit to this. Who, otherwise, would dare to approach Him so unworthily, with so many imperfections and with such lukewarm zeal?

Oh, we know not what we ask! How much better does His Wisdom know what we need! He reveals Himself to those who He knows will profit by His presence;[46] though unseen by bodily eyes, He has many ways of revealing Himself to the soul through deep inward emotions and by various other means. Delight to remain with Him; do not lose such an excellent time for talking with Him as the hour after Communion.[47] *Remember that this is a very profitable hour for the soul; if you spend it in the company of the good Jesus, you are doing Him a great service. Be very careful, then, daughters, not to lose it.* If you are compelled by obedience to do something else, try to leave your soul with the Lord. *For He is your Master, and, though it be in a way you may not understand, He will not fail to teach you.* But if you take your thoughts elsewhere, and pay no *more* attention to Him[48] *than if you had not received Him,* and care nothing for His being within you,[49] how can He make Himself known to you?

because He is not seen with these bodily eyes, He is quite hidden from His friends. Delight to remain with Him, etc."

[45] Luis de León's emendation of St. Teresa's "Beneath that bread," also found in T. Cf. pp. 224, 227, above, where St. Teresa herself uses that phrase.

[46] T. omits: "by His presence."

[47] E. omits: "Do not . . . Communion". The word translated "time" is *sazón*, rendered more conveniently as "opportunity" in a similar phrase on p. 228, l. 12, above. T. uses a much stronger word, *coyuntura*, which might be freely translated here as "Heaven-sent chance."

[48] E. has here: "to His being within you," which V. alters to: "and . . . within you" as in the text.

[49] T. ends the sentence: "you will not perceive the favours that He works."

You must complain, not of Him, but of yourself. This, then, is a good time for our Master to teach us and for us to listen to Him.[50] *I do not tell you to say no prayers at all, for if I did you would take hold of my words and say I was talking about contemplation, which you need practise only if the Lord brings you to it. No: you should say the Paternoster, realize that you are verily and indeed in the company of Him Who taught it you and kiss His feet in gratitude to Him for having desired to teach you and beg Him to show you how to pray and never to leave you.*

You may be in the habit of praying while looking at a picture of Christ,[51] but *at a time like this it seems foolish to me*[52] to turn away from *the living image*—the Person Himself—to look at His picture. Would it not be foolish if we had a portrait of someone whom we dearly loved and, when the person himself came to see us, we refused to talk with him and carried on our entire conversation with the portrait? Do you know when I find the use of a picture an excellent thing,[53] and take great pleasure in it? When the person is absent and we are made to feel his loss by our great aridity,[54] it is then that we find it a great comfort to look at the picture of Him Whom we have such reason to love.[55] *This is a great inspiration,* and *makes us* wish that, in whichever direction we turn our eyes, we could see the picture. What can we look upon that is better or more attractive to the sight[56] than upon Him Who so dearly loves us and contains within Himself all

---

[50] E. omits this sentence and in a few other minor respects differs from V. in this paragraph.

[51] So T. "Which we are looking at," adds V., redundantly and ungrammatically. E. reads: "If you are in the habit of praying to a picture of Christ, in Whose presence you are, do you not see, etc." (v. next note).

[52] E. makes this a question: "do you not see that it is foolish . . . ?"

[53] E.: "a good and very holy thing."

[54] "And . . . aridity" is not found in E.

[55] E.: "It is a great comfort to look at a picture of Our Lady, or of some saint to whom we have devotion—and how much more at a picture of Christ!"

[56] E. omits the rest of this sentence.

good things? Unhappy are those heretics, who through their own fault have lost this comfort, as well as others.[57]

When you have received the Lord, and are in His very presence, try to shut the bodily eyes and to open the eyes of the soul and to look into your own hearts. I tell you, and tell you again, for I should like to repeat[58] it often, that if you practise this habit *of staying with Him, not just once or twice, but* whenever you communicate, and strive to keep your conscience clear so that you can often rejoice in this your Good, He will not, as I have said, come so much disguised as to be unable to make His presence known to you in many ways, according to the desire which you have of seeing Him. So great, indeed, may be your longing for Him that He will reveal Himself to you wholly.

But if we pay no heed to Him save when we have received Him, and go away from Him in search of other and baser things, what can He do?[59] Will He have to drag us by force to look at Him *and be with Him* because He desires to reveal Himself to us? No; for when He revealed Himself to all men plainly,[60] and told them clearly who He was, they did not treat Him at all well—very few of them, indeed, even believed Him. So He grants us an exceeding great favour when He is pleased to show us that it is He Who is in the Most Holy Sacrament. But He will not reveal Himself openly and communicate His glories and bestow His treasures save on those who He knows greatly desire Him, for these are His true friends. I assure you that anyone who is not a true friend[61] and does not come to receive Him as such, after doing all in his power to prepare for Him, must never importune Him to reveal Himself to him. Hardly is the hour over which such a person has spent in fulfilling the Church's commandment

57 E.: "who lack this comfort and blessing among others."
58 E.: "I shall repeat."
59 T.: "away from Him to other, etc." E.: "But if you pay no heed to Him when you receive Him, though He is so near you, and go and look for Him elsewhere, or for other and base (*sic* things, what do you expect Him to do?"
60 E. omits: "plainly."
61 E.: "who offends Him."

than he goes home[62] and tries to drive Christ out of the house. What with all his other business and occupations and worldly[63] hindrances, he seems to be making all possible haste to prevent the Lord from taking possession of the house which is His own.[64]

CHAPTER 35

Describes the recollection which should be practised after Communion. Concludes this subject with an exclamatory prayer to the Eternal Father.

I have written at length about this, although, when writing of the Prayer of Recollection, I spoke of the great importance of our entering into solitude with God.[1] When you hear Mass without communicating, daughters, you may communicate spiritually, which is extremely profitable, and afterwards you may practise inward recollection in exactly the same way,[2] for this impresses upon us a deep love of the Lord. If we prepare to receive Him, He never fails to give, and He gives in many ways that we cannot understand. It is as if we were to approach a fire: it might be a very large one, but, if we remained a long way from it and covered our hands,[3]

---

[62] So E. V. has: "than he leaves his home and tries to drive Christ [*lit.*: "Him", both here and in E.] out of himself." The thought underlying each phrase is quite distinct; E. seems to me preferable.
[63] "Bodily," is the reading of T.
[64] In E. the final sentence reads: "So, if he enters within himself, it is to think of vanities in His very presence."
[1] "Since it is a very important thing indeed," adds T., which also has "being in" for "entering into" in the same sentence.
[2] V. is more explicit than E., which says merely: "and do the same."
[3] E.: "if we covered our hands." In both E. and V. the person changes abruptly from first to second in the course of the sentence. In the text above, the first person is kept throughout.

we should get little warmth from it,[4] although we should be warmer than if we were in a place where there was no fire at all. But when we try to approach the Lord there is this difference: if the soul is properly disposed, and comes with the intention of driving out the cold, and stays for some time where it is, it will retain its warmth for several hours,[5] *and if any little spark flies out, it will set it on fire.*

It is of such importance, daughters, for us to prepare ourselves in this way that you must not be surprised if I often repeat this counsel. If at first[6] you do not get on[7] with this practice (which may happen, for the devil will try to oppress and distress your heart, knowing what great harm he can do in this way),[8] the devil will make you think that you can find more devotion in other things and less in this.[9] But [trust me and] do not give up this method, for the Lord will use it to prove your love for Him. Remember that there are few souls who stay with Him and follow Him in His trials; let us endure something for Him and His Majesty will repay us. Remember, too, that there are actually people who not only have no wish to be[10] with Him but who insult Him and *with great irreverence* drive Him away *from their homes.*[11] We must endure something, therefore, to show Him that we have the desire to see Him. *In many places He is neglected and ill-treated, but* He suffers everything, and will continue to do so, if He finds but one single soul which will receive Him and

---

[4] E. continues: "You will remain cold, although that is better than not seeing the fire: one gets warmth by being near it. But when we try, etc."

[5] E. omits: "and comes with . . . several hours."

[6] So E. V. begins: "Remember, sisters, that if at first." T. has: "Do not trouble, sisters, if at first" and recasts this and the following sentence.

[7] E. reads: "If at first He does not reveal Himself to you, and you do not get on," and omits "which may happen."

[8] E. continues: "and if you find more devotion in other things and less in this do not give up, etc."

[9] T. omits: "and less in this."

[10] So E. V. reads: "who not only wish not to be."

[11] V.: "from themselves," as in p. 232, n. 62, above.

love to have Him as its Guest.[12] Let this soul be yours, then, for, if there were none, the Eternal Father would rightly refuse to allow Him to remain with us. Yet the Lord is so good a Friend to those who are His friends, and so good a Master to those who are His servants, that, when He knows it to be the will of His Beloved Son, He will not hinder Him in so excellent a work, in which His Son so fully reveals the love which He has for His Father,[13] *as this wonderful way which He seeks of showing how much He loves us and of helping us to bear our trials.*

Since, then, Holy Father, Who art in the Heavens, Thou dost will and accept this (and it is clear[14] that Thou couldst not deny us a thing which is so good for us) there must be someone, as I said at the beginning, who will speak for Thy Son, for He has never defended[15] Himself.[16] Let this be the task for us, daughters, though, having regard to what we are, it is presumptuous of us to undertake it. Let us rely, however, on Our Lord's command to us to pray to Him, and, in fulfilment of our obedience to Him, let us beseech His Majesty, in the name of the good Jesus, that, as He has left nothing undone that He could do for us in granting sinners so great a favour, He may be pleased of His mercy[17] to prevent Him from being so ill-treated. Since His Holy Son has given us this excellent way in which we can offer Him up frequently as a sacrifice, let us make use of this precious gift so that it may stay the advance of such terrible evil and irreverence as in many places is paid to this Most Holy Sacrament.[18] For these Lutherans[19] *seem to want to drive Him out of the world again: they* destroy churches, cause the loss of many

---

[12] *Lit.*: "and have Him within itself [cf. last note] with love." E. reads: "which will love to admit Him and keep Him company."

[13] T. omits: "which He has for His Father."

[14] T.: "certain."

[15] E.: "never been able to defend."

[16] E. continues: "and so I ask you, daughters, to help me beg our Holy Father, in His name, that, as He has left nothing undone, etc."

[17] E.: "of His majesty."

[18] E.: "as is committed in places where this Most Holy Sacrament is (found)."

[19] E. is less explicit: "For they."

priests and abolish the sacraments.[20] *And there is something of this even among Christians, who sometimes go to church meaning to offend Him rather than to worship Him.*

Why is this, my Lord and my God? Do Thou bring the world to an end or give us a remedy for such grievous wrongs, which even our wicked hearts cannot endure. I beseech Thee, Eternal Father, endure it no longer: quench this fire, Lord,[21] for Thou canst do so if Thou wilt. Remember that Thy Son is still in the world; may these dreadful things be stopped out of respect for Him, horrible and abominable and foul[22] as they are. With His beauty and purity He does not deserve to be in a house where such things happen.[23] Do this, Lord, not for our sake, for we do not deserve it, but for the sake of Thy Son. We dare not entreat Thee that He should no longer stay with us,[24] *for Thou hast granted His prayer to Thee to leave Him with us for to-day—that is, until the end of the world.*[25] If He were to go, what would become of us?[26] *It would be the end of everything.* If anything can placate Thee it is to have on earth such a pledge as this. Since some remedy must be found for this, then, my Lord, I beg Thy Majesty to apply it. *For if Thou wilt, Thou art able.*

O my God, if only I could indeed importune Thee! If only I had served Thee well so that I might be able to beg of Thee this great favour as a reward for my services, for Thou leavest no service unrewarded! But I have not served Thee, Lord; indeed, it may perhaps be for my sins, and because I have so greatly offended Thee, that so many evils come. What, then, can I do, my Creator, but present to Thee this most holy

---

[20] The sense of the verb here rendered "cause the loss of" is vague. Literally the phrase reads: "so many priests are lost." E. has: "They take Him out of the temples, cause the loss of so many priests and profane so many churches."
[21] E. ends the sentence here: the words which immediately follow in V. are found at the very end of the paragraph.
[22] E.: "horrible and foul."
[23] V. softens the phrase in E.: "where there are such evil stenches."
[24] E.: "We dare not ask Thee not to leave Him with us here."
[25] On this interpretation of "to-day", see p. 223, n. 5, above.
[26] This sentence is not found in E.

Bread,[27] which, though Thou gavest it to us, I return to Thee, beseeching Thee, by the merits of Thy Son,[28] to grant me this favour, which on so many counts He has merited? Do Thou, Lord,[29] calm this sea, and no longer allow this ship, which is Thy Church, to endure so great a tempest. Save us, my Lord, for we perish.[30]

CHAPTER 36

Treats of these words in the Paternoster: "Dimitte nobis debita nostra."[1]

Our good[2] Master sees that, if we have this heavenly food,[3] everything is easy for us, except when we are ourselves to blame, and that we are well able to fulfil our undertaking to the Father that His will shall be done in us. So He now asks Him to forgive us our debts, as we ourselves forgive others.[4] Thus, continuing the prayer which He is teaching us, He says these words:[5] "And forgive us, Lord, our debts, even as we forgive them to our debtors."

Notice, sisters, that He does not say: "as we shall forgive." We are to understand that anyone who asks for so great a gift as that just mentioned, and has already yielded his own will to the will of God, must have done this already. And so He says: "as we forgive our debtors." Anyone, then, who sincerely repeats this petition, "Fiat voluntas tua", must, at least in intention, have done this already. You see now why

[27] E.: "this blessed Bread."
[28] E.: "by Its (or "His") merits."
[29] T. repeats "Do Thou, Lord."
[30] St. Matthew viii, 25.
[1] "Forgive us our debts."
[2] E.: "precious."
[3] E.: "this sustenance."
[4] E.: "to forgive us as we forgive."
[5] The sentence "Thus . . . words" is not in E.

the saints rejoiced in insults and persecutions: it was because these gave them something to present to the Lord when they prayed to Him. What can a poor creature like myself do, who has had so little to forgive others and has so much to be forgiven herself?[6] This, sisters, is something which we should consider carefully; it is such a serious and important matter that God should pardon us our sins, which have merited eternal fire, that we must pardon all trifling things which have been done to us *and which are not wrongs at all, or anything else. For how is it possible, either in word or in deed, to wrong one who, like myself, has deserved to be plagued[7] by devils for ever? Is it not only right that I should be plagued in this world too?* As I have so few, Lord, even of these trifling things, to offer Thee,[8] Thy pardoning of me must be a free gift: there is abundant scope here for Thy mercy. *Thy Son must pardon me, for no one has done me any injustice, and so there has been nothing that I can pardon for Thy sake. But take my desire to do so, Lord, for I believe I would forgive any wrong if Thou wouldst forgive me and I might unconditionally do Thy will. True, if the occasion were to arise, and I were condemned without cause, I do not know what I should do. But at this moment I see that I am so guilty in Thy sight that everything I might have to suffer would fall short of my deserts, though anyone not knowing, as Thou knowest, what I am, would think I was being wronged.* Blessed be Thou, Who endurest one that is so poor: when Thy *most holy* Son makes this petition in the name of all mankind, I cannot be included, being such as I am and having nothing to give.[9]

And supposing, my Lord, that there are others who are like myself but have not realized that this is so? If there are

[6] E.: "What will sinners like myself do, who have so much to be forgiven?" In both E. and V. the rest of this paragraph is lightly crossed out and some editors omit it. It does not appear in T.
[7] *Lit.*: "ill-treated." The same verb is used in the following sentence.
[8] E. reads: "For this reason, then, my Lord, I have nothing to give Thee in begging Thee to forgive my debts," and begins a fresh sentence with "Thy Son must pardon me, etc."
[9] E. omits: "and having nothing to give", which, in V., reads literally: "and so (completely) without treasure."

any such, I beg them, in Thy name, to remember this truth, and to pay no heed to little things about which they think they are being slighted,[10] for, if they insist on these nice points of honour, they become like children building houses of straw. Oh, God help me, sisters! If we only knew what honour really is and what is meant by losing it! I am not speaking now about ourselves, for it would indeed be a bad business if we did not understand this; I am speaking of myself as I was when I prided myself on my honour without knowing what honour meant; I just followed the example of others.[11] Oh, how easily I used to feel slighted! I am ashamed to think of it now; and I was not one of those who worried most about such things either. But I never grasped the essence of the matter,[12] because I neither thought nor troubled about true honour, which it is good for us to have because it profits the soul. How truly has someone said: "Honour and profit cannot go together." I do not know if this was what that person was thinking of when he said it; but it is literally true, for the soul's profit and what the world calls honour can never be reconciled. Really, the topsy-turviness of the world is terrible.[13] Blessed be the Lord for taking us out of it! *May His Majesty grant that this house shall always be as far from it as it is now! God preserve us from religious houses where they worry about points of honour! Such places never do much honour to God.*

God help us, how absurd it is for religious to connect their honour with things so trifling that they amaze me! You know nothing about this, sisters, but I will tell you about it so that you may be wary. You see, sisters, the devil has not forgotten us.[14] He has invented honours of his own for religious houses

---

[10] E.: "to tiny slights."
[11] E. adds: "(going) by what I heard (them say)." On "honour", see Vol. I, p. 14, n. 2, above.
[12] E.: "But I went astray, like everyone, about the essence of the matter."
[13] E.: "Oh, God help me, how topsy-turvy the world is!"
[14] In E. this sentence is omitted and the following sentence reads: "Know that in religious houses there are also laws about honour: and the religious go up in rank, as in the world."

and has made laws by which we go up and down in rank, as people do in the world. Learned men have to observe this with regard to their studies (a matter of which I know nothing): anyone, for example, who has got as far as reading theology must not descend and read philosophy—that is their kind of honour, according to which you must always be going up and never going down. Even if someone were commanded by obedience to take a step down, he would *in his own mind* consider himself slighted; and then someone[15] would take his part [and say] it was an insult; next, the devil would discover reasons for this—and he seems to be an authority even in God's own law. Why, among ourselves,[16] anyone who has been a prioress is thereby incapacitated from holding any lower office[17] *for the rest of her life.* We must defer to the senior among us, and we are not allowed to forget it either: sometimes it would appear to be a positive merit for us to do this, because it is a rule of the Order.[18]

The thing is enough[19] to make one laugh—or, it would be more proper to say,[20] to make one weep. After all, the Order does not command us not to be humble: it commands us to do everything in due form. And in matters which concern my own esteem I ought not to be so formal as to insist that this detail of our Rule shall be kept[21] as strictly as the rest, which we may in fact be observing very imperfectly. We must not put all our effort into observing just this one detail: let my interests be looked after by others—I will forget about myself altogether. The fact is, although we shall never rise as far as Heaven in this way, we are attracted by the thought

15 E.: "many." V. continues: ". . . . would take his part, for it is an insult."
16 E.: "among nuns."
17 E.: "any other kind of office than that."
18 E.: "We must give precedence to seniority, and you need have no fear that that will be forgotten: apparently it is a merit, because it is a rule of the Order."
19 E.: "is funnier than can be imagined, and enough."
20 E.: "or, to put it better, and very properly."
21 E. omits the rest of the sentence and reads: "It may be that I observe all the rest imperfectly, whereas about this I never budge an inch: let my interests, etc."

of rising higher, and we dislike climbing down. O, Lord, Lord, art Thou our Example and our Master? Yes, indeed. And wherein did Thy honour consist,[22] O Lord, Who hast honoured us?[23] Didst Thou perchance[24] lose it when Thou wert humbled even to death? No, Lord, rather didst Thou gain it for all.[25]

For the love of God, sisters! We have lost our way; we have taken the wrong path from the very beginning.[26] God grant that no soul be lost through its attention to these wretched niceties about honour, when it has no idea wherein honour consists. We shall get to the point of thinking that we have done something wonderful because we have forgiven a person for some trifling thing,[27] which was neither a slight nor an insult nor anything else.[28] Then we shall ask the Lord to forgive us as people who have done something important, just because we have forgiven someone. Grant us, my God, to understand how little we understand ourselves[29] and how empty our hands are when we come to Thee that Thou, of Thy mercy, mayest forgive us.[30] For in truth, Lord, since all things have an end and punishment is eternal, I can see nothing meritorious which I may present to Thee that Thou mayest grant us so great a favour. Do it, then, for the

---

[22] E. completes the sentence with the words: "my King?"

[23] *Lit.*: "our Honourer"—*Honrador nuestro*: a rather unusual phrase which T. changes into the quite conventional *honrado Maestro*—"honoured Master."

[24] Thus E. V. has: "Certainly Thou didst not."

[25] E.: "gain it, and profit for all."

[26] In T. St. Teresa has made a long marginal addition to this sentence, but it has unfortunately been mutilated by the binder. As P. Silverio (III, 466) has reconstructed it from the Évora edition, it is a rambling digression which hardly merits reproduction.

[27] E.: "some mere nothing."

[28] E.: "nor had anything to do with a slight."

[29] E.: "Grant them, Lord, to understand that they know not what they say."

[30] E.: "and how empty their hands are when they come to beg of Thee, as I do. Do this of Thy mercy, and for Thine own sake." The rest of this paragraph is scored through by St. Teresa in V. It does not appear in T. nor in other early copies and editions.

sake of Him Who asks it of Thee, *and Who may well do so, for He is always being wronged and offended.*

How greatly the Lord must esteem this mutual love of ours one for another! *For, having given Him our wills, we have given Him complete rights over us, and we cannot do that without love. See, then, sisters, how important it is for us to love one another and to be at peace.*[31] The good Jesus might have put everything else before our love for one another, and said: "Forgive us, Lord, because we are doing a great deal of penance, or because we are praying often, and fasting, and because we have left all for Thy sake and love Thee greatly." But He has never said:[32] "Because we would lose our lives for Thy sake"; or any of these [numerous] other things which He might have said. He simply says: "Because we forgive." Perhaps *the reason He said* this *rather than anything else* was because He knew that our fondness for this dreadful honour made mutual love the hardest virtue for us to attain,[33] though it is the virtue dearest to His Father. *Because of its very difficulty* He put it where He did, and *after having asked for so many great gifts for us,* He offers it on our behalf to God.

Note particularly, sisters, that He says: "As we forgive." As I have said, He takes this for granted. And observe especially[34] with regard to it that unless, after experiencing the favours granted by God in the prayer that I have called perfect contemplation, a person is very resolute, and makes a point, if the occasion arises, of forgiving, not [only] these mere nothings which people call wrongs, but any wrong, how-

---

[31] E. continues: "For of the many things that we have given—or He has given in our name—to the Father, the Lord put in the first place none other than this. He might have said: 'Because we love Thee, and suffer trials, and desire to suffer them for Thee, or because of fasts and other good works, which are done by a soul that loves God and has given Him its will.' And yet He spoke only of this."

[32] T. omits this sentence and unites the two quotations with "and."

[33] The clause which follows was crossed out by the author and both T. and some of the editions omit it.

[34] E.: "And understand."

ever grave, you need not think much of that person's prayer.[35]
For wrongs have no effect upon a soul whom God draws to
Himself in such sublime prayer as this,[36] nor does it care if
it is highly esteemed or no.[37] That is not quite correct: it
does care, for honour distresses much more than dishonour
and it prefers trials to a great deal of rest and ease. For anyone to whom the Lord has really given His Kingdom no
longer wants a kingdom in this world, knowing that he is
going the right way to reign in a much more exalted manner,
and having already discovered by experience what great benefits the soul gains and what progress it makes[38] when it suffers for God's sake. For only very rarely does His Majesty
grant it such great consolations, and then only to those who
have willingly borne many trials for His sake. For contemplatives, as I have said elsewhere in this book, have to bear heavy
trials, and therefore the Lord seeks out for Himself souls of
great experience.

Understand, then, sisters, that as these persons have already learned to rate everything at its proper valuation, they
pay little attention to things which pass away. A great wrong,
or a great trial, may cause them some momentary distress,
but they will hardly have felt it when reason will intervene,
and will seem to raise its standard aloft, and drive away their
distress by giving them the joy of seeing how God has en-

[35] St. Teresa left this sentence uncompleted. Luis de León added:
"You need not . . . prayer" in his edition, since when it has always
been included. It figures as an anonymous correction in T.
[36] E.: "brings to that (point)." The word "brings" (llega) is that
translated "draws" in the text above.
[37] T. condenses, after "For a soul whom God . . . as this," and
reads: "is distressed much more by honour than by dishonour, etc."
E. continues: "it regrets honour, indeed, much more than dishonour.
So you may be sure that, unless they produce these effects, the favours are not of God, but of the devil: a kind of indulgence and
illusion which he makes you think to be good, hoping that you will
then attach more importance to your honour. And as the good Jesus
well knows that He produces these effects wherever He goes, He
gives the Father a definite assurance that we are forgiving our debtors." This takes us to the end of the present chapter.
[38] T.: "discovered by experience the good which comes to it and
the progress it makes."

trusted them with the opportunity of gaining, in a single day, more lasting favours and graces in His Majesty's sight[39] than they could gain in ten years by means of trials which they sought on their own account. This, as I understand (and I have talked about it with many contemplatives), is quite usual, and I know for a fact that it happens.[40] Just as other people prize gold and jewels, so these persons prize and desire trials, for they know quite well that trials will make them rich.

Such persons would never on any account esteem themselves:[41] they want their sins to be known and like to speak about them to people who they see have any esteem for them. The same is true of their descent, which they know quite well will be of no advantage to them in the kingdom which has no end. If being of good birth were any satisfaction to them, it would be because this would enable them to serve God better. If they are not well born, it distresses them when people think them better than they are, and it causes them no distress to disabuse them, but only pleasure. The reason for this is that those to whom God grants the favour of possessing such humility and great love for Him forget themselves when there is a possibility of rendering Him greater services, and simply cannot believe that others are troubled by things which they themselves do not consider as wrongs at all.

These last effects which I have mentioned are produced in persons who have reached a high degree of perfection and to whom the Lord commonly grants the favour of uniting them to Himself by perfect contemplation. But the first of these effects—namely, the determination to suffer wrongs even though such suffering brings distress—is very quickly seen in anyone to whom the Lord has granted this grace of prayer as far as the stage of union.[42] If these effects are not produced in a soul and it is not strengthened by prayer, you may take it that this was not Divine favour but indulgence and illusion

---

39 T. omits: "in His Majesty's sight."
40 T. omits: "and I know for a fact that it happens."
41 T. varies here, but I think through a misapprehension, so I do not give its reading.
42 T.: "this grace of attaining union."

coming from the devil, *which he makes us think to be good*, so that we may attach more importance to our honour.

It may be that, when the Lord first grants these favours, the soul will not immediately attain this fortitude. But, if He continues to grant them, He will soon give it fortitude—certainly, at least, as regards forgiveness, if not in the other virtues as well. I cannot believe that a soul which has approached so nearly to Mercy Itself, and has learned to know itself and the greatness of God's pardon, will not immediately and readily forgive, and be mollified and remain on good terms with a person who has done it wrong. For such a soul remembers the consolation and grace which He has shown it, in which it has recognized the signs of great love, and it is glad that the occasion presents itself for showing Him some love in return.

I repeat that I know many persons to whom Our Lord has granted the grace of raising them to supernatural experiences and of giving them this prayer, or contemplation, which has been described; and although I may notice other faults and imperfections in them, I have never seen such a person who had this particular fault, nor do I believe such a person exists, if the favours he has received are of God. If any one of you receives high favours, let her look within herself and see if they are producing these effects, and, if they are not, let her be very fearful,[43] and believe that these consolations are not of God, Who, as I have said, when He visits the soul, always enriches it. That is certain; for, although the grace and the consolations may pass quickly, it can be recognized in due course through the benefits which it bestows on the soul. And, as the good Jesus knows this well, He gives a definite assurance to His Holy Father that we are forgiving our debtors.

[43] T. omits: "If any one . . . fearful," and continues: "Otherwise, believe that these consolations, etc."

CHAPTER 37

Describes the excellence of this prayer called the Paternoster, and the many ways in which we shall find consolation in it.

The sublimity of the perfection of this evangelical prayer is something for which we should give great praise to the Lord.[1] So well composed by the good Master was it, daughters, that each of us may[2] use it in her own way. I am astounded when I consider that in its few words are enshrined all contemplation and perfection,[3] so that if we study it no other book seems necessary. For thus far in the Paternoster the Lord has taught us the whole method of prayer and of high contemplation,[4] from the very beginnings of mental prayer, to Quiet and Union.[5] With so true a foundation to build upon, I could write a great book on prayer if only I knew how to express myself.[6] As you have seen, Our Lord is beginning here to explain to us the effects which it produces, when the favours come from Him.

I have wondered why His Majesty did not expound such obscure and sublime subjects in greater detail so that we might all[7] have understood them. It has occurred to me

[1] E.: "is an amazing thing."
[2] E.: "It is (perfect), indeed, like the Master Who teaches it to us; so it is right, daughters, that each of us should."
[3] E.: "I was astounded to-day when I found all contemplation and perfection hidden in its few words."
[4] E.: "the whole of the highest method of contemplation."
[5] E.: "to the greatest heights of perfect contemplation." The change in V. is significant.
[6] E. reads: "if I had not written about it elsewhere, and also because I dare not enlarge upon it, for if I did it would be wearisome," and completes the paragraph with the sentence: "The Lord, too, is gradually showing us here the effects produced by prayer and contemplation, when they are of God."
[7] E. omits: "obscure and" and "all."

that, as this prayer[8] was meant to be a general one for the use of all, so that everyone could interpret it as he thought right, ask for what he wanted and find comfort in doing so, He left the matter in doubt;[9] and thus contemplatives, who no longer desire earthly things, and persons greatly devoted to God, can ask for the heavenly favours which, through the great goodness of God, may be given to us on earth. Those who still live on earth, and must conform to the customs of their state, may also ask for the bread which they need for their own maintenance and for that of their households, as is perfectly just and right, and they may also ask for other things according as they need them.

(*Blessed be His name for ever and ever. Amen. For His sake I entreat the Eternal Father to forgive my debts and grievous sins: though no one has wronged me, and I have therefore no one to forgive,[10] I have myself need for forgiveness every day. May He give me grace so that every day I may have some petition to lay before Him.*)

The good Jesus, then, has taught us a sublime method of prayer, and begged that, in this our life of exile, we may be like the angels, if we endeavour, with our whole might, to make our actions conform to our words—in short, to be like the children of such a Father, and the brethren of such a Brother. His Majesty knows that if, as I say, our actions and our words are one, the Lord will unfailingly fulfil our petitions, give us His kingdom and help us by means of supernatural gifts, such as the Prayer of Quiet, perfect contemplation and all the other favours which the Lord bestows on our trifling efforts—and everything is trifling which we can achieve and gain by ourselves alone.

It must be realized, however, that these two things—sur-

---

[8] T.: "this doctrine and prayer."
[9] *Lit.*: "He left it thus confused." Here follows in E., in place of the rest of this paragraph, a passage which interrupts the trend of the thought, and therefore, in the text above, is printed in italics and in brackets at the end of this paragraph.
[10] The words "though . . . forgive" are crossed out in the manuscript, as is the following sentence "May He . . . before Him."

rendering our will to God and forgiving others[11]—apply to all. True, some practise them more and some less, as has been said: those who are perfect will surrender their wills like the perfect souls they are and will forgive others with the perfection that has been described.[12] For our own part, sisters, we will do what we can, and the Lord will accept it all. It is as if He were to make a kind of agreement on our behalf with His Eternal Father, and to say: "Do this, Lord, and My brethren shall do that." It is certain that He for His own part will not fail us. Oh, how well He pays us and how limitless are His rewards!

We may say[13] this prayer only once, and yet in such a way that He will know that there is no duplicity about us and that we shall do what we say; and so He will leave us rich. We must never be insincere with Him, for He loves us, in all our dealings with Him, to be honest,[14] and to treat Him frankly and openly, never saying one thing and meaning another; and then He will always give us more than we ask for. Our good Master knows that those who attain real perfection in their petitions will reach this high degree through the favours which the Father will grant them, and is aware that those who are already perfect, or who are on the way to perfection,[15] do not and cannot fear, for they say they have trampled the world beneath their feet, and the Lord of the world is pleased with them. They will derive the greatest hope of His Majesty's pleasure[16] from the effects which He produces in their

11 T. omits "and forgiving others"—presumably by an oversight, as it is essential to the sense.

12 E. omits the foregoing part of this paragraph and reads: "by ourselves alone. But, if we do what we can, it is very certain that the Lord will help us, since His Son begs this (favour) for us, and it is as if, etc."

13 E.: "You, daughters, may say." Throughout the first half of this paragraph, the second person plural is used in E.

14 E.: "for He loves us not to try to bargain with Him, and if we do so we cannot succeed, as He knows everything." The simplified version of V. has greater unity of thought and seems distinctly preferable to E.

15 E., more vaguely: "that those who are here."

16 T.: "derive hope of His pleasure." "Majesty's" is scored through in the text.

souls; absorbed in these joys, they wish they were unable to remember that there is any other world at all, and that they have enemies.

O Eternal Wisdom! O good Teacher! What a wonderful thing it is, daughters, to have a wise and prudent Master who foresees our perils! This is the greatest blessing that the spiritual soul *still on earth* can desire, because it brings complete[17] security. No words could ever exaggerate the importance of this. The Lord, then, saw it was necessary to awaken such souls and to remind them that they have enemies, and how much greater danger they are in if they are unprepared,[18] and, since if they fall it will be from a greater height, how much more help they need from the Eternal Father. So, lest they should fail to realize their danger and suffer deception, He offers these petitions so necessary to us all while we live in this exile: "And lead us not, Lord, into temptation, but deliver us from evil."

CHAPTER 38

Treats of the great need which we have to beseech the Eternal Father to grant us what we ask in these words: "Et ne nos inducas in tentationem, sed libera nos a malo."[1] Explains certain temptations. This chapter is noteworthy.

There are great things here for us to meditate upon,[2] sisters, and to learn to understand as we pray. Remember I

---

[17] Thus E. V.: "great."
[18] E. ends the chapter thus: "and how much more help they need from the eternal Father if they are not to fall, or walk without finding themselves deceived. So He makes these petitions." In E., the petition "And lead . . . evil" stands at the beginning of the following chapter.
[1] "And lead us not into temptation, but deliver us from evil."
[2] T.: "to note."

consider it quite certain that those who attain perfection[3] do not ask the Lord to deliver them from trials, temptations, persecutions and conflicts[4]—and that is another sure and striking sign that these favours and this contemplation which His Majesty gives them[5] are coming from the Spirit of the Lord and are not illusions. For, as I said a little way back,[6] perfect souls *are in no way repelled by trials, but rather* desire them and pray for them and love them. They are like soldiers: the more wars there are, the better they are pleased, because they hope to emerge from them with the greater riches.[7] If there are no wars, they serve for their pay,[8] but they know they will not get very far on that.

Believe me, sisters, the soldiers of Christ—namely, those who experience contemplation and practise prayer[9]—are always ready for the hour of conflict. They are never very much[10] afraid of their open enemies, for they know who they are and are sure that their strength can never prevail against the strength which they themselves have been given by the Lord: they will always be victorious and gain great riches,[11] so they will never turn their backs on the battle. Those whom they fear, and fear rightly, and from whom they always beg the Lord to deliver them, are enemies who are treacherous, devils who[12] transform themselves and come and visit them in the disguise of angels of light. The soul fails to recognize them until they have done it a great deal of harm; they suck our life-blood and put an end to our virtues[13] and we go on

---

[3] E.: "attain this point of prayer."
[4] T. omits "persecutions."
[5] E.: "that these (things)."
[6] E. omits: "as . . . back."
[7] *Lit.*: "gains", as also in the next paragraph. E. has: "because they have hopes of becoming rich." The reference in both manuscripts is, of course, to the spoils and booty of war.
[8] E.: "they remain (content) with their pay."
[9] E.: "who practise prayer." T.: "who experience contemplation."
[10] "Very much" is not in E.
[11] T. has "emerge" for "be." E.: "and with gains, and rich." V.: "and with great gains." Cf. p. 249, n. 7 above.
[12] E.: "are devils who are treacherous and."
[13] E.: "to our lives."

yielding to temptation without knowing it. From these enemies let us pray the Lord often, in the Paternoster, to deliver
us: may He not allow us to run into temptations which deceive us; may their poison be detected; and may light and
truth[14] not be hidden from us. How rightly does our good
Master teach us to pray for this and pray for it in our name!

Consider, daughters, in how many ways these enemies do
us harm. Do not suppose that the sole danger lies in their
making us believe that the consolations and the favours
which they can counterfeit to us come from God.[15] This, I
think, in a way, is the least harmful thing they can do;[16] it
may even help some whom this sensible devotion entices to
spend more time in prayer and thus to make greater progress.[17] Being ignorant that these consolations come from the
devil, and knowing themselves to be unworthy of such favours, they will never cease to give thanks to God and will
feel the greater obligation to serve Him; further, they will
strive to prepare themselves for more favours which the Lord
may grant them, since they believe them to come from His
hand.[18]

Always strive after humility, sisters, and try to realize that
you are not worthy of these graces, and do not seek them. It
is because many souls do this, I feel sure, that the devil loses
them: he thinks that he has caused their ruin, but out of the
evil which he has been trying to do the Lord brings good. For
His Majesty regards our intention, which is to please Him
and serve Him and keep near to Him in prayer, and the Lord
is faithful. We shall do well to be cautious, and not to let
our humility break down or to become in any way vainglori-

---

[14] E.: "and may truth." Throughout this paragraph E. prefers the
second person plural to the first.

[15] E.: "believe, when they give us consolations, that these come
from God."

[16] E.: " This is the least harmful thing."

[17] E. reads: "often, indeed, they will lead you to make greater
progress and to spend more time in prayer," and continues: "Where
they can do great harm to ourselves and to others is in making us
believe, etc." (See next footnote but one).

[18] "This is doctrine of St. Augustine," adds P. Báñez in the margin.

ous. Entreat the Lord to deliver you from this, daughters, and you need then have no fear that His Majesty will allow you to be comforted much by anyone but Himself.

Where the devil can do great harm without our realizing it is in making us believe[19] that we possess virtues which we do not: that is pestilential. For, when consolations and favours come to us, we feel that we are doing nothing but receive, and have the greater obligation to serve; but when we suffer from this other delusion we think that we are giving and serving, and that the Lord will be obliged to reward us; and this, little by little, does us a great deal of harm. On the one hand, our humility is weakened, while, on the other, we neglect to cultivate that virtue, believing we have already acquired it. *We think we are walking safely, when, without realizing it, we stumble, and fall into a pit from which we cannot escape. Though we may not consciously have committed any mortal sin which would have sent us infallibly to hell, we have sprained our ankles and cannot continue on that road which I began to speak about and which I have not forgotten. You can imagine how much progress will be made by anyone who is at the bottom of a huge pit: it will be the end of him altogether and he will be lucky if he escapes falling right down to hell: at best, he will never get on with his journey. This being so, he will be unable to help either himself or others. It will be a bad thing for others, too, for, once the pit has been dug, a great many passers-by may fall into it. Only if the person who has fallen in gets out of it and fills it up with earth will further harm to himself and others be prevented. But I warn you that this temptation is full of peril. I know a great deal about it from experience, so I can describe it to you, though not as well as I should like. What can we do about it, sisters? To me the best thing seems to be what our Master teaches us: to pray, and to beseech the Eternal Father not to allow us to fall into temptation.*[20]

[19] E. takes up the thread here.
[20] No more of what follows in the V. text of this chapter is found in E. The paragraphs in italics at the end of the chapter, however, represent the continuation in E.: they were inserted in the text by

There is something else, too, which I want to tell you. If we think the Lord has given us a certain grace, we must understand that it is a blessing which we have received but which He may take away from us again, as indeed, in the great providence of God, often happens. Have you never observed this yourselves, sisters? I certainly have: sometimes I think I am extremely detached, and, in fact, when it comes to the test, I am; yet at other times I find I have such attachment to things which the day before I should perhaps have scoffed at that I hardly know myself. At some other time I seem to have so much courage that I should not quail at anything I was asked to do in order to serve God, and, when I am tested, I find that I really can do these things. And then on the next day I discover that I should not have the courage to kill an ant for God's sake if I were to meet with any opposition about it. Sometimes it seems not to matter in the least if people complain or speak ill of me, and, when the test comes, I still feel like this—indeed, I even get pleasure from it. And then there come days when a single word distresses me and I long to leave the world altogether, for everything in it seems to weary me. And I am not the only person to be like this, for I have noticed the same thing in many people better than myself, so I know it can happen.

That being so, who can say that he possesses any virtue, or that he is rich, if at the time when he most needs this virtue he finds himself devoid of it? No, sisters: let us rather think of ourselves as lacking it and not run into debt without having the means of repayment. Our treasure must come from elsewhere and we never know when God will leave us in this prison of our misery without giving us any. If others, thinking we are good, bestow favours and honours upon us, both they and we shall look foolish when, as I say, it becomes clear that our virtues are only lent us. The truth is that, if we serve the Lord with humility, He will sooner or later succour us in our needs. But, if we are not strong in this virtue, the Lord

Luis de León, who omitted the paragraph beginning: "The devil has yet another temptation."

will leave us to ourselves, as they say, at every step. This is a great favour on His part, for it helps us to realize fully that we have nothing which has not been given us.

And now you must take note of this other piece of advice. The devil makes us believe that we have some virtue—patience, let us say—because we have determination and make continual resolutions to suffer a great deal for God's sake. We really and truly believe that we would suffer all this, and the devil encourages us in the belief, and so we are very pleased. I advise you to place no reliance on these virtues: we ought not to think that we know anything about them beyond their names, or to imagine that the Lord has given them to us, until we come to the test. For it may be that at the first annoying word which people say to you your patience will fall to the ground. Whenever you have frequently to suffer, praise God for beginning to teach you this virtue, and force yourself to suffer patiently, for this is a sign that He wants you to repay Him for the virtue which He is giving you, and you must think of it only as a deposit, as has already been said.

The devil has yet another temptation, which is to make us appear very poor in spirit: we are in the habit of saying that we want nothing and care nothing about anything: but as soon as the chance comes of our being given something, even though we do not in the least need it, all our poverty of spirit disappears. Accustoming ourselves to saying this goes far towards making us think it true. It is very important always to be on the watch and to realize that this is a temptation, both in the things I have referred to and in many others. For when the Lord really gives one of these solid virtues, it seems to bring all the rest in its train: that is a very well-known fact. But I advise you once more, even if you think you possess it, to suspect that you may be mistaken;[21] for the person who is truly humble is always doubtful about his own virtues; very often they seem more genuine and of greater worth when he sees them in his neighbours.

[21] T.: "deceived."

The devil makes you think you are poor,[22] *and he has some reason for doing so, because you have made (with the lips, of course) a vow of poverty, as have some other people who practise prayer. I say "with the lips" because, if before making the vow we really meant in our hearts what we were going to say, the devil could not possibly lead us into that temptation —not even in twenty years, or in our entire lifetime—for we should see that we were deceiving the whole world, and ourselves into the bargain. Well, we make our vow of poverty, and then one of us, believing herself all the time to be keeping it, says: "I do not want anything, but I am having this because I cannot do without it: after all, if I am to serve God, I must live, and He wants us to keep these bodies of ours alive." So the devil, in his angelic disguise, suggests to her that there are a thousand different things which she needs and that they are all good for her. And all the time he is persuading her to believe that she is still being true to her vow and possesses the virtue of poverty and that what she has done is no more than her duty.*

And now let us take a test case, for we can only get to the truth of this by keeping a continual watch on ourselves: then, if there is any cause for anxiety on our part, we shall at once recognize the symptoms. Here is someone who has a larger income than he needs—I mean, needs for the necessaries of life—and, though he could do with a single manservant, he keeps three. Yet, when he is sued in the courts in connection with a part of his property, or some poor peasant omits to pay him his dues, he gets as upset and excited about it as if his life were at stake. He says he must look after his property or he will lose it, and considers that that justifies him. I do not suggest that he ought to neglect his property: whether or no things go well with him, he should look after it. But a person whose profession of poverty is a genuine one makes so little account of these things that, although for various reasons he attends to his own interests, he never worries about them, because he never supposes he will lose everything he has; and, even if he should do so, he would consider it of no

---

[22] Cf. p. 251, n. 20, above.

great moment, for the matter is one of secondary importance to him and not his principal concern. His thoughts rise high above it and he has to make an effort to occupy himself with it at all.

Now monks and nuns are demonstrably poor—they must be so, for they possess nothing: sometimes because there is nothing for them to possess. But if a religious of the type just mentioned is given anything, it is most unlikely that he will think it superfluous. He always likes to have something laid by; if he can get a habit of good cloth, he will not ask for one of coarse material. He likes to have some trifle, if only books, which he can pawn or sell, for if he falls ill he will need extra comforts. Sinner that I am! Is this the vow of poverty that you took? Stop worrying about yourself and leave God to provide for you, come what may. If you are going about trying to provide for your own future, it would be less trouble for you to have a fixed income. This may not involve any sin, but it is as well that we should learn to recognize our imperfections, so that we can see how far we are from possessing the virtue of poverty, which we must beg and obtain from God. If we think we already possess it, we shall grow careless, and, what is worse, we shall be deceiving ourselves.

The same thing happens with regard to humility.[23] We think that we have no desire for honour and that we care nothing about anything; but as soon as our honour comes to be slighted in some detail our feelings and actions at once show that we are not humble at all. If an opportunity occurs for us to gain more honour, we do not reject it; even those who are poor, and to whom I have just referred, are anxious to have as much profit as possible—God grant we may not go so far as actually to seek it! We always have phrases on our lips about wanting nothing, and caring nothing about anything, and we honestly think them to be true, and get so used to repeating them that we come to believe them more and more firmly. But when, as I say, we keep on the watch, we

---

[23] It will be noticed that this paragraph is similar to the last paragraph in the text of V. (p. 254, above). The differences, however, are so wide that each of the two is given as it stands.

realize that this is a temptation, as regards both the virtue I have spoken of and all the rest; for when we really have one of these solid virtues, it brings all the rest in its train: that is a very well-known fact.

CHAPTER 39

Continues the same subject and gives counsels concerning different kinds of temptation. Suggests two remedies by which we may be freed from temptations.[1]

Beware also, daughters, of certain kinds of humility which the devil inculcates in us and which make us very uneasy about the gravity of our *past* sins.[2] There are many ways in which he is accustomed to depress us so that in time we withdraw from Communion and give up our private prayer, because the devil suggests to us that we are not worthy to engage in it. When we come to the Most Holy Sacrament, we spend the time during which we ought to be receiving grace in wondering whether we are properly prepared or no. The thing gets to such a pass that a soul can be made to be-

[1] A marginal addition made, in the autograph, to the title by another hand reads: "This chapter is very noteworthy, both for those tempted by false kinds of humility and for confessors." This is found in T. and in most of the editions.
[2] E. puts the suggestions, vividly but bluntly and briefly, in *oratio recta*, and abbreviates what follows, continuing thus: ". . . past sins. 'Am I worthy to approach the Sacrament?' 'Am I in a good disposition?' 'I am not fit to live among good people.' Things like these, when they come with tranquillity, joy and pleasure, and are suggested by our own knowledge of ourselves, are to be highly esteemed. But if they are accompanied by turmoil, unrest and depression of soul, and you cannot quiet your thoughts, you may be sure it is a temptation, and you must not count yourselves humble, for it does not come from humility at all. This is what happens, etc. (p. 257)."

lieve that, through being what it is, it has been forsaken by God, and thus it almost doubts His mercy. Everything such a person does appears to her to be dangerous, and all the service she renders, however good it may be, seems to her fruitless. She loses confidence and sits with her hands in her lap because she thinks she can do nothing well and that what is good in others is wrong in herself.

Pay great attention, daughters, to this point which I shall now make, because sometimes thinking yourselves so wicked may be humility and virtue and at other times a very great temptation. I have had experience of this, so I know it is true. Humility, however deep it be, neither disquiets nor troubles nor disturbs the soul; it is accompanied by peace, joy and tranquillity. Although, on realizing how wicked we are, we can see clearly[3] that we deserve to be in hell, and are distressed by our sinfulness, and rightly think that everyone should hate us, yet, if our humility is true,[4] this distress is accompanied by an interior peace and joy of which we should not like to be deprived. Far from disturbing or depressing the soul, it enlarges it and makes it fit to serve God better. The other kind of distress only disturbs and upsets the mind and troubles the soul, so grievous is it. I think the devil is anxious for us to believe that we are humble, and, if he can, to lead us to distrust God.

When you find yourselves in this state, cease thinking, so far as you can, of your own wretchedness, and think of the mercy of God and of His love and His sufferings for us. If your state of mind is the result of temptation, you will be unable to do even this, for it will not allow you to quiet your thoughts or to fix them on anything but will only weary you the more: it will be a great thing if you can recognize it as a temptation. This is what happens[5] when we perform excessive penances in order to make ourselves believe[6] that, be-

---

[3] T. omits: "clearly."
[4] T.: "if this distress is true humility."
[5] Here E. continues (see p. 256, n. 2, above). T. reads: "Thus, if (it is a question of) performing excessive penances, he [the devil?] will contrive to make us believe, etc."
[6] E.: "to put it into our minds."

cause of what we are doing, we are more penitent than others. If we conceal our penances from our confessor or superior, or if we are told to give them up and do not obey, that is a clear case of temptation.[7] Always try to obey, however much it may hurt you to do so, for that is the greatest possible perfection.[8]

There is another very dangerous kind of temptation: a feeling of security caused by the belief that we shall never again return to our past faults and to the pleasures of the world. "I know all about these things now," we say, "and I realize that they all come to an end and I get more pleasure from the things of God." If this temptation comes to beginners it is very serious; for, having this sense of security, they think nothing of running once more into occasions of sin. They soon come up against these—and then God preserve them from falling back farther than before![9] The devil, seeing that here are souls which may do him harm and be of great help to others, does all in his power to prevent them from rising again.[10] However many consolations and pledges of love the

[7] E.: "If, when your confessor or superior tells you not to do a thing, (his advice) hurts you and you do it again, that is a clear case of temptation. This, as I say, is so in everything: but be specially careful not to forget this particular thing." V., as well as E., has the second person in this passage, but as V. has the first person earlier in the paragraph, this is continued in the translation for the sake of uniformity.

[8] This sentence is not found in E.

[9] E. begins this paragraph: "There is also a feeling of security [caused by] the belief that I shall never again return to the past, that I know now what the world is. This temptation is the worst of all, especially if it comes to beginners, for it makes you run into occasions of sin, and thus you come up against them, and then God grant that you rise after this fall!"

[10] T., after omitting "and be of great help to others" has "does all in his power to deceive them". E. continues: "Now as to consolations, if the Lord brings you to contemplation, and gives you a special share in Himself, and pledges of His love for you, take care to begin and end with self-examination, to walk warily and to discuss everything with someone who understands you; for here he [the devil] is wont to launch his attacks in different ways. There are many books full of such advice as this, but all of them together cannot give complete security, for we cannot understand ourselves." This

Lord may give you, therefore, you must never be so sure of yourselves that you cease to be afraid of falling back again, and you must keep yourselves from occasions of sin.

Do all you can to discuss these graces and favours with someone who can give you light and have no secrets from him. However sublime your contemplation may be, take great care both to begin and to end every period of prayer with self-examination. If these favours come from God, you will do this more frequently, without either taking or needing any advice from me, for such favours bring humility with them and always leave us with more light by which we may see our own unworthiness. I will say no more here, for you will find many books which give this kind of advice. I have said all this because I have had experience of the matter and have sometimes found myself in difficulties of this nature. Nothing that can be said about it, however, will give us complete security.

What, then, Eternal Father, can we do but flee to Thee and beg Thee not to allow these enemies of ours to lead us into temptation?[11] If attacks are made upon us publicly, we shall easily surmount them, with Thy help.[12] But how can we be ready for these treacherous assaults,[13] my God? We need constantly to pray for Thy help. Show us, Lord, some way of recognizing them and guarding against them.[14] Thou knowest that there are not many who walk along this road, and if so many fears are to beset them, there will be far fewer.

What a strange thing it is! You might suppose that the devil never tempted those who do not walk along the road of prayer![15] People get a greater shock when deception overtakes a single one of the many persons who are striving to be perfect[16] than when a hundred thousand others are deceived

---

passage stands for the remainder of the paragraph and the whole of the next.

11 E.: "Then, Eternal Father, lead us not into this temptation."

12 E.: "Let attacks be made on us publicly if we have Thy help."

13 *Lit.*: "these treasons." T.: "these temptations."

14 E.: "some sign, so that we may be able to walk without always being surprised."

15 E.: "who do not practise prayer."

16 E.: "a single one on this road."

and fall into open sin, whom there is no need to look at in order to see if they are good or evil, for Satan can be seen at their side a thousand leagues away.[17] But as a matter of fact people are right about this, for very few who say the Paternoster in the way that has been described[18] are deceived by the devil, so that, if the deception of one of them causes surprise, that is because it is a new and an unusual thing. For human nature is such that we scarcely notice what we see frequently[19] but are astounded at what we see seldom or hardly at all.[20] And the devils themselves encourage this astonishment, for if a single soul attains perfection it robs them of many others.

It is so strange, I repeat, that I am not surprised if people are amazed at it; for, unless they are altogether at fault, they are much safer on this road than on any other, just as people who watch a bull-fight from the grand-stand are safer than the men who expose themselves to a thrust from the bull's horns. This comparison, which I heard somewhere, seems to me very exact. Do not be afraid to walk on these roads, sisters, for there are many of them in the life of prayer—and some people get most help by using one of them and others by using another, as I have said. This road is a safe one and you will the more readily escape from temptation if you are near the Lord than if you are far away from Him. Beseech and entreat this of Him, as you do so many times each day in the Paternoster.[21]

----

[17] E.: "than when a hundred thousand are seen to be making, by other roads, straight for hell."
[18] E.: "who say the Paternoster with this attentiveness."
[19] E.: "what we see daily."
[20] E.: "at what has never happened."
[21] This paragraph, from E., was included by Luis de León in his edition.

CHAPTER 40

Describes how, by striving always to walk in the love and fear of God, we shall travel safely amid all these temptations.

Show us, then, O our good Master, some way in which we may live through this most dangerous warfare without frequent surprise. The best way that we can do this, daughters, is to use the love and fear given us by His Majesty. For love will make us quicken our steps, while fear will make us look where we are setting our feet so that we shall not fall on a road where there are so many obstacles. Along that road all living creatures must pass, and if we have these two things we shall certainly not be deceived.[1]

You will ask me how you can tell if you *really* have these two very, very great virtues.[2] You are right to ask, for we can never be quite definite and certain about it; if we were sure that we possessed love, we should be sure that we were in a state of grace.[3] But you know, sisters, there are some indications which are in no way secret but so evident that even a blind man, as people say, could see them.[4] You may not wish

[1] E. begins the chapter: "And take this advice, which comes, not from me, but from your Master. Strive to walk with love and fear, and I guarantee your safety: love will make you quicken your steps; fear will make you look where you are setting your feet so that you may not fall. With these two things, it is quite certain that you will not be deceived."

[2] *Lit.*: "these two virtues, so great, so great." This repetition does not occur in T., which reads "these very great virtues," nor in E., which continues: "It becomes evident at once: even a blind man, as people say, could see them: they are not things which are in any way secret. You may not wish, etc."

[3] "Which is not possible save by special privilege," adds P. Báñez, marginally. He also adds words in several places in this chapter to complete the sense of its rather numerous ellipses. These are not noted except where they affect the translation.

[4] V. has: "which even blind men seem to see." The reading in the text is based on E.

to heed them, but they cry so loud for notice that they make quite an uproar, for there are not many who possess them to the point of perfection[5] and thus they are the more readily noticed. Love and fear of God! These are two strong castles whence we can wage war on the world and on the devils.

Those who really love God love all good, seek all good, help forward all good, praise all good, and invariably join forces with good men and help and defend them.[6] They love only truth and things worthy of love. Do you think it possible that anyone who really and truly loves God can love vanities, riches, worldly pleasures[7] or honours? Can he engage in strife or feel envy? No; for his only desire is to please the Beloved. Such persons die with longing for Him to love them and so they will give their lives to learn how they may please Him better.[8] Will they hide their love? No: if their love for God is genuine love they cannot.[9] Why, think of Saint Paul or the Magdalen. One of these—Saint Paul—found in three days that he was sick with love. The Magdalen discovered this on the very first day.[10] And how certain of it they were! For there are degrees of love for God, which shows itself in proportion to its strength. If there is little of it, it shows itself but little; if there is much, it shows itself a great deal.[11] But it always shows itself, whether little or much, provided it is real love for God.

But to come to what we are chiefly treating of now[12]—the deceptions and illusions practised against contemplatives by the devil[13]—such souls have no little love; for had they not a

---

[5] "To the point of [*lit*.: "With"] perfection" is not found in E.

[6] E.: "and join forces with good men and invariably defend them."

[7] E.: "worldly things." In the next sentence T. omits "or feel envy."

[8] T. continues: "For their love for God, if it is genuine love, cannot possibly be very much concealed. Why, etc."

[9] E.: "No, it is impossible."

[10] E.: "in one [day]."

[11] E. ends the paragraph here.

[12] E.: "to what we are speaking of now." T.: "to what we are treating of now."

[13] E.: "against those who rise to perfect contemplation and to high things."

great deal they would not be contemplatives,[14] and so their love shows itself plainly and in many ways. Being a great fire, it cannot fail to give out a very bright light. If they have not much love, they should proceed with many misgivings and realize that they have great cause for fear; and they should try to find out what is wrong with them, say their prayers, walk in humility and beseech the Lord not to lead them into temptation, into which, I fear, they will certainly fall[15] unless they bear this sign. But if they walk humbly and strive to discover the truth and do as their confessor bids them and tell him the plain truth, then *the Lord is faithful, and,* as has been said, by using the very means with which he had thought to give them death, the devil will give them life, with however many fantasies and illusions he tries to deceive them.[16] *If they submit to the teaching of the Church, they need not fear; whatever fantasies and illusions the devil may invent, he will at once betray his presence.*

But if you feel this love for God which I have spoken of, and the fear which I shall now describe, you may go on your way with happiness and tranquillity. In order to disturb the soul and keep it from enjoying these great blessings, the devil will suggest to it a thousand false fears and will persuade other people to do the same; for if he cannot win souls he will at least[17] try to make them lose something, and among the losers will be those who might have gained greatly had they believed that such great favours, bestowed upon so miserable a creature, come from God,[18] and that it is possible for them to be thus bestowed, for sometimes we seem to forget His past mercies.

Do you suppose that it is of little use to the devil to sug-

14 "For . . . contemplatives" is not found in E.
15 The verb, in both E. and V., is in the present tense. E. is more downright than V., omitting "I fear". T. has "see" for "bear."
16 E.: "and do as their confessor bids them, the Lord is faithful: be sure that, if you walk without malice and feel no pride, the devil will give you life by using the very means with which he had thought to give you death." T. has "things" (*cosas*) for "fantasies" (*cocos*).
17 T. has "does not try to" for "cannot" and omits "at least."
18 E. ends the paragraph here.

gest these fears?[19] No, it is most useful to him,[20] for there are two *well-known* ways in which he can make use of this means to harm us, *to say nothing of others*. First, he can make those who listen to him[21] fearful of engaging in prayer, because they think that they will be deceived. Secondly, he can dissuade many from approaching God who, as I have said, see that He is so good that He will hold intimate converse with sinners.[22] Many such souls think that He will treat them in the same way, and they are right:[23] I myself know certain persons inspired in this way who began the habit of prayer and in a short time became truly devout and received[24] great favours from the Lord.

Therefore, sisters, when you see someone to whom the Lord is granting these favours, praise Him fervently,[25] yet do not imagine that she is safe, but aid her with more prayer, for no one can be safe in this life amid the engulfing dangers of this stormy sea.[26] Wherever this love is, then, you will not fail to recognize it; I do not know how it could be concealed. For they say that it is impossible for us to hide our love even for creatures, and that, the more we try to conceal it, the more clearly is it revealed. And yet this is so worthless that it hardly deserves the name of love, for it is founded upon nothing at all:[27] *it is loathsome, indeed, to make this comparison.* How, then, could a love *like God's*[28] be con-

---

[19] E.: "to throw doubt on this."

[20] E. begins this sentence: "He gains a very great deal."

[21] "And fear him," adds P. Báñez, marginally.

[22] E.: "that He can hold such close converse with a wicked person."

[23] So E. V. is much less explicit: "He makes them covetous, and they are right [to be so], etc."

[24] E.: "persons who became truly devout and in a short time received."

[25] E.: "when you recognize this love in one of yourselves, praise God for it and give Him thanks." T.: "give fervent praise."

[26] E.: "of this sea on which she is sailing."

[27] E. is more detailed, but hardly, I think, so effective: "For it is impossible for the love of a mere man or woman to be hidden; the more they try to hide it, the clearer does it seem to become. And yet love for which there is no object but a worm does not deserve the name, for it is founded upon nothing at all."

[28] So E., and there is nothing in B. to suggest that this sense was

cealed—so strong, so righteous, continually increasing, never seeing cause for ceasing to manifest itself, and resting upon the firm foundation of the love which is its reward? As to the reality of this reward there can be no doubt, for it is manifest in Our Lord's great sorrows, His trials, the shedding of His blood and even the loss of His life.[29] Certainly, then, there is no doubt as to this love.[30] *It is indeed love, and deserves that name, of which worldly vanities have robbed it.* God help me! How different must the one love be from the other to those who have experience of both!

May His Majesty be pleased to grant us *to experience* this before He takes us from this life, for it will be a great thing at the hour of death, *when we are going we know not whither*, to realize that we shall be judged by One Whom we have loved above all things,[31] *and with a passion that makes us entirely forget ourselves.* Once our debts have been paid we shall be able to walk in safety. We shall not be going into a foreign land, but into our own country, for it belongs to Him Whom we have loved so truly[32] and Who Himself loves us. *For this love of His, besides its other properties, is better than all earthly affection in that, if we love Him, we are quite sure that He loves us too.* Remember, my daughters, the greatness of the gain which comes from this love, and of our loss if we do not possess it, for in that case we shall be delivered into the hands of the tempter, hands so cruel and so hostile to all that is good, and so friendly to all that is evil.

What will become of the poor soul when it falls into these hands after emerging from all the pains and trials of death? How little rest it will have![33] How it will be torn as it goes down to hell! What swarms and varieties of serpents it will

---

later rejected. But the context in both E. and V. would favour a reading "love like that *for* God."

29 P. Báñez adds: "for our sakes."

30 E.: "so strong, resting upon such a foundation, having so much to love, and so many causes for loving?"

31 E.: "to have loved . . . the Lord Who is to judge us."

32 E. ends the sentence here.

33 E. is more forcible, with its characteristically Teresan repetition: "Miserable (*negro*) the rest it will have—miserable!"

meet! How dreadful is that place! How miserable that lodging! Why, a pampered person (and most of those who go to hell are that) can hardly bear to spend a single night in a bad inn: what, then, will be the feelings of that wretched soul when it is condemned to such an inn as this and has to spend eternity there?[34] Let us not try to pamper ourselves, daughters. We are quite well off here: there is only a single night for us to spend in this bad inn. Let us praise God[35] and strive to do penance in this life. How sweet will be the death of those who have done penance for all their sins and have not to go to purgatory! It may be that they will begin to enjoy glory even in this world, and will know no fear, but only peace.

Even if we do not attain to this, sisters, let us beseech God that, if in due course we must suffer these pains,[36] it may be with a hope of emerging from them. Then we shall suffer them willingly and lose neither the friendship nor the grace of God. May He grant us these in this life so that we may not unwittingly fall into temptation.

CHAPTER 41

Speaks of the fear of God and of how we must keep ourselves from venial sins.

How I have enlarged on this subject! Yet I have not said as much about it as I should like; for it is a delightful thing to

---

[34] *Lit.*: "to an inn for ever, *ever*, for eternity." The repetition of "ever" (*siempre*) reminds one of the famous reminiscence of St. Teresa's childhood, to be found in her *Life*, Chap. I (Vol. I, p. 11, above).

[35] E. ends the chapter thus: "Let us praise God and ever be careful to beseech Him to keep us, and all sinners, in His hand, and not to lead us into these hidden temptations."

[36] T.: "And if it is possible to attain to this, sisters, it will be very cowardly (of us) not to do so. Let us beseech God that, if we must go and suffer (these) pains."

talk about this love *of God*. What, then, must it be to possess it? May the Lord, for His own sake, give it me![1] *May I not depart from this life till there is nothing in it that I desire, till I have forgotten what it is to love anything but Thee and till I deny the name of love to any other kind of affection—for all love is false but love of Thee, and, unless the foundations of a building are true, the building itself will not endure.* I do not know why it surprises us to hear people say: "So-and-so has made me a poor return for something." "Someone else does not like me." I laugh to myself when I hear that. What other sort of return do you expect him to make you? And why do you expect anyone to like you? These things will show you what the world is; your love itself becomes your punishment, and the reason why you are so upset about it is that your will strongly resents your involving it in such childish pastimes.[2]

Let us now come to the fear of God—*though I am sorry not to be able to say a little about this worldly love, which, for my sins, I know well and should like to acquaint you with, so that you may free yourself from it for ever.* But I am straying from my subject and shall have to pass on.

This fear of God is another thing with which those who possess it and those who have to do with them[3] are very familiar. But I should like you to realize that at first it is not very deep, save in a few people, to whom, as I have said, the Lord grants such great favours as to make them rich in virtues *and to raise them, in a very short time, to great heights of prayer.*[4] It is not recognizable, therefore, at first, in everyone.[5] As it increases, it grows stronger each day, and then, of course, it can be recognized, for those who possess it forsake sin, and occasions of sin, and bad company, and other

---

[1] E.: "O my Lord, do Thou give it me."
[2] Though not occurring in V., this graphic and effective passage is found in all the printed editions in the *Way of perfection*.
[3] E.: "those who are around them."
[4] E. differs considerably in the wording of this sentence, but the thought is almost identical with that of V.
[5] E.: "[In these persons], of course, it is easily recognizable."

signs of it are visible in them.[6] When at last the soul attains to contemplation, of which we are chiefly treating at the moment, its fear of God is plainly revealed, and its love is not dissembled even outwardly. However narrowly we watch such persons, we shall not find them growing careless; for, close as our watch on them may be, the Lord so preserves them that they would not[7] knowingly commit one venial sin even to further their own interests, and, as for mortal sin, they fear it like fire. These are the illusions, sisters, which I should like you always to fear; let us always beseech God that temptation may not be strong enough for us to offend Him[8] but that He may send it to us in proportion to the strength which He gives us to conquer it. *If we keep a pure conscience, we can suffer little or no harm.*[9] That is the important point; and that is the fear which I hope will never be taken from us, for it is that fear which will stand us in good stead.

Oh, what a great thing it is not to have offended the Lord, so that the servants and slaves of hell[10] may be kept under control! In the end, whether willingly or no, we shall all serve Him—they by compulsion and we with our whole heart. So

[6] E.: "But where favours do not increase in the way I have described, where after one visit [from God] the soul is left rich in all the virtues, they increase little by little. But the love and fear of God always reveal themselves the more as they become more excellent, for those who possess them forsake sin, and occasions of sin, and bad company, and other signs of it are visible in them."

[7] E.: "But when the soul has attained the growth in prayer of which we are now speaking, its fear of God is not dissembled, but becomes very evident, and it will not be found to be growing careless in outward things, however narrowly it may be watched, but God so preserves it that its great anxiety not to offend Him is clearly evident. For they would not."

[8] E. ends the sentence here.

[9] E. adds: "Everything will be a source of fresh loss to him." By "him" must be meant the devil, who has not, however, been previously mentioned in this paragraph.

[10] *Lit.* "the infernal slaves." In E. and in V. the sentence ends here. The five words which follow appear only in T. and were adopted by Luis de León to complete the sense. T. has "vassals the devils" for "slaves of hell", which it substitutes for a deleted phrase "animal slaves," probably an error of the copyist for "infernal slaves."

that, if we please Him, they will be kept at bay and will do nothing that can harm us, however much they lead us into temptation and lay secret snares for us.[11]

Keep this in mind, for it is very important advice, so do not neglect it[12] until you find you have such a fixed determination not to offend the Lord that you would rather lose a thousand lives, *and be persecuted by the whole world*, than commit one mortal sin,[13] and until you are most careful not to commit venial sins. I am referring now to sins committed knowingly:[14] as far as those of the other kind are concerned, who can fail to commit them frequently? But it is one thing to commit a sin knowingly and after long deliberation, and quite another to do it so suddenly that the knowledge of its being a venial sin and its commission are one and the same thing, and we hardly realize[15] what we have done, *although we do to some extent realize it*. From any sin, however small, committed with full knowledge, may God deliver us,[16] especially since we are sinning against so great a Sovereign and realizing that He is watching us! That seems to me to be a sin committed of malice aforethought; it is as though one were to say: "Lord, although this displeases Thee, I shall do it. I know that Thou seest it and I know that Thou wouldst not have me do it; but, though I understand this, I would rather follow my own whim and desire[17] than Thy will." If we commit a sin in this way, however slight,[18] it seems to me that our offence is not small but very, very great.

---

11 E.: "nothing that will not bring us greater advantage."
12 E.: "Keep this in mind as to interior matters and do not neglect it." The words "and [so] do not neglect it" are not found in the Spanish but were added by Luis de León.
13 E. reads "venial" for "mortal" and ends the sentence at "sin".
14 E.: "[committed] after definite consideration—I mean knowingly."
15 E.: "that until some little fault has been committed—until it is done—we seem not to have realized."
16 E. ends the sentence here and continues: "I do not know how we are bold enough to sin against so great a Lord, even in the smallest thing—though nothing is small when it is committed against so great a Sovereign, and we realize, etc."
17 E. omits: "and desire."
18 E. omits: "however slight."

For the love of God, sisters, *never be careless about this—and, glory be to the Lord, you are not so at present.* If you would gain this fear of God, *remember the importance of habit and of starting to realize what a serious thing it is to offend Him. Do your utmost to learn this and to turn it over in your minds;*[19] for our life, and much more than our life, depends upon this virtue being firmly planted in our souls. Until you are conscious within your soul of possessing it,[20] you need always to exercise very great care and to avoid all occasions of sin and any kind of company which will not help you to get nearer to God. Be most careful, in all that you do, to bend your will to it; see that all you say tends to edification; flee from all places where there is conversation which is not pleasing to God. Much care is needed if this fear *of God* is to be thoroughly impressed upon[21] the soul; though, if one has true love, it is quickly acquired.[22] Even when the soul has that firm inward determination which I have described, not to offend God[23] for the sake of any creature, or *from fear of a thousand deaths,* it may subsequently fall from time to time,[24] for we are weak and cannot trust ourselves, and, the more determined we are, the less self-confidence we should have, for confidence must come from God.[25] But, when we find ourselves in this state, we need not feel constrained or depressed, for the Lord will help us and the habits we have formed will be of assistance to us so that we shall not offend Him;[26] we shall be able to walk in holy freedom, and asso-

---

[19] V. reads: "If you would gain this fear of God, think how serious a thing it is to offend God, and turn it over often in your minds." E. ends the sentence: "so that you may keep planting in your hearts a very wholesome fear of God."

[20] So E. V. has: "Until you (are really conscious that you) possess it. The bracketed words were deleted by the author.

[21] E.: "is to be planted in."

[22] E.: "His Majesty quickly bestows it."

[23] E.: "not to commit a venial sin."

[24] E.: "it may subsequently do so."

[25] "Do not be discouraged," interpolates T. here, "for perhaps He permits it so that we may know ourselves better; but try to [i.e., see that you] beg forgiveness immediately."

[26] E.: "for the Lord, and the habit [we have formed] will help us not to offend Him."

ciate with anyone, as seems right to us, even with dissolute people.[27] *These will do you no harm, if you hate sin.*[28] Before we had this true fear of God worldly people would have been poisonous to us and would have helped to ruin our souls; but now they will often help us[29] to love God more and to praise Him for having delivered us from what we see to be a notorious danger. And whereas we for our part may previously have helped to foster their weaknesses, we shall now be helping to repress them, because they will restrain themselves in our presence, and this is a compliment which they will pay us without our desiring it.

I often praise the Lord (though I also wonder why it should be so) that merely by his presence, and without saying a word, a servant of God should frequently prevent people from speaking against Him. It may be as it is in worldly intercourse: a person is always spoken of with respect, even in his absence, before those who are known to be his friends, lest they should be offended. Since this servant of God is in a state of grace, this grace must cause him to be respected, however lowly his station, for people will not distress him in a matter about which they know him to feel so strongly as giving offence to God. I really do not know the reason for this but I do know that it very commonly happens. Do not be too strict with yourselves, then, for, if your spirit begins to quail,[30] it will do great harm to what is good in you and may sometimes lead to scrupulosity, which is a hindrance to progress both in yourselves and in others. Even if things are not as bad as this, a person, however good in herself, will not lead many souls to God if they see that she is so strict and timorous. Human nature is such that these characteristics will frighten and oppress it[31] and lead people to avoid the road

27 E. is even more liberal: "and associate with anyone we meet, more particularly (*mejor*) with dissolute people."
28 E. then continues: "Rather they will help you to further your good resolutions, for they will show you the difference between the one and the other. And if your spirit begins to quail, etc."
29 T.: "give us an opportunity."
30 Here E. takes up the argument again. See n. 28, above.
31 E. reads: "will at once oppress it," and completes the paragraph

you are taking, even if they are quite clear it is the best one.

Another source of harm is this: we may judge others unfavourably, though they may be holier than ourselves, because they do not walk as we do, but, in order to profit their neighbours, talk freely and without restraint.[32] You think such people are imperfect; and if they are good and yet at the same time of a lively disposition, you think them dissolute. This is especially true of those of us who are unlearned and are not sure what we can speak about without committing sin. It is a very dangerous state of mind, leading to great uneasiness and to continual temptation, because it is unfair to our neighbour. It is very wrong to think that everyone who does not follow in your own timorous footsteps has something the matter with her. Another danger is that, when it is your duty to speak, and right that you should speak, you may not dare to do so lest you say too much and may perhaps speak well[33] of things that you ought to hate.[34]

Try, then, sisters, to be as pleasant as you can, without offending God, and to get on as well as you can with those you have to deal with, so that they may like talking to you and want to follow your way of life and conversation, and not be frightened and put off by virtue. This is very important for nuns: the holier they are, the more sociable they should be with their sisters.[35] Although you may be very sorry if all your sisters' conversation is not just as you would like it to be, never keep aloof from them if you wish to help them and to have their love. We must try hard to be pleasant, and to humour the people we deal with and make them like us, especially our sisters.[36]

---

thus: "and, lest they should find themselves similarly trammelled, people will no longer have the desire to draw near to the path of virtue."

[32] E.: "talk without restraint." *Lit.* (as in V.): "without those restraints"—i.e., those just referred to.

[33] E.: "lest you offend God and (you) may speak well."

[34] The paragraph which follows is not found in E.

[35] This sentence was originally written with the nouns in the masculine and corrected by the author to read as in the text.

[36] T. omits: "especially our sisters."

So try, my daughters, to bear in mind that God does not pay great attention to all the trifling matters which occupy you, and do not allow these things to make your spirit quail and your courage fade, for if you do that you may lose many blessings. As I have said, let your intention be upright and your will determined not to offend God. But do not let your soul dwell in seclusion, or, instead of acquiring holiness, you will develop many imperfections, which the devil will implant in you in other ways, in which case, as I have said, you will not do the good that you might, either to yourselves or to others.[37]

You see that, with these two things—love and fear of God —we can travel along this road in peace and quietness,[38] *and not think at every step that we can see some pitfall, and that we shall never reach our goal.*[39] *Yet we cannot be sure of reaching it,*[40] so fear will always lead the way, and then we shall not grow careless, for, as long as we live, we must never feel completely safe or we shall be in great danger. And that was our Teacher's meaning when at the end of this prayer He said these words to His Father,[41] knowing how necessary they were: *"But deliver us from evil. Amen."*

---

37 E.: "in which case, as I say, you will do good neither to yourselves nor to others."

38 E.: "along this road quietly."

39 Or "for [if we do this] we shall never reach our goal."

40 E. continues: "[though] it is true that we have these two things, which are very necessary. As the Lord has pity on us because we live a life of such uncertainty, and [are] among so many temptations and dangers, His Majesty does well to teach us to ask for ourselves what He asks for Himself: 'But deliver us from evil. Amen.'"

41 T. ends the sentence here.

CHAPTER 42

Treats of these last words of the Paternoster: "Sed libera nos a malo. Amen." "But deliver us from evil. Amen."[1]

I think the good Jesus was right to ask this for Himself, for we know[2] how weary of this life He was when at the Supper He said to His Apostles: "With desire I have desired to sup with you"[3]—and that was the last supper of His life. From this it can be seen how weary He must have been of living;[4] yet nowadays people are not weary even at a hundred years old, but always want to live longer. It is true, however, that we do not live so difficult a life or suffer such trials or such poverty as His Majesty had to bear.[5] What was His whole life but a continuous death, with the picture of the cruel death that He was to suffer always before His eyes? And this was the least important thing, with so many offences being[6] committed against His Father and such a multitude of souls being lost.[7] If to any human being full of charity this is a great torment, what must it have been to the boundless and measureless charity[8] of the Lord? And how right He was to beseech the Father to deliver Him from so many evils and trials

---

[1] T. begins this chapter: "As our good Master knows the perils and trials of this life, He makes this petition for us. He had indeed proved by experience how distressing it is, for we can see how weary of it He was when at the Supper, etc."
[2] E.: "I say that He asks this for Himself, because it is quite evident."
[3] St. Luke xxii, 15.
[4] T.: "how delectable death would be to Him."
[5] E.: "that we do not live a life so full of trials and poverty as did the good Jesu."
[6] T.: "offences which He saw being."
[7] E.: "but a cross, with our ingratitude always before His eyes, and the sight of so many offences being committed against His Father and so many souls being lost."
[8] E.: "to the charity."

and to give Him rest for ever[9] in His Kingdom, of which He was the true heir.

By the word "Amen," as it comes at the end of every prayer,[10] I understand that the Lord is begging that we may be delivered from all evil for ever. *It is useless, sisters, for us to think that, for so long as we live, we can be free from numerous temptations and imperfections and even sins; for it is said that whosoever thinks himself to be without sin deceives himself, and that is true. But if we try to banish bodily ills and trials—and who is without very many and various trials of such kinds?—is it not right that we should ask to be delivered from sin?*

Still, let us realize that what we are asking here—this deliverance from all evil—seems an impossibility, whether we are thinking of bodily ills, as I have said, or of imperfections and faults in God's service. I am referring, not to the saints, who, as Saint Paul said, can do all things in Christ,[11] but to sinners like myself. When I find myself trammelled by weakness, lukewarmness, lack of mortification and many other things, I realize that I must beg for help from the Lord.

You, daughters, must ask as you think best. Personally, I shall find no redress in this life, so I ask the Lord to deliver me from all evil "for ever." What good thing shall we find in this life, sisters, in which we are deprived of our great Good and are absent from Him? Deliver me, Lord, from this shadow of death; deliver me from all these trials; deliver me from all these pains; deliver me from all these changes, from all the formalities with which we are forced to comply for as long as we live, from all the many, many, many things which weary and depress me, and the enumeration of all of which would weary the reader if I were to repeat them. This life is unendurable. The source of my own depression must be my own wicked life and the realization that even now I am not living as I should, so great are my obligations.

---

[9] E. ends the paragraph here.
[10] V., T. have "of all things", though the reference is probably to prayers. E.: "of all things and arguments."
[11] Philippians iv, 13.

I beseech the Lord,[12] then, to deliver me from all evil for ever, since I cannot[13] pay what I owe, and may perhaps run farther into debt each day. And the hardest thing to bear, Lord, is that I cannot know with any certainty if I love Thee and if my desires are acceptable in Thy sight. O my God and Lord, deliver me[14] from all evil and be pleased to lead me to that place where all good things are to be found. What can be looked for on earth by those to whom Thou hast given[15] some knowledge of what the world is and those who have a living faith[16] in what the Eternal Father has laid up for them *because His Son asks it of Him and teaches us to ask Him for it too?*[17]

When contemplatives ask for this with fervent desire and full determination it is a *very* clear sign that *their contemplation is genuine and that* the favours which they receive in prayer are from God.[18] Let those who have these favours,[19] then, prize them highly. But if I myself make this request it is not for that reason (I mean, it must not be taken as being for that reason); it is because I am wearied by so many trials and because my life has been so wicked that I am afraid of living any longer. It is not surprising if those who share in the favours of God should wish to pass to a life where they no longer enjoy mere sips at them: *being already partakers in some knowledge of His greatness, they would fain see it in*

---

[12] T.: "I beseech His Majesty."

[13] T.: "I do not believe I can." The addition, deleted and then rewritten, is in St. Teresa's hand.

[14] E. begins the paragraph here, with: "O my Lord, deliver me, etc."

[15] E.: "by those of us who have."

[16] E.: "have some faith."

[17] E. begins the next paragraph with the words: "Believe that it is not good for us to live unless we desire to be free of all evil." These words, however, are crossed out in the MS. and do not appear in V.

[18] E. substitutes an impersonal subject for "contemplatives" and ends the sentence "and that it is God Who draws the soul to Himself." It then continues: "Being already partakers, etc." T. continues: "(their aim) being not to flee from trials, but only to enjoy Him. Let those to whom Our Lord gives (these favours), then, etc."

[19] *Lit.*: "Let those who are so."

its entirety. They have no desire to remain where[20] there are so many hindrances to the enjoyment of so many blessings; nor that they should desire to be where the Sun of justice never sets. Henceforward all the things they see on earth seem dim to them and I wonder that they can live *for even an hour.* No one[21] can be content to do so who has begun to enjoy such things, and has been given the Kingdom of God on earth, and must live to do, not his own will, but the will of the King.

Oh, far other must be that life in which we no longer desire death! How differently shall we then incline our wills towards the will of God![22] His will is for us to desire[23] truth, whereas we desire falsehood; His will is for us to desire the eternal, whereas we prefer that which passes away; His will is for us to desire great and sublime things, whereas we desire the base things of earth; He would have us desire only what is certain, whereas here on earth we love what is doubtful.[24] What a mockery it all is, my daughters, unless we beseech God to deliver us from these perils for ever and to keep us from all evil![25] And although our desire for this may not be perfect, let us strive to make the petition. What does it cost us to ask it, since we ask it of One Who is so powerful? *It would be insulting a great emperor to ask him for a farthing.* Since we have already given Him our will, let us leave the giving to His will, so that we may be the more surely heard; and may His name be for ever hallowed in the Heavens and on the earth and may His will be ever done in me. Amen.

You see now, friends, what is meant by perfection in vocal

20 V. reads: "mere sips at them, and where."
21 E. begins: "They cannot be content to do so," and continues: "A fine world is this to please one who has begun to enjoy God, and has been given, etc."
22 E.: "How differently will the will of God incline towards our own!"
23 Throughout this sentence E. has "His will desires" and not "His will is for us to desire".
24 The words which follow, "What a mockery . . . our will", are lightly crossed out by St. Teresa in V. They do not appear in T., but were included by Luis de León in his edition.
25 E.: "to deliver us for ever from all evil."

prayer, in which we consider and know to Whom the prayer is being made, Who is making it and what is its object. When you are told that it is not good for you to practise any but vocal prayer, do not be discouraged, but read this with great care and beg God to explain to you anything about prayer which you cannot understand. For no one can deprive you of vocal prayer or make you say the Paternoster hurriedly, without understanding it. If anyone tries to do so, or advises you to give up your prayer, take no notice of him. You may be sure he is a false prophet; and in these days, remember, you must not believe everyone, for, though you may be told now that you have nothing to fear, you do not know what is in store for you. I had intended, as well as saying this, to talk to you a little about how you should say the Ave Maria, but I have written at such length that that will have to be left over. If you have learned how to say the Paternoster well, you will know enough to enable you to say all the other vocal prayers you may have to recite.

Now let us go back and finish the journey which I have been describing, for the Lord seems to have been saving me labour[26] by teaching both you and me the Way which I began to outline to you and by showing me how much we ask for when we repeat this evangelical prayer.[27] May He be for ever blessed, for it had certainly never entered my mind that there were such great secrets in it. You have now seen that it comprises the whole spiritual road,[28] right from the beginning, until God absorbs the soul and gives it to drink abundantly of the fountain of living water which I told you was at the end of the road.[29] It seems, sisters, that the Lord's will has been to teach us what great consolation is comprised in it, and this is a great advantage to those who cannot read. If they understood this prayer, they could derive a great deal

[26] Thus E. V. begins the paragraph: "See, now, sisters, what labour the Lord has saved me."
[27] E.: "both you and me what we have to ask for in this prayer."
[28] E.: "that there was such a great secret in this evangelical prayer that it comprises the whole spiritual road."
[29] E. reads: "water of which we spoke," and continues, parenthetically: "And so, having finished this prayer, I cannot go any farther."

of sound instruction from it and would find it a real comfort.[30] *Our books may be taken from us, but this is a book which no one can take away, and it comes from the lips of the Truth Himself, Who cannot err.*

As we repeat the Paternoster so many times daily, then, as I have said, let us delight in it and strive to learn from so excellent a Master the humility with which He prays, and all the other things that have been described. May His Majesty forgive me for having dared to speak of such high matters. Well does His Majesty know that *I should not have ventured to do so, and that* my understanding would not have been capable of it, had He not taught me what I have said.[31] Give thanks to Him for this, sisters, for He must have done it because of the humility with which you asked me to write it for you in your desire to be instructed by one so unworthy.[32]

Well, sisters, Our Lord seems not to want me to write any more, for, although I had intended to go on, I can think of nothing to say. The Lord has shown you the road and has taught me what I wrote in the book which, as I say, I have already written.[33] *This tells you how to conduct yourselves on reaching this fount of living water and what the soul experiences when there, and how God satiates it and takes away its thirst for earthly things, and makes it grow in things pertaining to God's service. This will be very helpful to those who have reached the fount, and will give them a great deal of light.*

Before you see this book I shall give it to my confessor, Father Presentado Domingo Báñez[34] *of the Order of Saint Dominic. If he thinks you will benefit by it, and gives it you to read, and if you find it of any comfort, I, too, shall be comforted. If he gives you this book, he will give you the*

---

[30] V. continues: "Let us learn, then, sisters, from the humility with which it is taught us by this our good Master. Beseech Him to forgive me, etc."
[31] E.: "had He not put it before me."
[32] This sentence is not found in E.
[33] The *Life.*
[34] P. Báñez deletes his own name in V. T. has "Master" for "Presentado" and adds " of the Order of Saint Dominic."

other[35] *as well.* Should it be found unsuitable for anyone to read, you must take[36] the will for the deed, as I have obeyed your command by writing it.[37] I consider myself well repaid for my labour in writing, though it has certainly been no labour to me to think about what I have been going to say, *as the Lord has taught me the secrets of this evangelical prayer, which has been a great comfort to me.* Blessed and praised be the Lord, from Whom comes all the good that we speak and think and do. Amen.[38]

[35] The *Life.* I do not know what reason St. Teresa had to suppose this, but the Spanish of E. ("también os dará el otro") is quite definite. The sentence does not appear in either V. or T. Cf. the last paragraph of the Prologue (p. 35, above).
[36] E. begins the sentence: "If he does not, take."
[37] *Lit.*: "you will take my will, as I have obeyed your command with the work" [i.e. in deed]. T. has: "with the happiness [? blessing] of my confessor" for "with the work."
[38] E.: "Blessed and praised be He for ever. Amen. Jesus."